Mometrix

TEST PREPARATION

AFCT

Secrets Study Guide

Part 2 of 2

DEAR FUTURE EXAM SUCCESS STORY

First of all, **THANK YOU** for purchasing Mometrix study materials!

Second, congratulations! You are one of the few determined test-takers who are committed to doing whatever it takes to excel on your exam. **You have come to the right place.** We developed these study materials with one goal in mind: to deliver you the information you need in a format that's concise and easy to use.

In addition to optimizing your guide for the content of the test, we've outlined our recommended steps for breaking down the preparation process into small, attainable goals so you can make sure you stay on track.

We've also analyzed the entire test-taking process, identifying the most common pitfalls and showing how you can overcome them and be ready for any curveball the test throws you.

Standardized testing is one of the biggest obstacles on your road to success, which only increases the importance of doing well in the high-pressure, high-stakes environment of test day. Your results on this test could have a significant impact on your future, and this guide provides the information and practical advice to help you achieve your full potential on test day.

Your success is our success

We would love to hear from you! If you would like to share the story of your exam success or if you have any questions or comments in regard to our products, please contact us at **800-673-8175** or **support@mometrix.com**.

Thanks again for your business and we wish you continued success!

Sincerely,
The Mometrix Test Preparation Team

Need more help? Check out our flashcards at:
http://MometrixFlashcards.com/AFCT

Written and edited by the Mometrix Exam Secrets Test Prep Team
Printed in the United States of America

Table of Contents

Mathematics Knowledge

3D Shapes

Solids

The **surface area of a solid object** is the area of all sides or exterior surfaces. For objects such as prisms and pyramids, a further distinction is made between base surface area (B) and lateral surface area (LA). For a prism, the total surface area (SA) is $SA = LA + 2B$. For a pyramid or cone, the total surface area is $SA = LA + B$.

The **surface area of a sphere** can be found by the formula $A = 4\pi r^2$, where r is the radius. The volume is given by the formula $V = \frac{4}{3}\pi r^3$, where r is the radius. Both quantities are generally given in terms of π.

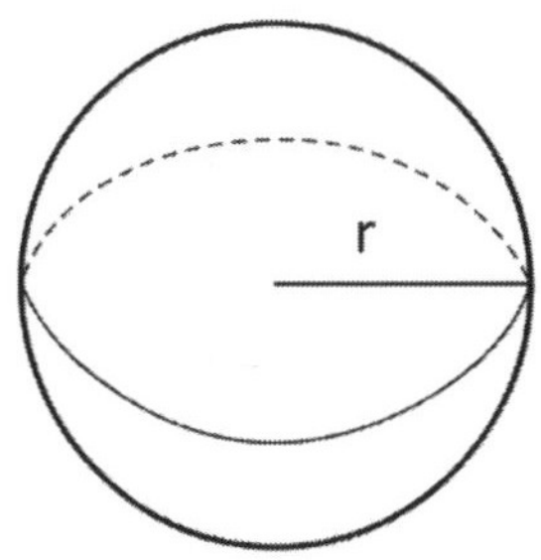

Review Video: Volume and Surface Area of a Sphere
Visit mometrix.com/academy and enter code: 786928

Review Video: How to Calculate the Volume of 3D Objects
Visit mometrix.com/academy and enter code: 163343

The **volume of any prism** is found by the formula $V = Bh$, where B is the area of the base, and h is the height (perpendicular distance between the bases). The surface area of any prism is the sum of the areas of both bases and all sides. It can be calculated as $SA = 2B + Ph$, where P is the perimeter of the base.

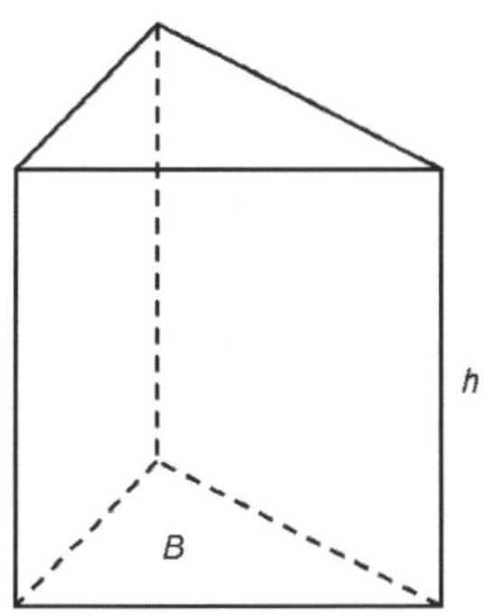

Review Video: Volume and Surface Area of a Prism
Visit mometrix.com/academy and enter code: 420158

For a **rectangular prism**, the volume can be found by the formula $V = lwh$, where V is the volume, l is the length, w is the width, and h is the height. The surface area can be calculated as $SA = 2lw + 2hl + 2wh$ or $SA = 2(lw + hl + wh)$.

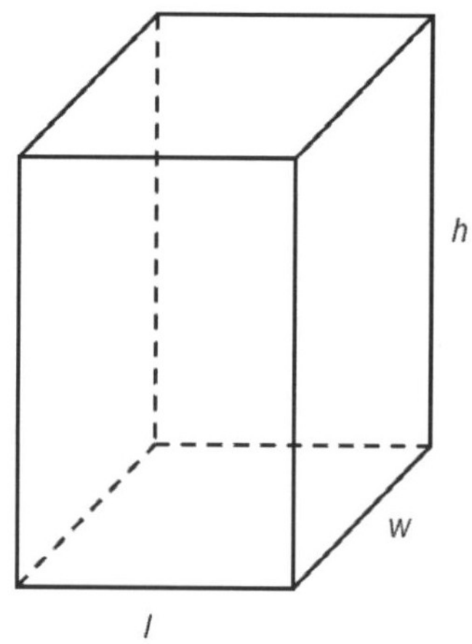

Review Video: Volume and Surface Area of a Rectangular Prism
Visit mometrix.com/academy and enter code: 282814

The **volume of a cube** can be found by the formula $V = s^3$, where s is the length of a side. The surface area of a cube is calculated as $SA = 6s^2$, where SA is the total surface area and s is the length of a side. These formulas are the same as the ones used for the volume and surface area of a rectangular prism, but simplified since all three quantities (length, width, and height) are the same.

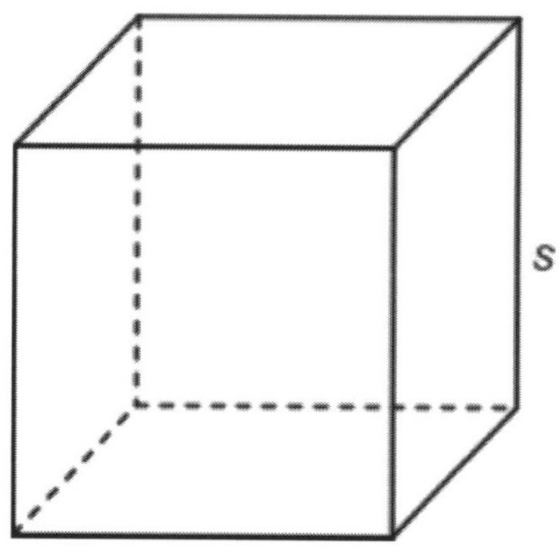

Review Video: Volume and Surface Area of a Cube
Visit mometrix.com/academy and enter code: 664455

The **volume of a cylinder** can be calculated by the formula $V = \pi r^2 h$, where r is the radius, and h is the height. The surface area of a cylinder can be found by the formula $SA = 2\pi r^2 + 2\pi rh$. The first term is the base area multiplied by two, and the second term is the perimeter of the base multiplied by the height.

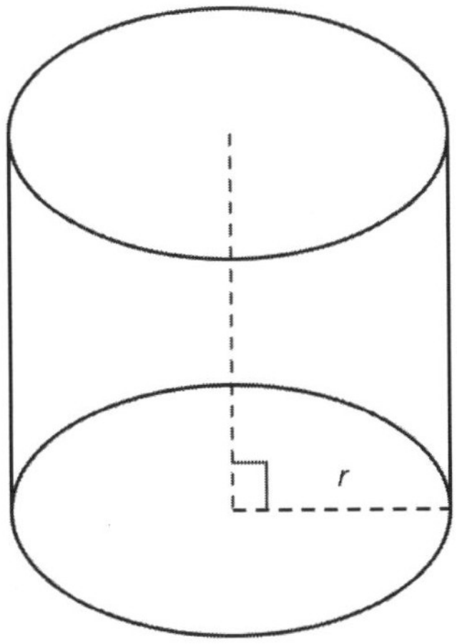

Review Video: Volume and Surface Area of a Right Circular Cylinder
Visit mometrix.com/academy and enter code: 226463

The **volume of a pyramid** is found by the formula $V = \frac{1}{3}Bh$, where B is the area of the base, and h is the height (perpendicular distance from the vertex to the base). Notice this formula is the same as $\frac{1}{3}$ times the volume of a prism. Like a prism, the base of a pyramid can be any shape.

Finding the **surface area of a pyramid** is not as simple as the other shapes we've looked at thus far. If the pyramid is a right pyramid, meaning the base is a regular polygon and the vertex is directly over the center of that polygon, the surface area can be calculated as $SA = B + \frac{1}{2}Ph_s$, where P is the perimeter of the base, and h_s is the slant height (distance from the vertex to the midpoint of one side of the base). If the pyramid is irregular, the area of each triangle side must be calculated individually and then summed, along with the base.

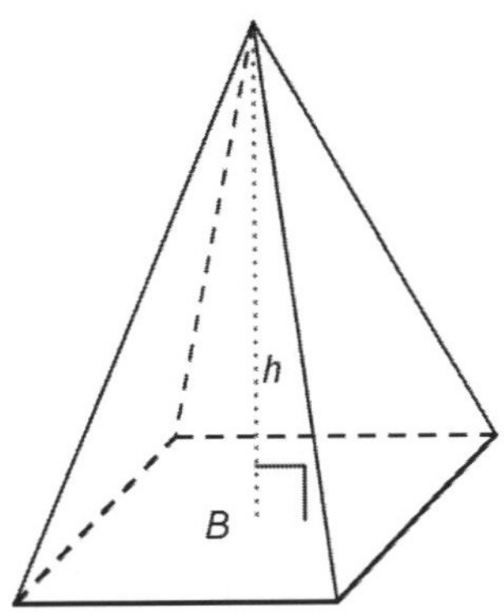

Review Video: Volume and Surface Area of a Pyramid
Visit mometrix.com/academy and enter code: 621932

The **volume of a cone** is found by the formula $V = \frac{1}{3}\pi r^2 h$, where r is the radius, and h is the height. Notice this is the same as $\frac{1}{3}$ times the volume of a cylinder. The surface area can be calculated as

$SA = \pi r^2 + \pi rs$, where s is the slant height. The slant height can be calculated using the Pythagorean theorem to be $\sqrt{r^2 + h^2}$, so the surface area formula can also be written as $SA = \pi r^2 + \pi r\sqrt{r^2 + h^2}$.

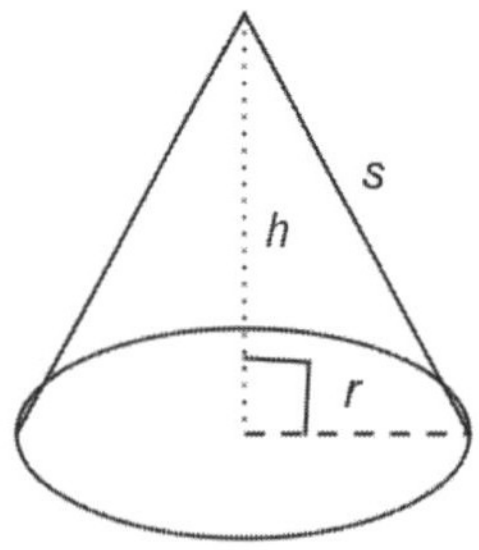

Review Video: Volume and Surface Area of a Right Circular Cone
Visit mometrix.com/academy and enter code: 573574

Trigonometry

Pythagorean Theorem

The side of a triangle opposite the right angle is called the **hypotenuse**. The other two sides are called the legs. The Pythagorean theorem states a relationship among the legs and hypotenuse of a right triangle: $(a^2 + b^2 = c^2)$, where a and b are the lengths of the legs of a right triangle, and c is the length of the hypotenuse. Note that this formula will only work with right triangles.

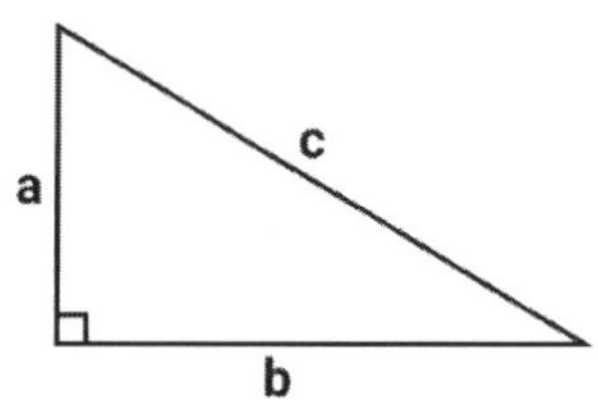

Review Video: Pythagorean Theorem
Visit mometrix.com/academy and enter code: 906576

Trigonometric Formulas

In the diagram below, angle C is the right angle, and side c is the hypotenuse. Side a is the side opposite to angle A and side b is the side opposite to angle B. Using ratios of side lengths as a means to calculate the sine, cosine, and tangent of an acute angle only works for right triangles.

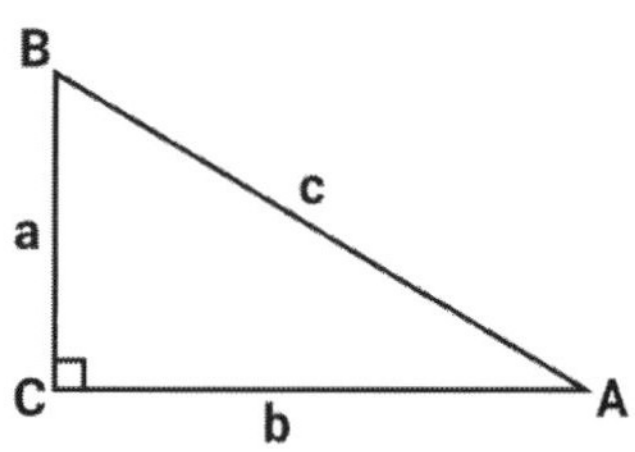

$$\sin A = \frac{\text{opposite side}}{\text{hypotenuse}} = \frac{a}{c} \qquad \csc A = \frac{1}{\sin A} = \frac{\text{hypotenuse}}{\text{opposite side}} = \frac{c}{a}$$

$$\cos A = \frac{\text{adjacent side}}{\text{hypotenuse}} = \frac{b}{c} \qquad \sec A = \frac{1}{\cos A} = \frac{\text{hypotenuse}}{\text{adjacent side}} = \frac{c}{b}$$

$$\tan A = \frac{\text{opposite side}}{\text{adjacent side}} = \frac{a}{b} \qquad \cot A = \frac{1}{\tan A} = \frac{\text{adjacent side}}{\text{opposite side}} = \frac{b}{a}$$

Laws of Sines and Cosines

The **law of sines** states that $\frac{\sin A}{a} = \frac{\sin B}{b} = \frac{\sin C}{c}$, where A, B, and C are the angles of a triangle, and a, b, and c are the sides opposite their respective angles. This formula will work with all triangles, not just right triangles.

The **law of cosines** is given by the formula $c^2 = a^2 + b^2 - 2ab(\cos C)$, where a, b, and c are the sides of a triangle, and C is the angle opposite side c. This is a generalized form of the Pythagorean theorem that can be used on any triangle.

Review Video: Law of Sines
Visit mometrix.com/academy and enter code: 206844

Review Video: Law of Cosines
Visit mometrix.com/academy and enter code: 158911

Statistics

Probability

Probability is the likelihood of a certain outcome occurring for a given event. An **event** is any situation that produces a result. It could be something as simple as flipping a coin or as complex as launching a rocket. Determining the probability of an outcome for an event can be equally simple or complex. As such, there are specific terms used in the study of probability that need to be understood:

- **Compound event**—an event that involves two or more independent events (rolling a pair of dice and taking the sum)
- **Desired outcome** (or success)—an outcome that meets a particular set of criteria (a roll of 1 or 2 if we are looking for numbers less than 3)
- **Independent events**—two or more events whose outcomes do not affect one another (two coins tossed at the same time)
- **Dependent events**—two or more events whose outcomes affect one another (two cards drawn consecutively from the same deck)
- **Certain outcome**—probability of outcome is 100% or 1
- **Impossible outcome**—probability of outcome is 0% or 0
- **Mutually exclusive outcomes**—two or more outcomes whose criteria cannot all be satisfied in a single event (a coin coming up heads and tails on the same toss)
- **Random variable**—refers to all possible outcomes of a single event which may be discrete or continuous.

Review Video: Intro to Probability
Visit mometrix.com/academy and enter code: 212374

Sample Space

The total set of all possible results of a test or experiment is called a **sample space**, or sometimes a universal sample space. The sample space, represented by one of the variables S, Ω, or U (for universal sample space) has individual elements called outcomes. Other terms for outcome that may be used interchangeably include elementary outcome, simple event, or sample point. The number of outcomes in a given sample space could be infinite or finite, and some tests may yield multiple unique sample sets. For example, tests conducted by drawing playing cards from a standard deck would have one sample space of the card values, another sample space of the card suits, and a third sample space of suit-denomination combinations. For most tests, the sample spaces considered will be finite.

An **event**, represented by the variable E, is a portion of a sample space. It may be one outcome or a group of outcomes from the same sample space. If an event occurs, then the test or experiment will generate an outcome that satisfies the requirement of that event. For example, given a standard deck of 52 playing cards as the sample space, and defining the event as the collection of face cards, then the event will occur if the card drawn is a J, Q, or K. If any other card is drawn, the event is said to have not occurred.

For every sample space, each possible outcome has a specific likelihood, or probability, that it will occur. The probability measure, also called the **distribution**, is a function that assigns a real number probability, from zero to one, to each outcome. For a probability measure to be accurate, every outcome must have a real number probability measure that is greater than or equal to zero and less than or equal to one. Also, the probability measure of the sample space must equal one, and the probability measure of the union of multiple outcomes must equal the sum of the individual probability measures.

Probabilities of events are expressed as real numbers from zero to one. They give a numerical value to the chance that a particular event will occur. The probability of an event occurring is the sum of the probabilities of the individual elements of that event. For example, in a standard deck of 52 playing cards as the sample space and the collection of face cards as the event, the probability of drawing a specific face card is $\frac{1}{52} = 0.019$, but the probability of drawing any one of the twelve face cards is $12(0.019) = 0.228$. Note that rounding of numbers can generate different results. If you multiplied 12 by the fraction $\frac{1}{52}$ before converting to a decimal, you would get the answer $\frac{12}{52} = 0.231$.

Theoretical and Experimental Probability

Theoretical probability can usually be determined without actually performing the event. The likelihood of an outcome occurring, or the probability of an outcome occurring, is given by the formula:

$$P(A) = \frac{\text{Number of acceptable outcomes}}{\text{Number of possible outcomes}}$$

Note that $P(A)$ is the probability of an outcome A occurring, and each outcome is just as likely to occur as any other outcome. If each outcome has the same probability of occurring as every other possible outcome, the outcomes are said to be equally likely to occur. The total number of acceptable outcomes must be less than or equal to the total number of possible outcomes. If the two are equal, then the outcome is certain to occur and the probability is 1. If the number of acceptable outcomes is zero, then the outcome is impossible and the probability is 0. For example, if there are 20 marbles in a bag and 5 are red, then the theoretical probability of randomly selecting a red marble is 5 out of 20, $\left(\frac{5}{20} = \frac{1}{4}, 0.25, \text{or } 25\%\right)$.

If the theoretical probability is unknown or too complicated to calculate, it can be estimated by an experimental probability. **Experimental probability**, also called empirical probability, is an estimate of the likelihood of a certain outcome based on repeated experiments or collected data. In other words, while theoretical probability is based on what *should* happen, experimental probability is based on what *has* happened. Experimental probability is calculated in the same way as theoretical probability, except that actual outcomes are used instead of possible outcomes. The more experiments performed or datapoints gathered, the better the estimate should be.

Theoretical and experimental probability do not always line up with one another. Theoretical probability says that out of 20 coin-tosses, 10 should be heads. However, if we were actually to toss 20 coins, we might record just 5 heads. This doesn't mean that our theoretical probability is incorrect; it just means that this particular experiment had results that were different from what was predicted. A practical application of empirical probability is the insurance industry. There are no set functions that define lifespan, health, or safety. Insurance companies look at factors from hundreds of thousands of individuals to find patterns that they then use to set the formulas for insurance premiums.

Review Video: Empirical Probability
Visit mometrix.com/academy and enter code: 513468

Objective and Subjective Probability

Objective probability is based on mathematical formulas and documented evidence. Examples of objective probability include raffles or lottery drawings where there is a pre-determined number of possible outcomes and a predetermined number of outcomes that correspond to an event. Other cases of objective probability include probabilities of rolling dice, flipping coins, or drawing cards. Most gambling games are based on objective probability.

In contrast, **subjective probability** is based on personal or professional feelings and judgments. Often, there is a lot of guesswork following extensive research. Areas where subjective probability is applicable include sales trends and business expenses. Attractions set admission prices based on subjective probabilities of attendance based on varying admission rates in an effort to maximize their profit.

Complement of an Event

Sometimes it may be easier to calculate the possibility of something not happening, or the **complement of an event**. Represented by the symbol $\bar{A}$, the complement of A is the probability that event A does not happen. When you know the probability of event A occurring, you can use the formula $P(\bar{A}) = 1 - P(A)$, where $P(\bar{A})$ is the probability of event A not occurring, and $P(A)$ is the probability of event A occurring.

Addition Rule

The **addition rule** for probability is used for finding the probability of a compound event. Use the formula $P(A \cup B) = P(A) + P(B) - P(A \cap B)$, where $P(A \cap B)$ is the probability of both events occurring to find the probability of a compound event. The probability of both events occurring at the same time must be subtracted to eliminate any overlap in the first two probabilities.

Conditional Probability

Given two events A and B, the **conditional probability** $P(A|B)$ is the probability that event A will occur, given that event B has occurred. The conditional probability cannot be calculated simply from $P(A)$ and $P(B)$; these probabilities alone do not give sufficient information to determine the conditional probability. It can, however, be determined if you are also given the probability of the intersection of events A and B, $P(A \cap B)$, the probability that events A and B both occur.

Specifically, $P(A|B) = \frac{P(A \cap B)}{P(B)}$. For instance, suppose you have a jar containing two red marbles and two blue marbles, and you draw two marbles at random. Consider event A being the event that the first marble drawn is red, and event B being the event that the second marble drawn is blue. If we want to find the probability that B occurs given that A occurred, $P(B|A)$, then we can compute it using the fact that $P(A)$ is $\frac{1}{2}$, and $P(A \cap B)$ is $\frac{1}{3}$. (The latter may not be obvious, but may be determined by finding the product of $\frac{1}{2}$ and $\frac{2}{3}$). Therefore $P(B|A) = \frac{P(A \cap B)}{P(A)} = \frac{1/3}{1/2} = \frac{2}{3}$.

CONDITIONAL PROBABILITY IN EVERYDAY SITUATIONS

Conditional probability often arises in everyday situations in, for example, estimating the risk or benefit of certain activities. The conditional probability of having a heart attack given that you exercise daily may be smaller than the overall probability of having a heart attack. The conditional probability of having lung cancer given that you are a smoker is larger than the overall probability of having lung cancer. Note that changing the order of the conditional probability changes the meaning: the conditional probability of having lung cancer given that you are a smoker is a very different thing from the probability of being a smoker given that you have lung cancer. In an extreme case, suppose that a certain rare disease is caused only by eating a certain food, but even then, it is unlikely. Then the conditional probability of having that disease given that you eat the dangerous food is nonzero but low, but the conditional probability of having eaten that food given that you have the disease is 100%!

> **Review Video: Conditional Probability**
> Visit mometrix.com/academy and enter code: 397924

INDEPENDENCE

The conditional probability $P(A|B)$ is the probability that event A will occur given that event B occurs. If the two events are independent, we do not expect that whether or not event B occurs should have any effect on whether or not event A occurs. In other words, we expect $P(A|B) = P(A)$.

This can be proven using the usual equations for conditional probability and the joint probability of independent events. The conditional probability $P(A|B) = \frac{P(A \cap B)}{P(B)}$. If A and B are independent, then $P(A \cap B) = P(A)P(B)$. So $P(A|B) = \frac{P(A)P(B)}{P(B)} = P(A)$. By similar reasoning, if A and B are independent then $P(B|A) = P(B)$.

MULTIPLICATION RULE

The **multiplication rule** can be used to find the probability of two independent events occurring using the formula $P(A \cap B) = P(A) \times P(B)$, where $P(A \cap B)$ is the probability of two independent events occurring, $P(A)$ is the probability of the first event occurring, and $P(B)$ is the probability of the second event occurring.

The multiplication rule can also be used to find the probability of two dependent events occurring using the formula $P(A \cap B) = P(A) \times P(B|A)$, where $P(A \cap B)$ is the probability of two dependent events occurring and $P(B|A)$ is the probability of the second event occurring after the first event has already occurred.

Use a **combination of the multiplication** rule and the rule of complements to find the probability that at least one outcome of the element will occur. This is given by the general formula $P(\text{at least one event occurring}) = 1 - P(\text{no outcomes occurring})$. For example, to find the probability that at least one even number will show when a pair of dice is rolled, find the probability that two odd numbers will be rolled (no even numbers) and subtract from one. You can always use a tree diagram or make a chart to list the possible outcomes when the sample space is small, such as in the dice-rolling example, but in most cases it will be much faster to use the multiplication and complement formulas.

Review Video: Multiplication Rule
Visit mometrix.com/academy and enter code: 782598

UNION AND INTERSECTION OF TWO SETS OF OUTCOMES

If A and B are each a set of elements or outcomes from an experiment, then the **union** (symbol ∪) of the two sets is the set of elements found in set A or set B. For example, if $A = \{2,3,4\}$ and $B = \{3,4,5\}$, $A \cup B = \{2,3,4,5\}$. Note that the outcomes 3 and 4 appear only once in the union. For statistical events, the union is equivalent to "or"; $P(A \cup B)$ is the same thing as $P(A \text{ or } B)$. The **intersection** (symbol ∩) of two sets is the set of outcomes common to both sets. For the above sets A and B, $A \cap B = \{3,4\}$. For statistical events, the intersection is equivalent to "and"; $P(A \cap B)$ is the same thing as $P(A \text{ and } B)$. It is important to note that union and intersection operations commute. That is:

$$A \cup B = B \cup A \text{ and } A \cap B = B \cap A$$

MEASURES OF CENTRAL TENDENCY

A **measure of central tendency** is a statistical value that gives a reasonable estimate for the center of a group of data. There are several different ways of describing the measure of central tendency. Each one has a unique way it is calculated, and each one gives a slightly different perspective on the data set. Whenever you give a measure of central tendency, always make sure the units are the same. If the data has different units, such as hours, minutes, and seconds, convert all the data to the same unit, and use the same unit in the measure of central tendency. If no units are given in the data, do not give units for the measure of central tendency.

MEAN

The **statistical mean** of a group of data is the same as the arithmetic average of that group. To find the mean of a set of data, first convert each value to the same units, if necessary. Then find the sum of all the values, and count the total number of data values, making sure you take into consideration each individual value. If a value appears more than once, count it more than once. Divide the sum of the values by the total number of values and apply the units, if any. Note that the mean does not have to be one of the data values in the set, and may not divide evenly.

$$\text{mean} = \frac{\text{sum of the data values}}{\text{quantity of data values}}$$

For instance, the mean of the data set $\{88, 72, 61, 90, 97, 68, 88, 79, 86, 93, 97, 71, 80, 84, 89\}$ would be the sum of the fifteen numbers divided by 15:

$$\frac{88+72+61+90+97+68+88+79+86+93+97+71+80+84+89}{15} = \frac{1242}{15} = 82.8$$

While the mean is relatively easy to calculate and averages are understood by most people, the mean can be very misleading if it is used as the sole measure of central tendency. If the data set has outliers (data values that are unusually high or unusually low compared to the rest of the data values), the mean can be very distorted, especially if the data set has a small number of values. If unusually high values are countered with unusually low values, the mean is not affected as much. For example, if five of twenty students in a class get a 100 on a test, but the other 15 students have an average of 60 on the same test, the class average would appear as 70. Whenever the mean is skewed by outliers, it is always a good idea to include the median as an alternate measure of central tendency.

A **weighted mean**, or weighted average, is a mean that uses "weighted" values. The formula is weighted mean $= \frac{w_1x_1+w_2x_2+w_3x_3...+w_nx_n}{w_1+w_2+w_3+\cdots+w_n}$. Weighted values, such as $w_1, w_2, w_3, ... w_n$ are assigned to each member of the set $x_1, x_2, x_3, ... x_n$. When calculating the weighted mean, make sure a weight value for each member of the set is used.

Review Video: All About Averages
Visit mometrix.com/academy and enter code: 176521

MEDIAN

The **statistical median** is the value in the middle of the set of data. To find the median, list all data values in order from smallest to largest or from largest to smallest. Any value that is repeated in the set must be listed the number of times it appears. If there are an odd number of data values, the median is the value in the middle of the list. If there is an even number of data values, the median is the arithmetic mean of the two middle values.

For example, the median of the data set {88, 72, 61, 90, 97, 68, 88, 79, 86, 93, 97, 71, 80, 84, 88} is 86 since the ordered set is {61, 68, 71, 72, 79, 80, 84, **86**, 88, 88, 88, 90, 93, 97, 97}.

The big disadvantage of using the median as a measure of central tendency is that is relies solely on a value's relative size as compared to the other values in the set. When the individual values in a set of data are evenly dispersed, the median can be an accurate tool. However, if there is a group of rather large values or a group of rather small values that are not offset by a different group of values, the information that can be inferred from the median may not be accurate because the distribution of values is skewed.

MODE

The **statistical mode** is the data value that occurs the greatest number of times in the data set. It is possible to have exactly one mode, more than one mode, or no mode. To find the mode of a set of data, arrange the data like you do to find the median (all values in order, listing all multiples of data values). Count the number of times each value appears in the data set. If all values appear an equal number of times, there is no mode. If one value appears more than any other value, that value is the mode. If two or more values appear the same number of times, but there are other values that appear fewer times and no values that appear more times, all of those values are the modes.

For example, the mode of the data set {**88**, 72, 61, 90, 97, 68, **88**, 79, 86, 93, 97, 71, 80, 84, **88**} is 88.

The main disadvantage of the mode is that the values of the other data in the set have no bearing on the mode. The mode may be the largest value, the smallest value, or a value anywhere in between in the set. The mode only tells which value or values, if any, occurred the greatest number of times. It does not give any suggestions about the remaining values in the set.

Review Video: Mean, Median, and Mode
Visit mometrix.com/academy and enter code: 286207

Displaying Information

Frequency Tables

Frequency tables show how frequently each unique value appears in a set. A **relative frequency table** is one that shows the proportions of each unique value compared to the entire set. Relative frequencies are given as percentages; however, the total percent for a relative frequency table will not necessarily equal 100 percent due to rounding. An example of a frequency table with relative frequencies is below.

Favorite Color	Frequency	Relative Frequency
Blue	4	13%
Red	7	22%
Green	3	9%
Purple	6	19%
Cyan	12	38%

Review Video: Data Interpretation of Graphs
Visit mometrix.com/academy and enter code: 200439

Circle Graphs

Circle graphs, also known as *pie charts*, provide a visual depiction of the relationship of each type of data compared to the whole set of data. The circle graph is divided into sections by drawing radii to create central angles whose percentage of the circle is equal to the individual data's percentage of the whole set. Each 1% of data is equal to 3.6° in the circle graph. Therefore, data represented by a 90° section of the circle graph makes up 25% of the whole. When complete, a circle graph often looks like a pie cut into uneven wedges. The pie chart below shows the data from the frequency table referenced earlier where people were asked their favorite color.

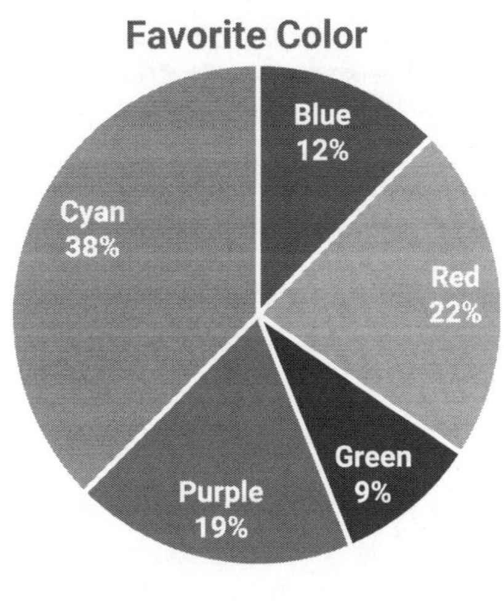

PICTOGRAPHS

A **pictograph** is a graph, generally in the horizontal orientation, that uses pictures or symbols to represent the data. Each pictograph must have a key that defines the picture or symbol and gives the quantity each picture or symbol represents. Pictures or symbols on a pictograph are not always shown as whole elements. In this case, the fraction of the picture or symbol shown represents the same fraction of the quantity a whole picture or symbol stands for. For example, a row with $3\frac{1}{2}$ ears of corn, where each ear of corn represents 100 stalks of corn in a field, would equal $3\frac{1}{2} \times 100 = 350$ stalks of corn in the field.

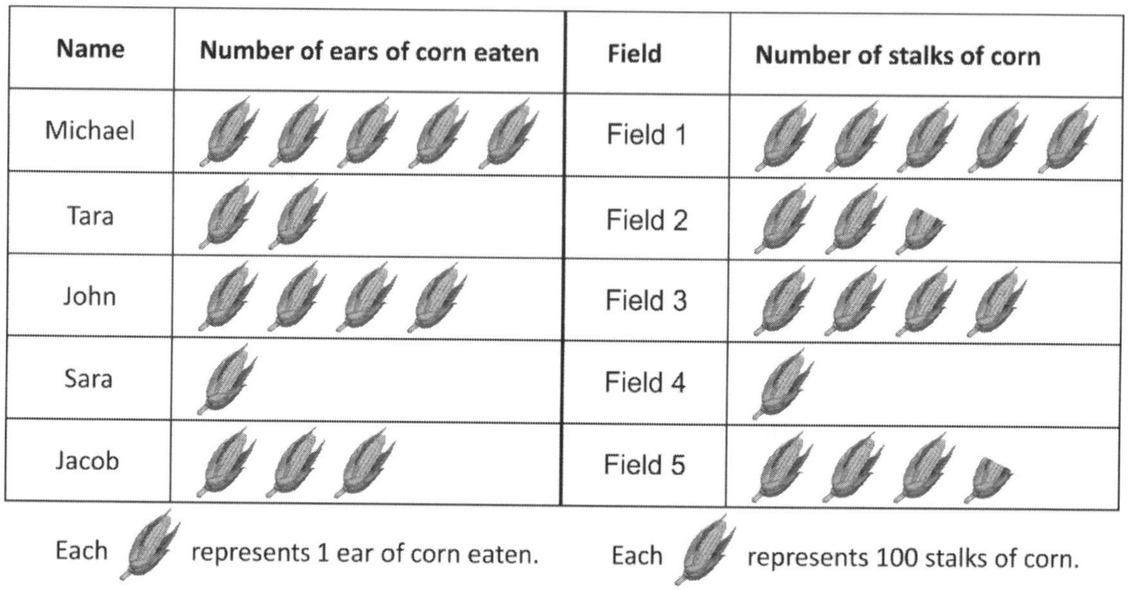

Review Video: Pictographs
Visit mometrix.com/academy and enter code: 147860

LINE GRAPHS

Line graphs have one or more lines of varying styles (solid or broken) to show the different values for a set of data. The individual data are represented as ordered pairs, much like on a Cartesian plane. In this case, the x- and y-axes are defined in terms of their units, such as dollars or time. The individual plotted points are joined by line segments to show whether the value of the data is increasing (line sloping upward), decreasing (line sloping downward), or staying the same (horizontal line). Multiple sets of data can be graphed on the same line graph to give an easy visual comparison. An example of this would be graphing achievement test scores for different groups of students over the same time period to see which group had the greatest increase or decrease in performance from year to year (as shown below).

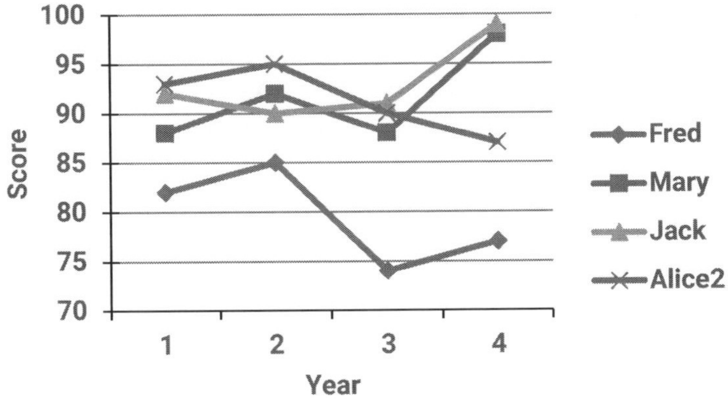

Review Video: How to Create a Line Graph
Visit mometrix.com/academy and enter code: 480147

Line Plots

A **line plot**, also known as a *dot plot*, has plotted points that are not connected by line segments. In this graph, the horizontal axis lists the different possible values for the data, and the vertical axis lists the number of times the individual value occurs. A single dot is graphed for each value to show the number of times it occurs. This graph is more closely related to a bar graph than a line graph. Do not connect the dots in a line plot or it will misrepresent the data.

Review Video: Line Plot
Visit mometrix.com/academy and enter code: 754610

Stem and Leaf Plots

A **stem and leaf plot** is useful for depicting groups of data that fall into a range of values. Each piece of data is separated into two parts: the first, or left, part is called the stem; the second, or right, part is called the leaf. Each stem is listed in a column from smallest to largest. Each leaf that has the common stem is listed in that stem's row from smallest to largest. For example, in a set of two-digit numbers, the digit in the tens place is the stem, and the digit in the ones place is the leaf. With a stem and leaf plot, you can easily see which subset of numbers (10s, 20s, 30s, etc.) is the largest. This information is also readily available by looking at a histogram, but a stem and leaf plot also allows you to look closer and see exactly which values fall in that range. Using a sample set of test scores (82, 88, 92, 93, 85, 90, 92, 95, 74, 88, 90, 91, 78, 87, 98, 99), we can assemble a stem and leaf plot like the one below.

Test Scores

7	4	8							
8	2	5	7	8	8				
9	0	0	1	2	2	3	5	8	9

Review Video: Stem and Leaf Plots
Visit mometrix.com/academy and enter code: 302339

Bar Graphs

A **bar graph** is one of the few graphs that can be drawn correctly in two different configurations – both horizontally and vertically. A bar graph is similar to a line plot in the way the data is organized on the graph. Both axes must have their categories defined for the graph to be useful. Rather than placing a single dot to mark the point of the data's value, a bar, or thick line, is drawn from zero to the exact value of the data, whether it is a number, percentage, or other numerical value. Longer bar lengths correspond to greater data values. To read a bar graph, read the labels for the axes to find the units being reported. Then, look where the bars end in relation to the scale given on the corresponding axis and determine the associated value.

The bar chart below represents the responses from our favorite-color survey.

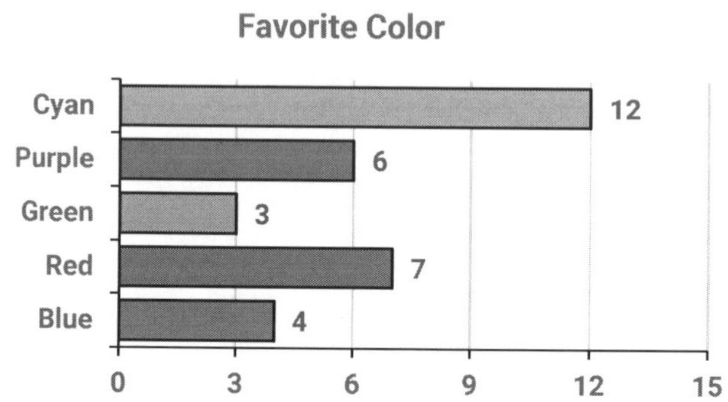

Histograms

At first glance, a **histogram** looks like a vertical bar graph. The difference is that a bar graph has a separate bar for each piece of data and a histogram has one continuous bar for each *range* of data. For example, a histogram may have one bar for the range 0–9, one bar for 10–19, etc. While a bar graph has numerical values on one axis, a histogram has numerical values on both axes. Each range is of equal size, and they are ordered left to right from lowest to highest. The height of each column on a histogram represents the number of data values within that range. Like a stem and leaf plot, a histogram makes it easy to glance at the graph and quickly determine which range has the greatest quantity of values. A simple example of a histogram is below.

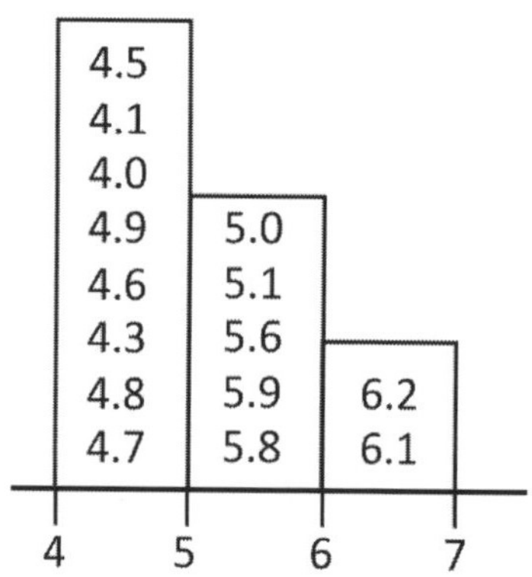

5-Number Summary

The **5-number summary** of a set of data gives a very informative picture of the set. The five numbers in the summary include the minimum value, maximum value, and the three quartiles. This information gives the reader the range and median of the set, as well as an indication of how the data is spread about the median.

Box and Whisker Plots

A **box-and-whiskers plot** is a graphical representation of the 5-number summary. To draw a box-and-whiskers plot, plot the points of the 5-number summary on a number line. Draw a box whose ends are through the points for the first and third quartiles. Draw a vertical line in the box through the median to divide the box in half. Draw a line segment from the first quartile point to the minimum value, and from the third quartile point to the maximum value.

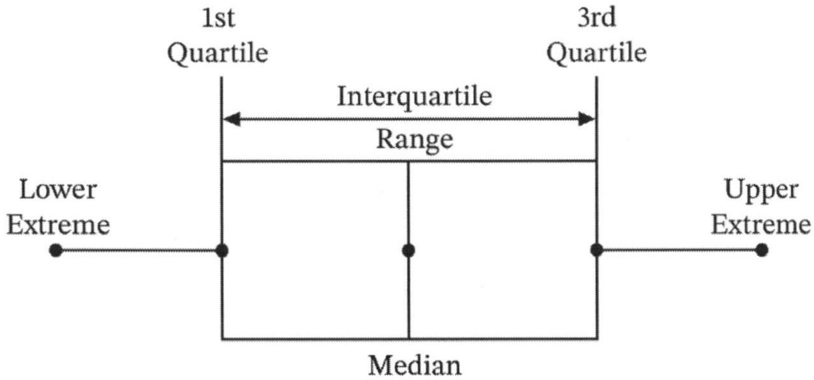

> **Review Video: Box and Whisker Plots**
> Visit mometrix.com/academy and enter code: 810817

Example

Given the following data (32, 28, 29, 26, 35, 27, 30, 31, 27, 32), we first sort it into numerical order: 26, 27, 27, 28, 29, 30, 31, 32, 32, 35. We can then find the median. Since there are ten values, we take the average of the 5th and 6th values to get 29.5. We find the lower quartile by taking the median of the data smaller than the median. Since there are five values, we take the 3rd value, which is 27. We find the upper quartile by taking the median of the data larger than the overall median, which is 32. Finally, we note our minimum and maximum, which are simply the smallest and largest values in the set: 26 and 35, respectively. Now we can create our box plot:

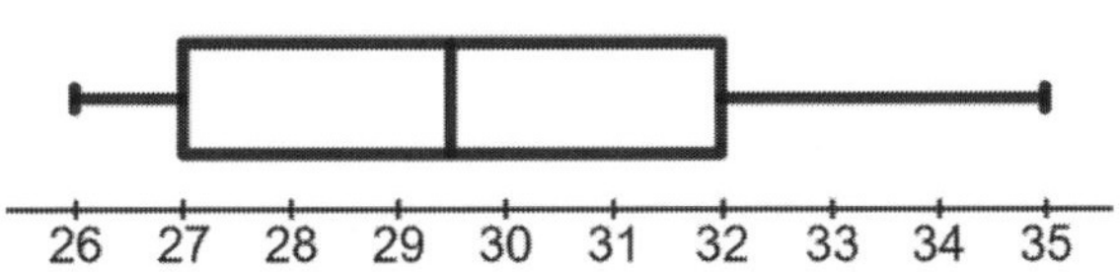

This plot is fairly "long" on the right whisker, showing one or more unusually high values (but not quite outliers). The other quartiles are similar in length, showing a fairly even distribution of data.

Interquartile Range

The **interquartile range, or IQR**, is the difference between the upper and lower quartiles. It measures how the data is dispersed: a high IQR means that the data is more spread out, while a low IQR means that the data is clustered more tightly around the median. To find the IQR, subtract the lower quartile value (Q_1) from the upper quartile value (Q_3).

EXAMPLE

To find the upper and lower quartiles, we first find the median and then take the median of all values above it and all values below it. In the following data set (16, 18, 13, 24, 16, 51, 32, 21, 27, 39), we first rearrange the values in numerical order: 13, 16, 16, 18, 21, 24, 27, 32, 39, 51. There are 10 values, so the median is the average of the 5th and 6th: $\frac{21+24}{2} = \frac{45}{2} = 22.5$. We do not actually need this value to find the upper and lower quartiles. We look at the set of numbers below the median: 13, 16, 16, 18, 21. There are five values, so the 3rd is the median (16), or the value of the lower quartile (Q_1). Then we look at the numbers above the median: 24, 27, 32, 39, 51. Again there are five values, so the 3rd is the median (32), or the value of the upper quartile (Q_3). We find the IQR by subtracting Q_1 from Q_3: $32 - 16 = 16$.

68-95-99.7 RULE

The **68–95–99.7 rule** describes how a normal distribution of data should appear when compared to the mean. This is also a description of a normal bell curve. According to this rule, 68 percent of the data values in a normally distributed set should fall within one standard deviation of the mean (34 percent above and 34 percent below the mean), 95 percent of the data values should fall within two standard deviations of the mean (47.5 percent above and 47.5 percent below the mean), and 99.7 percent of the data values should fall within three standard deviations of the mean, again, equally distributed on either side of the mean. This means that only 0.3 percent of all data values should fall more than three standard deviations from the mean. On the graph below, the normal curve is centered on the y-axis. The x-axis labels are how many standard deviations away from the center you are. Therefore, it is easy to see how the 68-95-99.7 rule can apply.

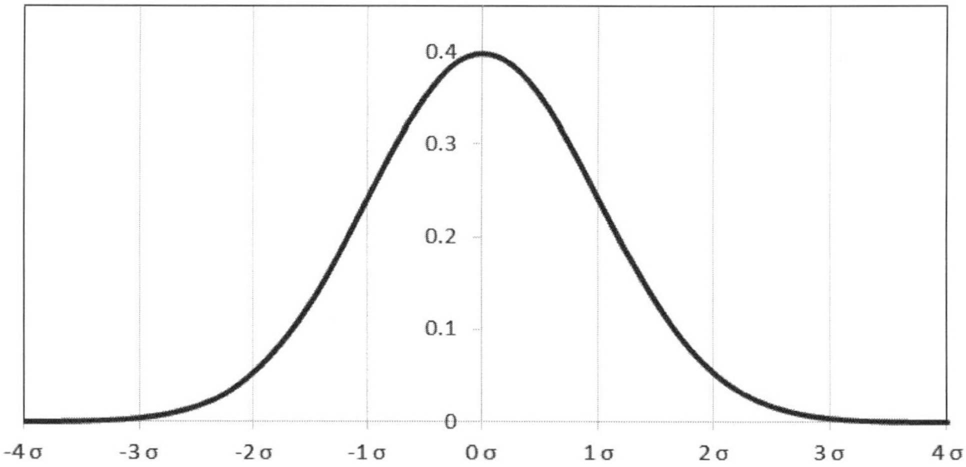

Chapter Quiz

Ready to see how well you retained what you just read? Scan the QR code to go directly to the chapter quiz interface for this study guide. If you're using a computer, simply visit the online resources page at **mometrix.com/resources719/afct** and click the Chapter Quizzes link.

Electronics Information

Circuits

Charge & Current

Charge is a physical property of protons (+1, positive charge), neutrons (0, neutral), and **electrons** (−1, negative charge), which together make up atoms. Like charges repel each other (positive and positive or negative and negative), and opposite charges attract (negative and positive). **Net charge** can be found by adding up the protons and electrons that make up an atom or molecule.

Electric **current** is the net rate of flow of charge (electrons) past a specific point, as in a wire or circuit. Current (represented by a capital I in equations) is measured in Amperes or Amps (A). An Ampere is equal to roughly 6.24×10^{18} electrons/second. Ammeters are tools that can be used to measure current.

Electron flow theory states that electrons (e^-) flow from the negative terminal to the positive terminal. **Electricity** is the form of energy that exists statically (potential energy) with an accumulation of protons or electrons or dynamically with their movement (current).

Ohm's Law & Circuit Components

Voltage (V in equations) is the electric potential energy per unit charge between two points which causes current. It is measured in volts, can be generated by batteries or generators, and can be measured by a **voltmeter**.

Resistance (R in equations) is a material's ability to resist current; it is measured in Ohms which are represented by the Greek letter Ω (omega). **Resistors** are electrical components designed to resist current in a **circuit** (a closed loop through which electrons can flow). Resistance can be measured with a tool called an **Ohmmeter**; it can also be determined for various materials using the following equation because resistance increases with greater material length (L) and resistivity (ρ) and decreases with a greater cross-sectional area. Resistivity (ρ) is the physical property of resistance of different materials and is usually given (example: aluminum or silver).

$$R = \frac{\rho L}{A}$$

Ohm's law describes the relationship between current (I), voltage (V), and resistance (R) in a circuit and can be written in the following ways:

$$V = I \times R \qquad I = \frac{V}{R}$$

As voltage increases or as resistance decreases, current increases.

Example: Find the current through a 6 Ω resistor if the voltmeter reads 12 V across the resistor.

$$I = \frac{V}{R}$$
$$I = \frac{12\,V}{6\,\Omega}$$
$$I = 2\,A$$

Series Circuits

A **series circuit** is a loop through which charge can flow along only one path. Resistance of resistors (labeled R_n) lined up in series is additive, so $R_{total} = R_1 + R_2 + R_3 + \cdots$ for all resistors in that series. Current (I) is consistent in all locations throughout a closed series circuit, so $I_{battery} = I_{R_1} = I_{R_2} = I_{R_3} = \cdots$, regardless of the number of elements in the series. Charge at the positive terminal of the battery experiences a **voltage drop** (ΔV), or loss of potential energy, as it passes through each resistor, such that its voltage will be zero at the negative terminal of the battery. Therefore, $\Delta V_{battery} = \Delta V_1 + \Delta V_2 + \Delta V_3 + \cdots$, where each ΔV_n represents the voltage drop across each resistor in series.

Problem Solving with Series Circuits

Using the labelled diagram of a series circuit, solve the following problems:

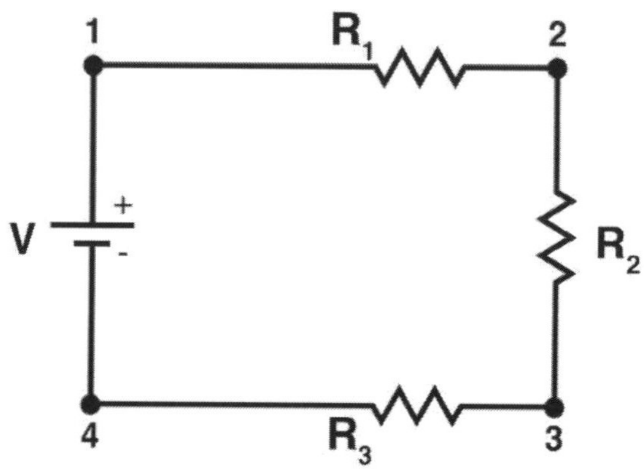

V = Voltage source (battery)

R = Resistor

Example 1: If each resistor is 3 Ω and the battery is 9 V, what is the current at each of the indicated corners?

Step 1:	Step 2:	Step 3:
Given: $R_1 = R_2 = R_3 = 3\ \Omega$ Equation: $R_{total} = R_1 + R_2 + R_3$ Solve: $R_{total} = 3\ \Omega + 3\ \Omega + 3\ \Omega = 9\ \Omega$	Given: $V_{battery} = 9\text{ V}$ Equation: $I = \frac{V}{R}$ Solve: $I_{battery} = \frac{9\text{ V}}{9\ \Omega} = 1\text{ A}$	Because current is the same throughout the circuit, current at each corner is the same: $I_{total} = I_1 = I_2 = I_3 = I_4 = 1\ A$

Example 2: If the current at point 3 is 4 Amps, and each resistor is 1 Ω, what is the battery voltage?

Step 1:	Step 2:	Step 3:
Given: $I_3 = 4\text{ A}$ The circuit is in series so current is the same throughout: $I_{total} = 4\text{ A}$	Given: $R_1 = R_2 = R_3 = 1\ \Omega$ Equation: $R_{total} = R_1 + R_2 + R_3$ Solve: $R_{total} = 1\ \Omega + 1\ \Omega + 1\ \Omega = 3\ \Omega$	Equation: $V_{total} = I_{total}(R_{total})$ Solve: $V_{total} = (4\text{ A})(3\ \Omega) = 12\text{ V}$

Parallel Circuits

Parallel circuits provide multiple pathways for current to follow, which adjusts the way that current, voltage, and resistance interact when compared to series circuits. Because current (I) can follow multiple pathways, it is divided among those pathways at each branch, so $I_{total} = I_1 + I_2 + I_3 + \cdots$, where 1, 2, and 3 represent each unique branch. In this example, there are 3.

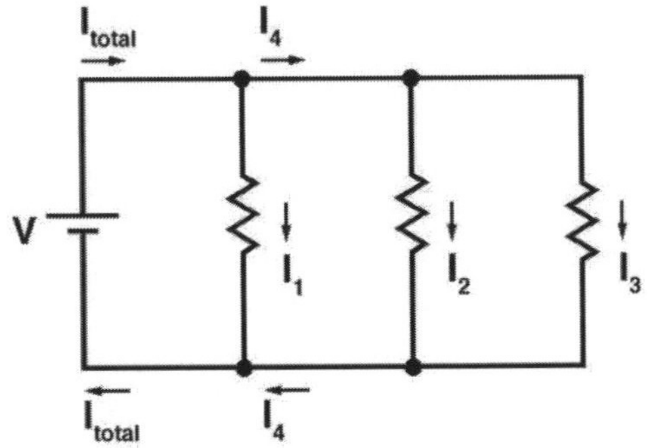

Equivalent resistance (R_{eq}) is the amount of resistance in a parallel circuit, represented as if there was only one resistor in series. All of the resistors in parallel can be simplified using the following equation:

$$\frac{1}{R_{eq}} = \frac{1}{R_1} + \frac{1}{R_2} + \frac{1}{R_3}$$

Because a charge will only pass through one resistor in the parallel circuit and not all three, the voltage drop across each resistor will be the same as that of the battery. Therefore, voltage drops for parallel circuits follow this rule:

$$\Delta V_{battery} = \Delta V_1 = \Delta V_2 = \Delta V_3 = \cdots$$

Note: If multiple resistors exist on a branch of a parallel circuit, they are in series and should be added together ($R_{total} = R_1 + R_2 + R_3 + \cdots$) before dealing with them as part of a parallel circuit.

Problem Solving with Parallel Circuits

Using the labelled diagram of a parallel circuit, solve the following problems:

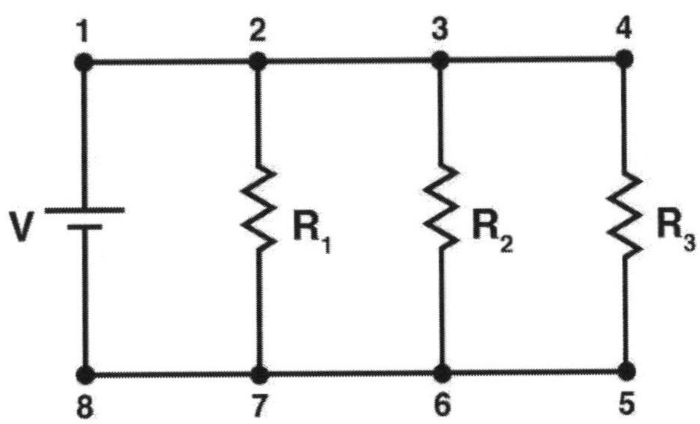

Example 1: If each resistor is 3 Ω and the battery is 9 V, what is the current at each of the indicated points (1-8) and each resistor?

Step 1:
Given: $R_1 = R_2 = R_3 = 3\ \Omega$
Equation: $\frac{1}{R_{eq}} = \frac{1}{R_1} + \frac{1}{R_2} + \frac{1}{R_3}$
Solve: $\frac{1}{R_{eq}} = \frac{1}{3\ \Omega} + \frac{1}{3\ \Omega} + \frac{1}{3\ \Omega}$

$$\frac{1}{R_{eq}} = \frac{3}{3\ \Omega}$$

$$R_{eq} = 1\ \Omega$$

Step 2:
Given: $V_{batt} = 9\text{ V}$
Equation: $I_{total} = \frac{V_{batt}}{R_{eq}}$
Solve: $I_{total} = \frac{9\text{ V}}{1\ \Omega} = 9\text{ A}$

Step 3:
Equation: $\Delta V_n = I_{R_n}(R_n)$
Solve: $I_{R_1} = \frac{9\text{ V}}{3\ \Omega} = 3\ A$
Current is the same for each branch in this example because $R_1 = R_2 = R_3 = 3\ \Omega$

Using this information and the additive properties of current in parallel circuits, the current through the following points and resistors is:

$$I_1 = I_2 = I_7 = I_8 = I_{total} = 9\text{ A}$$

$$I_3 = I_6 = 6\text{ A}$$

$$I_4 = I_5 = 3\text{ A}$$

$$I_{R_1} = I_{R_2} = I_{R_3} = 3\text{ A}$$

Example 2: If the current at point 4 is 4 Amps, and $R_1 = 3\ \Omega$; $R_2 = 2\ \Omega$; $R_3 = 6\ \Omega$, what is the total current?

Step 1:
Given: $R_3 = 6\ \Omega$; $I_4 = I_{R_3} = 4\ A$
Equation: $\Delta V_3 = I_{R_3}(R_3)$
Solve: $\Delta V_3 = (4\text{ A})(6\ \Omega) = 24\text{ V}$

Step 2:
Given: $R_1 = 3\ \Omega$; $R_2 = 2\ \Omega$
Equation: $I_n = \frac{V}{R_n}$
Solve: $I_1 = \frac{24\text{ V}}{3\ \Omega} = 8\text{ A}$

$$I_2 = \frac{24\text{ V}}{2\ \Omega} = 12\text{ A}$$

Step 3:
Equation: $I_{total} = I_1 + I_2 + I_3$
Solve: $I_{total} = 8\text{ A} + 12\text{ A} + 4\text{ A}$

$$I_{total} = 24\text{ A}$$

Electrical Power

Electrical power (P) is the rate energy is produced or absorbed in a circuit. For example, a light bulb absorbs electrical energy and converts it to light energy. Measured in Watts (W), it can be calculated with the formulas:

$$P = I \times V \qquad P = I^2 \times R \qquad P = \frac{V^2}{R}$$

For example, a 48 W lightbulb in a series circuit powered by a 24 V battery (with no other circuit components) would have a 2 A current and 12 Ω resistance. Using these numbers, practice with the equations.

Note: Horsepower (hp), used when electric power is used for motion, uses the following conversion to Watts: 1 hp = 746 W.

Structure of Electrical and Electronic Systems

AC vs. DC

In the previous examples, the circuits utilized **direct current** (DC), which is when current flows in only one direction, and voltage and current are constant. Direct current is supplied by batteries and is used in cell phones, ships, and planes. **Alternating current** (AC), in which current periodically reverses direction, can be produced using generators and is used for land-based applications (including in homes) because less power is lost when electricity travels long distances. In the United States, AC electricity is supplied most commonly at 120 V and 240 V.

Ground

Grounding is the process of neutralizing the charge of an object by removal of excess electrons to or donation of additional electrons by a much larger object (example: the earth). This ground or large object can seemingly infinitely donate or accept electrons without mathematically significant changes to its net voltage. Examples of grounds include lighting rods and the round component of a three-pronged plug, as used for home appliances. Current shouldn't usually flow through air, but lightning is the visible current that results when charge builds up in clouds; lightning rods provide a safe, low-resistance ground so the high-voltage current is less likely to be destructive. The round component of three-pronged plugs serves as one of the residential applications of this concept.

Electric and Electronic Components

Semiconductors

Resistivity is the physical property of resistance of different materials: metals, which easily conduct electricity, have low resistivity; insulators have high resistivity; and the resistivity of **semiconductors** falls in between (example: Silicon (Si). **Doping** is the process of mixing different semiconductor atoms in order to control conductivity of the material. **N-type semiconductors** have an excess of electrons as a result of the doping process; when an electric field is applied, a negative pole forms due to the buildup of negatively charged electrons (example: silicon doped with antimony). **P-type semiconductors** have a shortage of electrons; when an electric field is applied, a positive pole forms (example: Silicon doped with boron).

Diodes

Diodes are a basic component of circuits, but they can't be described using Ohm's law; they operate as an electrical "valve", only allowing current to pass in one direction. This allows them to rectify alternating current by converting it to direct current, which is preferred or necessary for some applications. A common example is the light-emitting diode (LED) bulb, which emits light when powered more efficiently than regular light bulbs.

A p-n junction diode is formed by fusing a p-type semiconductor and an n-type semiconductor. It is considered a solid-state device because electricity flows through solid material rather than a vacuum tube. The p-region of the junction is positively charged and the n-region is negatively charged. Reverse bias occurs when the diode is connected such that the positive voltage is applied to the n-region; forward bias occurs when the positive voltage is applied to the p-region.

Transistors

A bipolar junction transistor, p-n-p or n-p-n, consists of two p-n junction diodes arranged back-to-back with three electrical leads or terminals: the emitter, the collector, and the base. Transistors are used to boost electrical signals or switch them on or off at high speeds. A large current flows from the emitter to the collector, and a smaller current entering through the base lead can be used to control the larger collector current.

Electricity and Magnetism

Capacitors

Capacitors store charge between two conductor components (example: parallel metal plates) with insulation (example: air) between them. Because they store charge between them, capacitors also oppose voltage change across the two plates. Direct current can charge a capacitor but cannot flow through it. **Capacitance** is the measure of a capacitor's ability to store charge between the two plates.

They are used in circuits and have many applications, including preventing computer memory loss during a short power failure and protecting sensitive components during power surges.

Inductors

When current passes through a wire coil, a magnetic field develops. An **inductor** is an electrical component made of a coil of wire that can store energy and opposes the rate of change of alternating current flowing through it; however, direct current passes through easily. They can be used as filters, sensors, motors, and transformers.

Inductance is the measure of ability of an inductor to resist changes in current. **Faraday's law of induction describes the ways voltage** or electromagnetic frequency can be generated by changing the magnetic environment in a coil of wire by moving a magnet within it, changing the external magnetic field of the magnet, or changing the area of the coil.

Transformers

Transformers are devices made of two or more coils of wire that use induction to transfer electricity between circuits. A **step-up transformer**'s input (primary) voltage is lower than its output (secondary) voltage; and a **step-down transformer**'s input voltage is higher than its output voltage. This allows for electricity to be to be generated safely at a lower voltage (example: 12 kV), passed through a step-up transformer for transport through power lines at high voltage (example: 400 kV), and passed through step-down transformers for distribution and use (example: 240 V residential use).

Motors and Generators

Motors use electromagnetic induction to convert electrical energy (electricity) to mechanical energy (motion). In a **DC motor**, torque is produced by magnetic force, which results from current passing through coil located in a magnetic field. They have been around for more than 100 years and are simple, inexpensive, and easy to maintain. In **AC (synchronous) motors**, torque is produced the same way as in DC motors, but much higher current is required, and they are inefficient. **Induction (asynchronous) motors** are more common, and they rotate a magnetic field in order to induce alternating current.

Generators use electromagnetic induction to convert mechanical energy to electrical energy. **AC generators** mechanically turn a coil in a magnetic field to produce voltage output and induce alternating current.

Chapter Quiz

Ready to see how well you retained what you just read? Scan the QR code to go directly to the chapter quiz interface for this study guide. If you're using a computer, simply visit the online resources page at **mometrix.com/resources719/afct** and click the Chapter Quizzes link.

Auto Information

The Internal Combustion Engine Systems

Internal Combustion Engines

Combustion is the chemical reaction between fuel and air to release energy; spark ignition (SI)/gasoline **internal combustion engines** ignite gasoline (or a gasoline mixture) and air with a spark to do work. Diesel engines are also internal combustion engines, but they utilize compression ignition (CI) to ignite diesel, rather than a spark for gasoline. Core engine components are housed in the **engine block**.

Most gasoline engines operate with reciprocating pistons in cylinders. They use either a four-stroke or a two-stroke cycle; most automobiles in the United States utilize the four-stroke cycle. Four piston strokes make up the four-stroke cycle: intake, compression, power, and exhaust. In one cycle, the piston moves down and back up twice.

Electrical System

When a driver turns a key (or pushes a button) to start a car, an electrical circuit is completed. Electricity runs from the **battery** to the **starter motor (starter)**, which turns the crankshaft. In turn, the engine uses a pully system to turn the **alternator**, which recharges the battery and produces most of the electricity to the vehicle while it runs. The **solenoid** acts as a heavy-duty relay between the battery and the starter motor.

The electrical system also simultaneously fires up the fuel pump (in newer cars) and spark plugs (via a coil).

Common Electrical Problems

If a car won't start when the key is turned, this could be the result of a dead battery, faulty battery connections, or a problem with the starter motor or solenoid. If the alternator is bad, this may lead to a battery without a charge or headlights that are dim at low engine speeds.

Battery connections can be checked and improved by cleaning off corrosion with a wire brush and applying specialized grease to prevent further corrosion. A dead battery can be jumped to attempt to get the car running and help troubleshoot electrical problems. If it won't jump start, the problem might be with the starter; if it will start but won't stay running, the problem could be with the battery; if it will start and stays running, the problem could be with the alternator, or a light might have been left on in the vehicle.

Fuel System

When a gasoline car is started, the electrical system starts the fuel system, which stores and delivers fuel (gasoline or gasoline mixture, in this case) to the engine. In newer cars, the **fuel pump** is housed in the **fuel tank**. **Fuel filters** protect fuel injectors or carburetors by ensuring clean fuel, and they can be found on either side of the fuel pump. In newer cars, computer-controlled **fuel injectors** atomize fuel into the cylinder (part of the engine) through a tiny electric valve in order to feed the combustion process; the computerization allows for better fuel economy and lower emissions. Older vehicles use **carburetors**, which mix fuel and air without a computer.

Common Fuel System Problems

Fuel filters can clog and should be replaced at regular intervals. Clogged filters can prevent the vehicle from starting or cause it to sputter when traveling at high speed. Faulty fuel pumps can also prevent the car from starting; this could be an electrical problem or a problem with the pump itself due to regular wear-and-tear, contamination, or overheating. Fuel injectors can also clog, even with regular changing of the fuel filter. Signs of dirty or clogged injectors include increased emissions, decreased fuel economy, and poor idling and performance.

Ignition System

When a gasoline car is started, the electrical system starts the ignition system. **Ignition** is the generation of a spark or heating of an electrode to initiate combustion of fuel and air. The battery provides low voltage to a **coil**, which acts as a transformer and electromagnetically converts it to high voltage for use by the corresponding spark plug. **Spark plugs** force electricity to jump between electrodes across a gap, creating a spark. The alternator continues to produce electricity while the car is running, which allows the spark plugs to continue firing. There is one spark plug per cylinder in a spark-ignition internal combustion engine.

Common Ignition Problems

One of the most common ignition problems is spark plug fouling, which occurs when carbon builds up at the ignition point; it will cause engine misfiring and increased carbon emissions. Driving at highway speeds is good for spark plugs because the increased temperature of the engine helps burn off the excess fuel or ash. Spark plug fouling is more common with prolonged idling and city driving because the engine doesn't get as hot.

Common signs of faulty ignition coils include backfiring as a result of excess fuel in the combustion chamber, poor fuel economy, vibration when idling, and stalling.

Engine System

Piston and Cylinder

Most gasoline engines utilize a reciprocating piston and cylinder system for combustion, which functions to combust fuel (in this case, gasoline) and air. **Pistons**, together with their **rings**, act as plungers to take in and compress gas within the **cylinder**. Pistons are connected to the crankshaft via a hinged **connecting rod**. The **combustion chamber** is the space created by a piston where fuel and air mix and are ignited by the spark plug. Fuel delivery occurs by either a **fuel injector** or a **carburetor**.

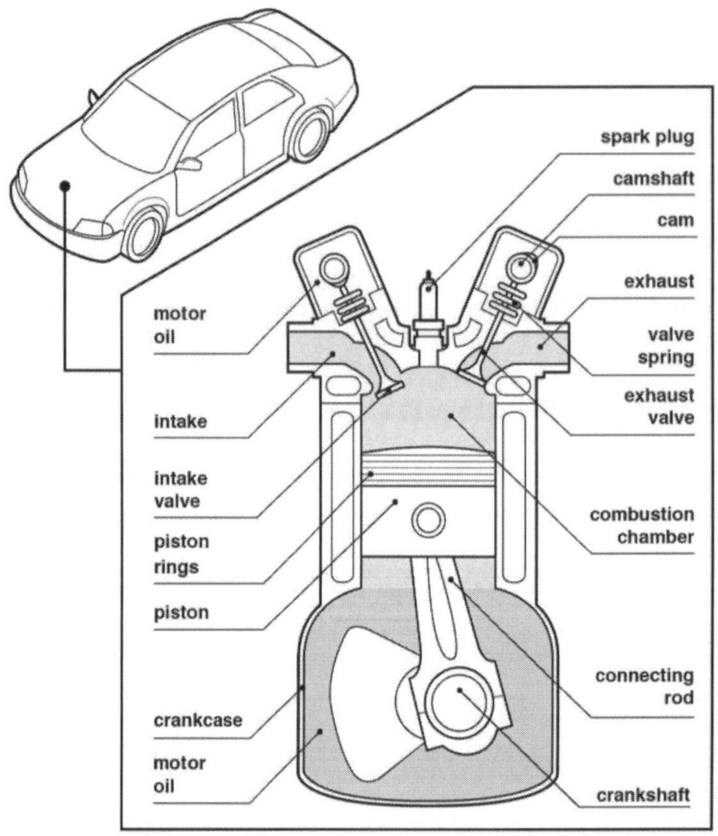

ENGINE BLOCK

Once the gasoline vehicle is started, the electrical, fuel, and ignition systems converge in the engine. The electrical system starts turning the crankshaft, fuel injectors atomize gasoline pre-combustion, and spark plugs create a spark.

The valvetrain coordinates the opening and closing of valves so that air-fuel entry and exhaust release are timed properly. The **camshaft** is a rotating shaft surrounded by oil with **cams** (specially shaped nodes) that depress or allow the release of the intake and exhaust valves as they rotate with the shaft. **Intake valves** regulate air-fuel mixture entry into the combustion chamber. **Exhaust valves** release gas byproducts of combustion to the exhaust manifold.

The **crankcase** is full of oil and houses the crankshaft and connecting rods. Each piston is hinged to a **connecting rod**, which is hinged to the crankshaft. The **crankshaft** rotates by combined, alternating motion of the pistons and their connecting rods. As it rotates, the crankshaft drives the camshaft by way of a **timing belt** or chain and gears.

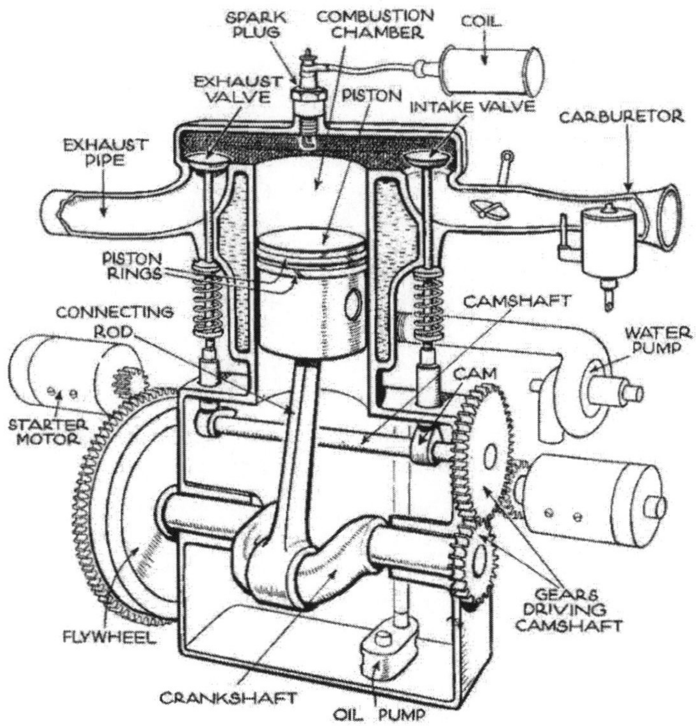

Common Engine Problems

Problems with the engine and the process of combustion can occur within the piston and cylinder unit or with the components that coordinate their functions. A broken or faulty timing belt will likely result in a ticking noise from the engine and will cause the vehicle to rough-idle or misfire. It can also lead to a decrease in oil pressure, smoke coming from the engine, or broken pistons or valves. Crankshaft problems will lead to difficulty starting the vehicle or intermittent stalling. Camshaft problems may cause rough idling, frequent stalling, poor fuel economy, slow accelerations, and difficulty starting. If the piston rings fail, oil will leak into the combustion chamber, causing the engine to smoke. Backfiring occurs when combustion takes place outside of the cylinders and can be the result of bad engine timing or improper fuel-air mixture ratios.

Exhaust System

The **exhaust system** transports gas products (exhaust) from the combustion process away from the engine and the vehicle. Exhaust from the combustion chamber is released by the exhaust valve towards the **exhaust manifold**, which collects gas byproducts from each cylinder and helps with noise control. Through the exhaust pipe, gas travels to the **catalytic converter**, which filters out pollutants and converts them to water vapor and carbon dioxide. From the catalytic converter, exhaust travels through the exhaust pipe to the **muffler**, which further reduces noise. From the muffler, the **tail pipe** releases gas away from the vehicle.

Common Exhaust Problems

Consistently short trips of less than 15 miles, such as driving in town without getting on the highway, don't allow the water condensed in the exhaust system to vaporize and escape, which can cause corrosion and rusting of the exhaust system.

If there is a faulty gasket, fluids such as coolant or oil can leak from the engine and clog the catalytic converter, causing poor engine performance or preventing it from running properly. Excessive heat or unused fuel coming off the engine can cause the catalytic converter to overheat. Other symptoms of catalytic converter trouble include reduced acceleration, dark exhaust smoke, more heat than usual under the vehicle, or exhaust that smells like sulfur.

LUBRICATION SYSTEM

Motor oil is used to prevent friction and corrosion within the engine. The **oil pan** is below the engine block and holds oil for pressurized distribution by the **oil pump** through the **oil galleries**, specialized channels throughout the engine. An **oil filter** helps keep the oil free of debris so that the moving parts in the engine don't get clogged. In addition to the galleries, the camshaft and the crankshaft are lubricated by motor oil; piston rings keep oil below the piston head and out of the combustion chamber.

COMMON LUBRICATION PROBLEMS

Besides friction reduction, oil also keeps the engine parts clean, and vehicles should have the oil and oil filter changed regularly to prevent overheating and wearing out of the engine. Motor oil is labelled with viscosity ratings at both low temperatures (example: 5W or 10W) and high temperatures (SAE 30 or SAE 40) so that it will be thin enough to be functional when it is very cold outside and thick enough when the engine is very hot. **Synthetic motor oil** is manufactured and is more consistent and will last longer than conventional motor oil.

COOLING SYSTEM

While running, the average engine temperature is 200 °F; the walls of the cylinders are between 350 °F and 600 °F, and the combustion chamber is roughly 3,000 °F. The cooling system helps keep the engine running within its ideal temperature range without overheating. **Coolant**, commonly made up of half antifreeze and half water, prevents overheating by circulating through **channels** throughout the engine by way of the **water pump**. The **thermostat** helps control engine temperature by sending coolant either to the engine or to the radiator if it needs to be cooled further. The **radiator** is a series of thin channels that allow air to remove heat from the coolant, aided by the **cooling fan**.

COMMON COOLING PROBLEMS

Problems with the cooling system can lead to engine overheating and damage. Broken or cracked coolant or radiator hoses can allow coolant to leak. Coolant breaks down over time and should be replaced according to the schedule given by the vehicle manufacturer. A thermostat stuck open will cause the engine to run cold and result in bad gas mileage; a thermostat stuck closed will cause the engine to overheat. The water pump and radiator cap both maintain the correct pressure range of the coolant in the system; a problem with either will prevent proper temperature regulation and lead to overheating. A broken or faulty fan belt or cooling fan will prevent the pumping of air into the radiator; if the car overheats, both should be checked for proper function.

Chassis Systems

DRIVETRAIN SYSTEM

The **drivetrain** translates power from the engine in order to move the vehicle forward. The crankshaft is attached to the **flywheel**, which stores rotational energy from the engine and smooths the motion of the pistons. The **clutch** allows for disengaging and re-engaging of the transmission and the flywheel/engine so that stopping the motion of the wheels doesn't also stop the engine. The

transmission multiplies engine torque to allow for a wide range of vehicle speeds, as well as acceleration and deceleration; it consists of a series of gears, and more gears translate to better engine efficiency. Most modern transmissions are automatic, but they can also be manual or constant velocity (CV). The **differential** splits the torque of the engine to allow the inside and outside wheels to spin at different speeds, as when turning.

Drivetrain Configurations

Drivetrains power the turning of the wheels of the vehicle through the transmission and axles in the following configurations:

- **Rear-wheel drive (RWD)** is found in trucks and older cars, and the transmission delivers power to the rear axle via the **driveshaft**.
- **Front wheel drive (FWD)** is found in most modern economy or compact cars; the **transaxle** combines the functionality of the transmission, front axle, and differential into one component. The engine weight is over the drive wheels, which allows for better traction.
- **All wheel drive (AWD)** is in most newer cars and SUVs and powers both axles using a **transfer case**, which distributes the engine torque to both the front and rear axles.
- **Four-wheel drive (4WD)** utilizes a specialized transfer case to accommodate different driving conditions; **Two-wheel drive** (2WD) offers better gas mileage for city and highway driving; **four-wheel drive high** (4WD-HI) allows for intermediate torque for off-road driving at higher speeds; **four-wheel drive low** (4WD-LO) provides maximum torque for off-road driving at lower speeds.

Common Drivetrain System Problems

In a manual transmission, hard shifting or grinding may be the result of clashing gears and worn out synchronizers. Automatic transmissions also wear out, which leads to transmission slipping and poor shifting. Transmission fluid should also be changed and levels maintained to prevent gear slippage and shifting problems. The clutch can jam, which may cause violent vehicle shaking and overheating in the transmission. Transfer case problems can lead to difficulty shifting gears, grinding noises, or jumping in and out of four-wheel drive.

Suspension System

The suspension system allows for a smooth, comfortable ride when driving, prevents components from stress or vibrating loose, keeps the vehicle upright, and allows for pivoting when steering. **Springs**, installed between the chassis or frame and the axels, absorb the impact of the road on the vehicle; most vehicles use coil springs or layered leaf springs:

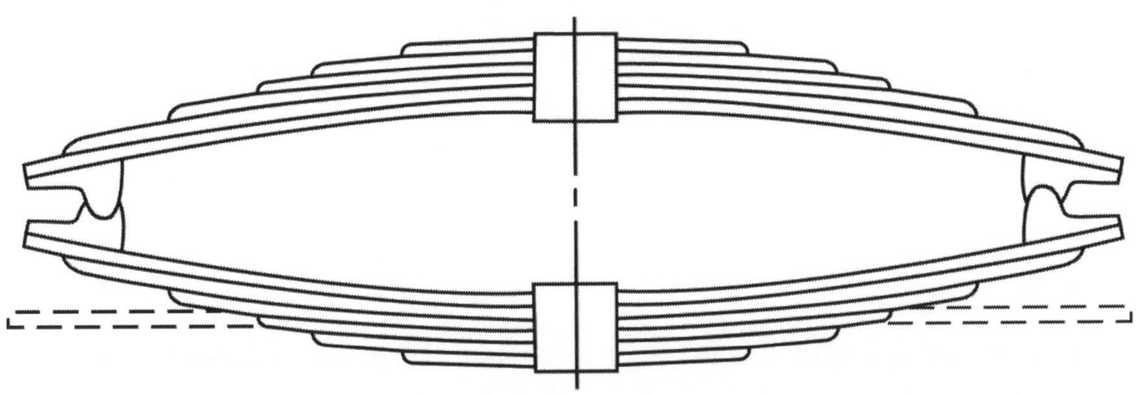

Shocks (shock absorbers or dampers) oppose the oscillating motion of the springs and dampen road vibration. **Struts** are a combination of springs and shocks. The **anti-roll bar** or **sway bar** keeps the vehicle from rolling over when turning and allows for better handling. The **spindles**, which should be parallel to the ground, are the center point of each wheel that connects to the upper and lower control arms via a sealed and greased ball joint. **Control arms** connect the suspension system to the frame of the vehicle through **bushings**, which are insulated joint linings that protect the jointed components from vibration or wear.

Common Suspension Problems

Worn shocks and struts can cause excessive bumping and bouncing, and oil leaking from either is a sign of wear. The bushings of the sway bar can also wear out, signaled by thumping or knocking when turning or taking bumps. Pickup trucks should normally sit with their bed slightly higher than the body of the truck to allow for heavy loads; if it sits level (without modifications), it could be a sign of a faulty spring. The same is true if one corner of the vehicle sits lower than the rest while on level ground.

Steering System

The steering system directs the vehicle while driving and minimizes the force required for such movement. The steering system engages either the modern, highly precise **rack-and-pinion system** or the older, less precise **steering-box system** to translate the turning of the **steering wheel** via small gears to the front wheels. **Power steering** supplies pressurized engine oil from a pump to the steering rack or steering box so that steering is easier and more responsive.

Car alignment, though it involves the suspension system, impacts vehicle steering; proper alignment is required for the vehicle to continue to travel straight when the steering wheel is temporarily released.

Common Steering Problems

Power steering fluid sometimes gets low and needs to be refilled. However, hoses associated with the steering system, like all vehicle hoses, can wear and crack over time and lead to leaking power steering fluid, requiring replacement. Low or leaking power steering fluid, a problem with the power steering pump, and even some suspension problems, such as worn control arm bushings, can make it difficult to steer the vehicle. Power steering problems can also cause a grinding or squealing noise when turning. Improper alignment can also cause passive steering problems. For example, when the steering wheel is temporarily released, the vehicle will pull to one side.

Brake System

The brake system is vital for motorist safety as it allows for slowing and stopping, even at high speeds. When the **brake pedal** is depressed, **brake fluid** is pushed from the **master cylinder** through the brake lines to each wheel's **brake caliper**. The fluid pressure causes friction, which forces the wheels to stop turning.

Most vehicles have **disc brakes** on the front wheels, and some have them on the rear wheels as well. When the brake fluid flows through the brake lines, it depresses a piston in the brake caliper, squeezing the inner and outer **brake pads**, which are materially hard and designed to withstand heat and friction. Brake pads squeeze against the cast iron **disc rotor**, which is held to the wheel at the wheel hub.

Vehicles that do not have disc brakes on the rear tires use **drum brakes**. The **wheel cylinder** forces the paired **brake shoes** against the inside walls of the bowl-shaped, cast iron **drum**.

Common Brake Problems

Brake pads encounter lots of friction, so they wear out and often need to be replaced; symptoms of this include grinding, squealing, and slow stopping when the brake pedal is applied. Rotors also encounter a lot of friction and can warp. If the vehicle experiences pulsing when slowing or stopping, it might be due to warped rotors. Sponginess or softness when the brake pedal is applied could signal a problem with the master cylinder or low brake fluid levels; this requires immediate attention. If the car pulls to one side when braking, the brake calipers might not be applying equal pressure to all the tires. A stuck brake caliper or engaged parking brake while driving can lead to overheating, will likely cause a sharp odor, and should also be addressed immediately.

Chapter Quiz

Ready to see how well you retained what you just read? Scan the QR code to go directly to the chapter quiz interface for this study guide. If you're using a computer, simply visit the online resources page at **mometrix.com/resources719/afct** and click the Chapter Quizzes link.

Shop Information

Measuring Tools

Rulers & Tape Measures

A **ruler** is a device with a straight edge used to measure length, generally in both centimeters (cm) and inches (in); these are generally subdivided into millimeters and sixteenths, respectively. A standard length for rulers is 12 inches (30 cm).

A **tape measure** is a flexible, often retractable, ruler used to measure length. Standard tape measures are measured in centimeters (with millimeter increments) on one edge of the tape and inches (with quarter-, eighth-, and sixteenth-inch increments) on the other. Some tape measures may include thirty-second-inch or even smaller increments, which are required for more detailed projects.

Calipers

Calipers are precise measuring devices with sliding jaws used to measure two-dimensional **inside measurements** (an empty distance between two points) and **outside measurements** (the width or thickness of an object). Calipers can be digital or analog; analog calipers measure relatively precisely using a vernier (a graduated, sliding measuring device) or a dial (using a rack and pinion). Both calipers pictured have jaws for inside and outside measurements. The bases of calipers also frequently have a pin that can measure offsets, such as the depth of holes.

Calipers are used widely in mechanical engineering, woodworking, machining, and metalworking.

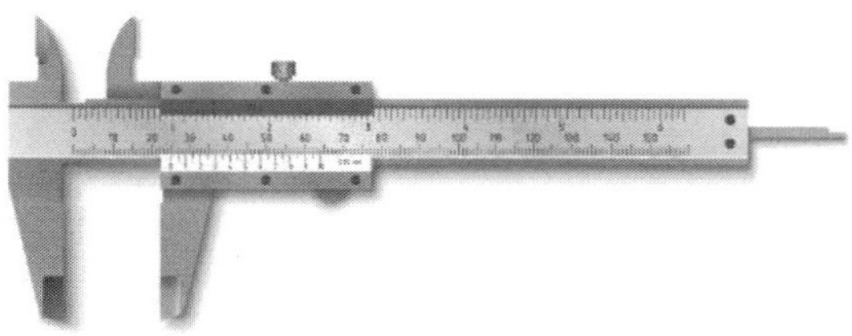

Vernier Caliper

Dial Caliper

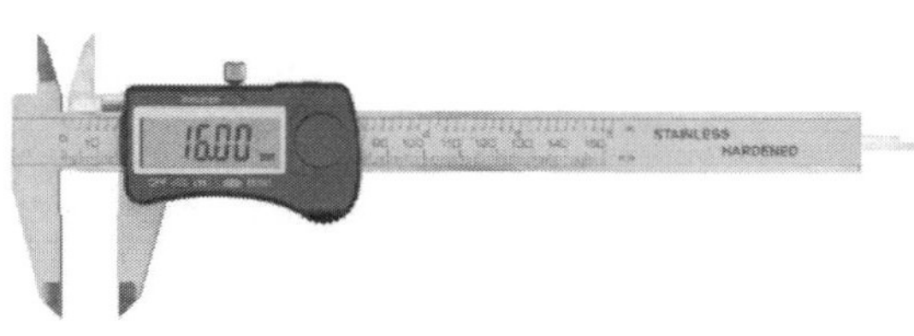

Digital Caliper

MICROMETERS

A type of caliper, **micrometers** are jawed devices used to measure the distance between two points. However, micrometers are much more precise, specialized, and difficult to use; they are most commonly used in machining applications and mechanical engineering. Micrometers can measure to 1/20,000 of an inch, which makes them sensitive to even temperature, and they must be handled with skill and caution. Like calipers, they can measure inside and outside measurements, but with their specialized jaws, they can be used for other, more difficult, measurements as well. Ball micrometers measure the thickness of curved parts, and offset centerline micrometers accurately measure the distance between the center of two holes.

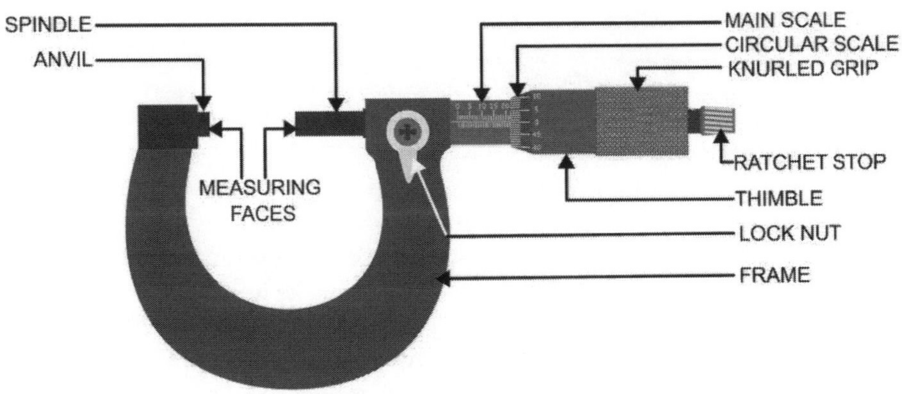

Simple outside micrometer

LEVELS

Levels are used to determine if an object's surface is horizontal (level; 0°), vertical (plumb; 90°), or occasionally at 45°relative to the Earth's gravitational pull, though this does not necessarily mean relative to the ground in the immediate area. There are several different types of levels:

- **Spirit or bubble level**: A tool containing or consisting of a small, clear tube filled with alcohol or another liquid and a small air bubble. The tube is very slightly bowed so that when the level is perfectly horizontal, the bubble will be in the middle; the less bow the tube has, the more accurate the level will be.
- **Laser level:** A tool utilizing a laser or series of lasers to establish a horizontal plane on the desired surface.
- **Optical level**: A tool used by builders to establish grade (a level base or specific slope) across a large area, such as for foundations of buildings.

- **Water level**: Clear, flexible tubing filled with water used to create a horizontal line between distant objects (such as fence posts) or a large surface (such as a deck). When both ends are held steady and upright, the water lines in each tube will be in line with one another horizontally.

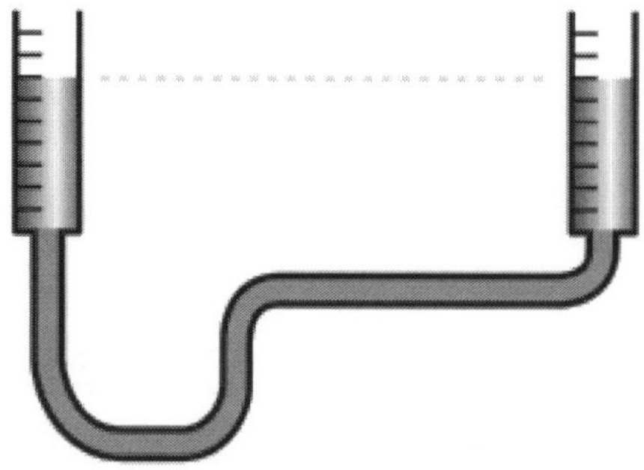

Diagram of water level

Plumb Bob

A **plumb bob** is a tool used to establish a vertical (plumb; 90°) reference line relative to the earth's surface, though this does not necessarily mean the ground in the immediate area. Laser plumb bobs work much like laser levels, but the simpler plumb bob, a weight with a point on the bottom hung from a string, can also be used to find the plumb-line or vertical reference line. To use the plumb bob, attach the end of the string to the upper point being measured. For example, tie the end of the string to a long nail at the top of a fence post. To be sure the fence post is upright, let the plumb bob swing unhindered until still. The bottom tip of the bob will hang perfectly vertically below the knot in the string above, and the line will be parallel to the fence post if it is plumb.

Squares

Squares consist of two straight edges set at 90° to each other and are used by carpenters, builders, and machinists, among others, to check for exact right (90°) angles. Perfect right angles are essential to the proper function of doors and windows and the soundness of buildings and other structures, among other uses. There are several different types of squares, depending on the project at hand. For example:

- **Speed square**: A small, right triangle-shaped tool that can be used to easily laying out 90° and 45° cuts. Speed squares usually have a pivot point and a scale for laying out other angles. Speed squares are commonly used for guiding saw cuts, marking angles, and squaring lines. Speed squares are often made of either aluminum or steel and come in 4", 6", and 12" sizes, depending on the purpose.
- **Framing** or **steel square**: An L-shaped square with graduated edges used for cutting stair stringers and laying out rafters. Framing squares come in a variety of sizes, but are most commonly 16" by 24".
- **Combination square**: A tool consisting of a ruler and interchangeable, sliding heads used most commonly in woodworking, stonemasonry, and metalworking. The square or standard head is the most common and is used to check 90° and 45° angles. Combination squares can be set to specific lengths to help lay out consistent markings on multiple pieces. Combination squares also frequently include a small bubble level and a small awl for scratching marks on wood.

- **Drywall square** or **T-Square**: Used for marking and cutting drywall for hanging, this T-shaped tool has graduated edges, the longest of which is 48 inches in order to accommodate squaring a standard sheet of drywall.
- **Engineer's Square:** A simple square that is only set to 90°. The main purpose of an engineer's square is that they are usually set to an extremely high degree of precision and are used for setting up other tools.
- **Bevel square, bevel gauge,** or **T-bevel:** A bevel square is a body that had an adjustable blade that can be set to any angle. These are not designed to be set to any particular angle and must be paired with a protractor to set a particular angle.

Striking Tools and Related Tasks

Striking tools are any tool used to hit another object to exert force. The most common term for a striking tool is a hammer, but other types include mallets and mauls. All of these are designed to hit other objects to exert force on them. **Hammers** are generally for driving nails and breaking objects. Hammers are used when the user is not concerned with protecting the object that is hit. A **mallet** is like a hammer, but generally has a soft or non-marring face so that it can exert force without harming the object it hits, such as when hitting a chisel. **Mauls** are large, heavy hammers that are used for driving wedges or posts and are also meant to be non-marring. Some specific types of hammers and mallets include:

- **Claw hammer**: Highly versatile, this hammer has a curved claw on the back side of the weighted head used for prying. This is very common for use with nail construction.
- **Ball-peen hammer**: A hammer with a rounded head on one side, made to peen, or spread, metal, such as on rivets.
- **Sledge hammer**: These typically have medium to long handles and heavy, hard heads. These are designed for driving stakes, breaking masonry, and other demolition tasks requiring heavy blows. (Note that sledge hammers are not the best implement for driving metal wedges because do so presents a safety risk. When hitting metal on metal, sharp pieces can fly off of the wedge and cause lacerations or eye injuries.)
- **Rubber mallet**: Commonly used in woodworking and upholstery, the rubber head delivers more insulated force so as not to damage the work surface.
- **Dead-blow mallet:** A mallet with loose weights inside that applies heavy force gently. The impact force of a dead-blow mallet happens inside the mallet instead of on the surface of the object that is hit, protecting the object.
- **Air hammer**: A pneumatic tool that applies force with the power of compressed air.
- **Nail gun**: Drives nails, powered most commonly by electricity or an air compressor.

Chisels

A **chisel** is a hand tool commonly used in woodworking and in other trades. Woodworking and masonry chisels look and work differently. Woodworking chisels have a flat back and a bevel on one side of the tip that produces the cutting angle. Chisels can be used for a variety of tasks, such as flush paring, chopping, and splitting. Chisels should be **extremely sharp** and the user should keep his or her hands out of the way of the blade when using them. Typically, this means having a two-handed grip on the chisel. One hand should guide while the other drives the chisel. If more force is needed, a mallet can be used to deliver the force to the end of the handle.

Chisel Operations

- **Paring cuts:** Chisels can be used across the grain, using one surface as a reference face to slice the wood and cut down to the same plane. This is useful when cutting wood joinery.

- **Splitting cuts:** Chisels can functionally act as a wedge and can easily split wood. Generally, carpenters and woodworkers should avoid using a chisel as a wedge because it can result in extreme breaks that are hard to control. To intentionally split wood, the blade can be inserted into the end-grain or along the face grain and struck. Most woods will fracture along the grain with minimal force. This can be used to quickly remove waste in a joint (such as a half-lap) if appropriate relief cuts are first used.
- **Chopping cuts**: Chisels can be used to chop holes (called mortises) or to shape wood. Chopping cuts require putting force directly into the body of the wood, which presents the issue of splitting. To prevent splitting, chopping cuts should be perpendicular to the wood grain. Chopping generally requires the use of a mallet to apply force.
- **Shaping cuts**: Chisels can be used to shape wood, especially when using specialized chisels with cutting geometry designed for carving. There are a variety of chisel types with v-shapes and rounded parts made specifically for shaping. Shaping requires a high degree of control and understanding of grain direction.

Common Types of Chisels

- **Bevel-edge chisels**: The most basic of chisels, beveled edge chisels have a relatively thin blade with a flat back. Its square blade end has 3 acute beveled edges on the front side.
- **Mortise chisels**: Sturdier than beveled edge chisels, mortise chisels have a thicker blade with a flat back. Its square end has just 1 beveled edge on the front side, which is less acute than that of a beveled edge chisel.
- **Butt chisels**: Butt chisels typically have shorter blades and shorter handles and are designed for comfortable, controlled use when paring.
- **Skew chisels**: These are chisels with a skew to the front of the blade and are designed to easily reach into the inside of angled surfaces to clean them out. The most common use is for cleaning out the waste in half-blind dovetails.
- **Cold chisels and Masonry Chisels**: These are chisels that can be used to cut or chip away at metal or masonry, such as tile or concrete. These are not sharpened like woodworking chisels, but use their acute tip to scratch and wedge apart materials.

Beveled edge chisel

Mortise chisel

Punches

Used in conjunction with a hammer and sometimes a chisel, a **punch tool** or **punch** is a hard metal hand tool with a blunted end and a specialized pointed end used to mark the center for drawing circles, punch precise holes in hard material such as sheet metal or leather, start holes for drilling, and more. Hollow punches have a hollow interior and are used to create holes in the workpiece, and solid punches have a solid interior and are used for marking, to remove material from an area, or to drive small components such as pins precisely into place.

Turning Tools

Screwdrivers

Screwdrivers are hand tools used to apply torque (a twisting force used to cause rotation); most commonly, they are used to turn screws using the groove patterns on the screw head with the corresponding shape at the end of the screwdriver.

The **Phillips-head screwdriver** forms a cross at the end of the screwdriver. The **flat head screwdriver** is a simple line shape, commonly tapered to a slight wedge. Other types of screwdrivers include JIS, which look similar to Phillips-head, but do not cam out of the screw when overtorqued, square-head (also called Robertson screws), and torx screws, which have a star-shaped driver. Square-head and torx screws are increasing in popularity because they easily lock onto driver bits and do not easily slip.

Power drills and **power screwdrivers** are battery-powered or corded tools used to drive screws, among other things. They are required when the project requires many screws or the materials being attached are hard to penetrate. Power or electric screwdrivers are more lightweight than drills and are easier to maneuver, but they are less powerful and therefore less versatile. **Impact drivers** are similar to power drills, but are specifically designed to apply torque for driving screws to prevent breaking and stripping screws.

Wrenches

Wrenches are hand tools used to apply torque, usually by gripping the outside of the bolt, nut, or screw with relative specificity.

Image	Tool Variation	Description & Uses
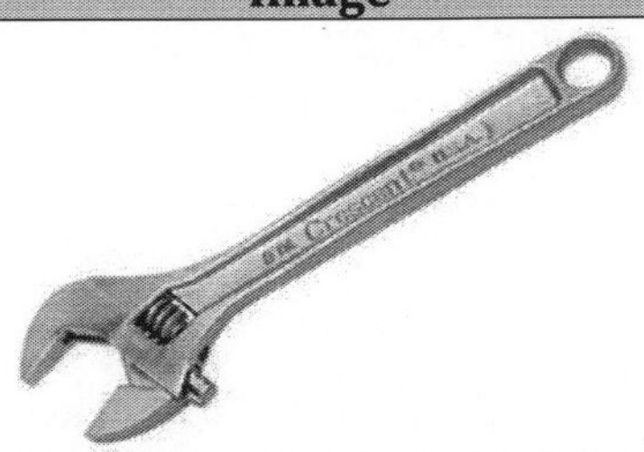	Crescent or adjustable wrench	Jaw diameter can be adjusted by turning the threaded worm to engage the corrugated edge of the non-fixed jaw. **Crescent wrenches** are highly versatile.

Image	Tool Variation	Description & Uses
	Pipe wrench	With serrated and adjustable jaws, the F-shaped **pipe wrench** is sturdy and commonly used for metal pipes.
	Lug wrench	Used to remove or replace lug nuts on cars, **lug wrenches** are either L-shaped (with a socket on one end) or X-shaped (with 4 different sockets).
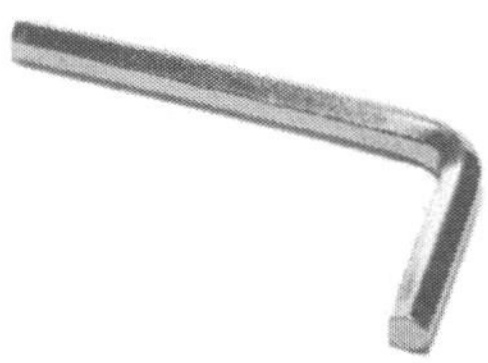	Allen wrench or Allen key	Used to apply torque to screws with a hexagonal recess in their head, **Allen wrenches** are L-shaped and have a hexagonal cross-section. They usually come in sets of various sizes.
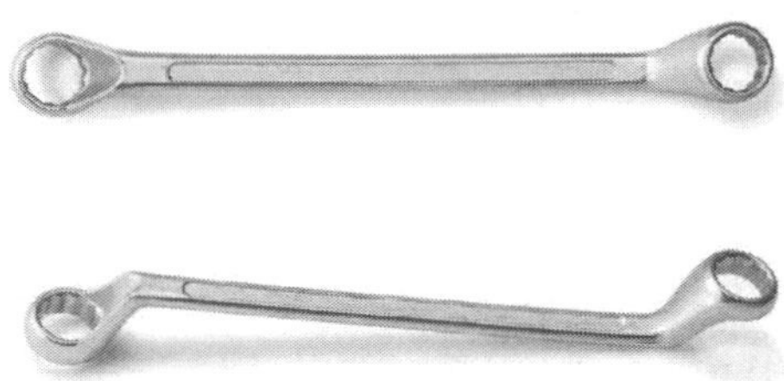	Box-ended wrench	The closed loops at either end of the **box wrench** can be used for square or hexagonal bolts, and the (sometimes present) raised ends allow for gripping of recessed nuts or bolts. The two ends are slightly different sizes. They usually come in sets of various sizes.
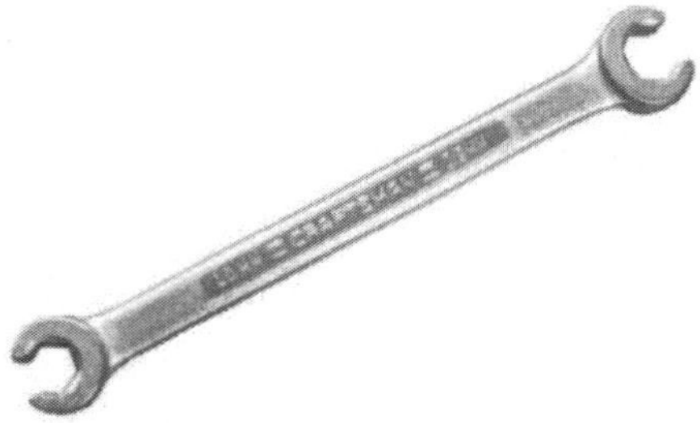	Open-ended wrench	A very common type of wrench, **open-ended wrenches** have U-shaped openings at each end, and the ends are slightly different sizes. The open ends are more likely to round the edges of a nut or bolt than closed ends. They usually come in sets of various sizes.

Image	Tool Variation	Description & Uses
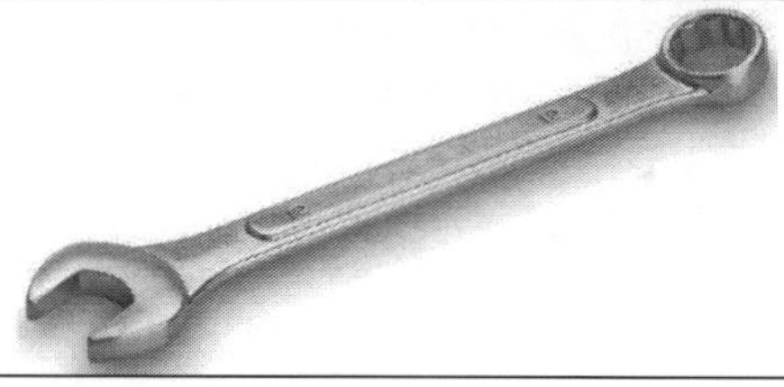	Combination wrench	A combination of box-ended and open-ended wrenches, **combination wrenches** have an open and a closed end. They usually come in sets of various sizes.
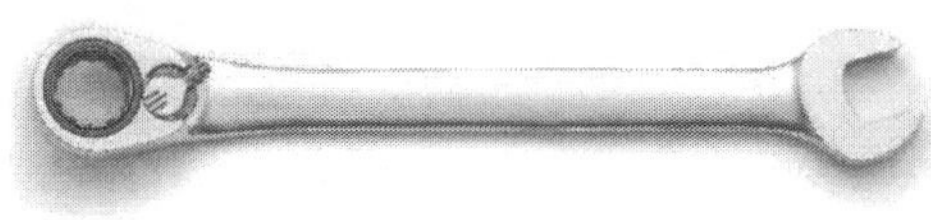	Ratcheting wrench	At least one end of the **ratcheting wrench** contains a ratcheting device so that loosening or tightening doesn't require a complete circular motion or removing and resetting the wrench if something is in the way. These wrenches are helpful in tight spaces.
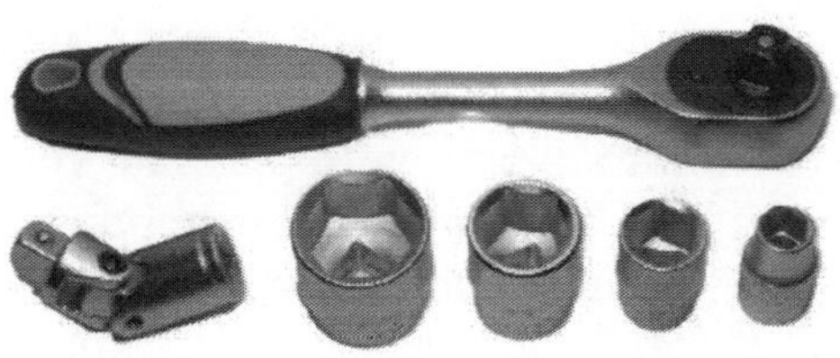	Socket wrench	**Socket wrenches** have a drive (the square-shaped fitting) attached to a ratchet on one end; various sockets can be attached to the drive to accommodate different size bolt heads. Sockets come in sets of various sizes.
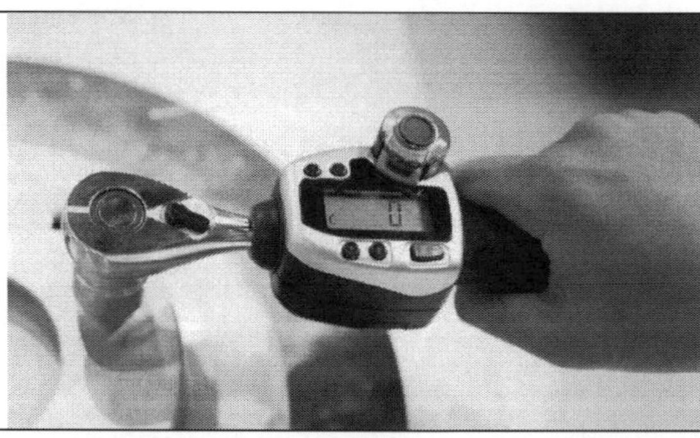	Torque wrench	Manual and digital **torque wrenches** help prevent overtightening because they can be calibrated in accordance with manufacturer specifications. These are commonly used in automotive work, among other things.

Wrench sizes for sets come in standard and metric, and size-range and specificity depend on the trade or project for which they are used. Common metric wrench sizes start at 4 millimeters (mm) and increase by 1 mm increments; common standard wrench sizes start at $^{5}/_{32}$ of an inch and increase by $^{1}/_{32}$ of an inch increments.

Like other wrenches, **Allen wrenches** come in fractional inch and metric sizes.

Socket sizes depend on the **drive size**, which is the square-shaped fitting on the ratchet at the end of the socket wrench. The larger the drive, the more torque it can handle, therefore the sockets will be larger. The most common drive sizes are $^{1}/_{4}$ inch, $^{3}/_{8}$ inch, and $^{1}/_{2}$ inch.

IMPACT TOOLS

Impact drivers operate much like power drills or power screwdrivers, but they sense when additional torque is needed and internally employ a spring, hammer, and anvil to provide more rotational force. Because of the additional torque, drill bits must have a **hex shank**, meaning the end of the bit inserted into the **chuck** (the drill's specialized clamp used to hold bits) must be hexagonal. Hex shanks are designed to withstand the stress of impact drivers. An example of when an impact driver might be necessary is when attempting to remove a screw that has rusted into place. They can be cordless with a battery or powered by an air compressor.

Impact wrenches use sockets (like the socket wrench) to remove stubborn nuts or bolts with the same spring, hammer, and anvil mechanism as impact drivers. They can be cordless with a battery or powered by an air compressor.

An **air compressor** pressurizes gas by reducing its volume, therefore converting power from a motor or an engine into pressurized air. They can be used to power pneumatic tools such as nail guns or impact wrenches, and they can also fill air up in tires.

Fastening and Joinery Tools

Nails

Nails are fasteners that do not have threads to help lock them in place. Nails can be straight or tapered, cylindrical or rectangular, and can have either flat or pointed heads depending on the purpose. Tapered nails can be particularly effective because of the wedging action when they are driven in, but they typically need to have pre-drilled holes to fit into to prevent splits. Nails come in a variety of gauges and lengths for different purposes, and they are common in construction and finish carpentry. Nails can come in a variety of materials for different properties, including steel, stainless steel, copper, brass, aluminum, iron, and galvanized steel. Steel is most common for general use while galvanized steel is commonly recommended for outdoor use, where rust is a concern.

Screws and Bolts

Bolts and screws are fasteners that have a cylindrical shaft and threads running along at least part of the shaft. These threads are intended to catch on the material or a nut that has the same thread pattern. The difference between screws and bolts are hard to define as the rules have many exceptions. In general, screws are used directly in a material while a bolt is used with a pre-threaded receiver, which can include nuts or a tapped hole.

Nuts, Bolts & Washers

A **nut** is a piece of hardware with a threaded hole and a typically hexagonal perimeter used in conjunction with a bolt; a **bolt** is a threaded rod with a head capable of being securely grasped. Together, a nut and a bolt are used to fasten multiple parts together. **Washers** are used when the hole through which the bolt passes is too large for the bolt head or the nut, or when the force of the nut-bolt load needs to be more widely distributed; they are typically flat, typically circular plates with circular holes in the center. The outside edge should be larger than the holes passing through the pieces to be attached; the hole in the middle of the washer should be just large enough for the bolt to pass through. Lock washers are a type of washer designed with teeth to help prevent slipping.

Adhesives and Resins

Adhesives have been around for a very long time, and adhesive technology continue to improve and find new applications. Every adhesive has its own set of properties and may not work equally well on different materials. The most common historical adhesive is **hide glue**, which is made from animal collagen. Woodworkers continue to use hide glue for particular purposes. **PVA glue** is the basis for white glue used in childrens' crafts, but it is also an extremely strong wood glue. **Cyanoacrylate glue** (CA glue), commonly called superglue, is an extremely fast drying glue that works on a variety of materials. **Two-part epoxies** have grown in development and use. They can range in dry-times, but are commonly extremely strong and cooperate with a variety of materials. Some epoxy resins can even be used as a building material by itself.

Riveting Tools

Riveting is the process of joining plates of metal by use of **rivets**, which are short metal pins with a head and a stem (which may be solid or hollow) that act as mechanical fasteners. Once passed through both metal sheets by drilling, placing, or punching, the rivets are smashed or pounded so as to flatten the head and expand the stem to complete the rivet joint.

Rivets support tensile loads (force that occurs in opposite directions along the same axis) and shear loads (force that produces sliding, which is a failure in the plane parallel to the direction of force). The most common modern applications include residential gutter construction, HVAC duct work, and aircraft manufacturing.

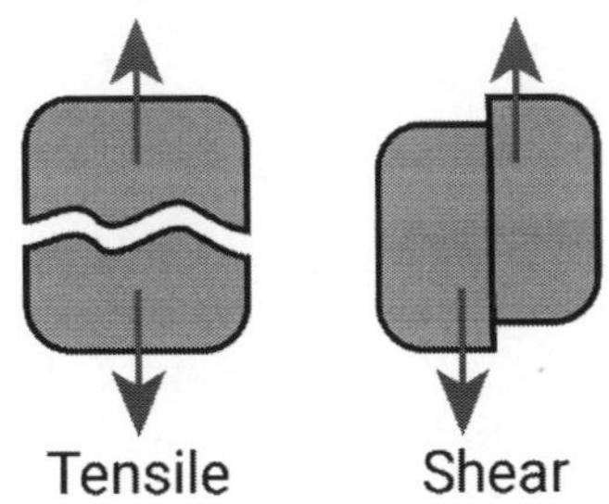

Retaining Rings

Retaining rings are a class of hardware used to reduce motion by stretching or compressing between mating pieces by fitting either on the inside of the exterior component or around the outside of the interior component. Common variations include:

- **Circlip rings** allow axial rotation while preventing lateral motion by snapping into a groove or onto a shaft.
- **Grooveless rings** do not require a groove to function properly and often have a low profile.
- **Spiral rings** are coiled into a groove and allow flexibility.
- **Beveled rings** are specifically beveled to provide a rigid, sturdy joint when complementary ends are locked.
- **Bowed rings** have one central tab and two projecting tabs so that they function like a spring.

Soldering Tools

Soldering is the process of melting **solder** (a metal alloy commonly made of lead and tin) to create a joint between two different metals without melting either of them; this process requires applying heat at roughly 600-840 °F. Solder comes as wire with common diameters of 0.032 and 0.062 inches, and it can be purchased with or without lead as part of the alloy. Soldering is commonly used to connect components on electronic circuit boards.

- **Soldering irons** are hand tools used to apply heat to melt solder.
- **Soldering guns** are heavier than soldering irons, but they heat and cool more quickly. They are used when soldering stained-glass windows and in heavy electronics.

- A **soldering station** allows precise temperature adjusting for soldering irons and include other safety features such as temperature sensors and password protection, depending on the device.
- A **solder sucker** or **de-soldering pump** is used to removed excess solder or to correct mistakes when soldering, even after the solder has solidified.

WELDING & WELDING TOOLS

Welding is the process of fusing two metals into one by melting the **base metal** (material to be welded or cut) through use of extreme heat (6500 °F) and sometimes other metals or gases, depending on the welding method.

Goggles, a helmet (auto-dimming is best), gloves, and long sleeves should be worn while welding to protect from heat and radiation. Never look at the welding arc with the naked eye; this could cause permanent eye damage.

Common arc welding processes include: Tungsten inert gas (TIG) welding, flux-cored arc welding (FCAW), stick welding, and metal inert gas (MIG) welding.

COMMON WELDING TERMINOLOGY & TOOLS

- A **cutting torch** is a tool that uses gas to pre-heat and cut metal.
- **Electrodes** in welding refer to the various current-conducting metals used between the electrode holder/stinger and welding arc.
- **Flux** is a cleaner used before welding or soldering to dissolve oxidation (rust); it can also be used during high-temperature welding to prevent oxidation.
- External **shielding gases** are inert or semi-inert gases that protect the welding arc and molten weld from atmospheric contamination.
- **Slag** is the solidified byproduct of some arc welding processes after the area cools.
- A **stinger** or **electrode holder** is an insulated clamp that holds the electrode securely in position.
- A **welder** or **welding machine** is the power source for the electrical current and heat source.
- The **welding arc** is the discharge of electrons between the electrode and the base metal.

Gripping Tools

PLIERS

Pliers are a class of hinged hand tool with handles and specialized jaws used especially for gripping and pulling. There are many different types of pliers, including:

Image	Tool Variation	Description & Uses
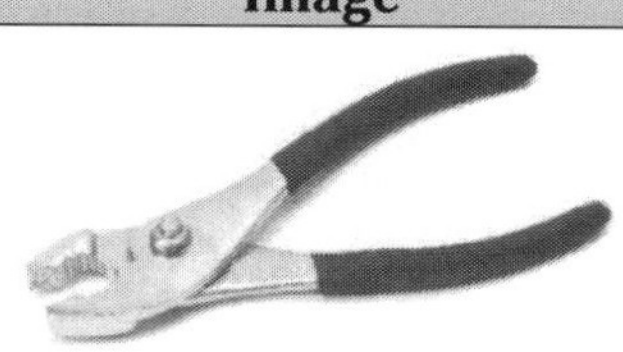	Slip-joint pliers	Highly versatile, the adjustable fulcrum allows the corrugated jaws to lock at two or more working widths.

Image	Tool Variation	Description & Uses
	Needle Nose Pliers	Elongated, often corrugated jaws allow for increased precision when bending and shaping wire.
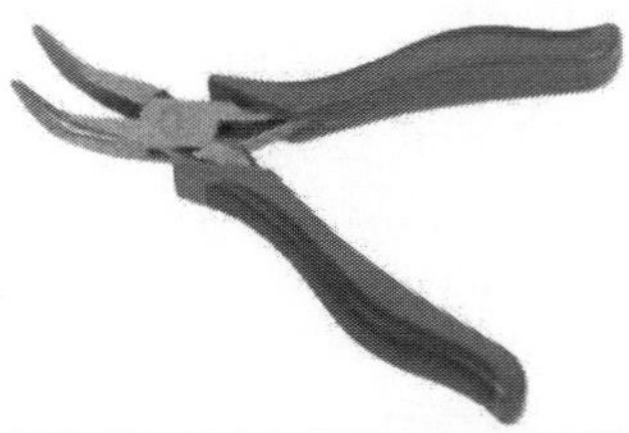	Bent Nose Pliers	A variation of needle nose pliers with bent jaws, they are used for delicate tasks or working at difficult angles.
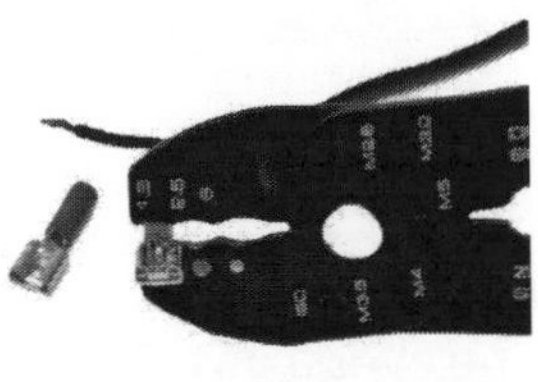	Crimping pliers	Specialized jaws allow for breaking plastic coating on wire and crimping wires together; this makes them ideal for telecommunications technicians.
	Diagonal pliers (Wire cutters)	Acutely angled jaws enable cutting of wire and nails.
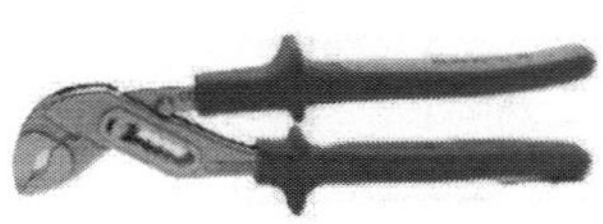	Tongue and Groove Pliers (Channel Locks)	Various grooves on the upper jaw allow for an adjustable, locking fulcrum and a highly versatile tool.
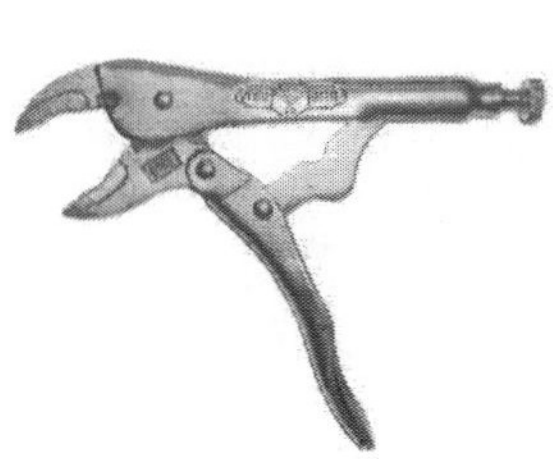	Locking Pliers or Vise Grips	These have handles like pliers and corrugated jaws for a firm, biting grip. Unlike normal pliers, when these are fully closed, the handle locks in place, acting more like a handheld vise. Vise-grips can be used as clamps, pliers, wrenches, and more; their versatility makes them useful for most trades and projects.

CLAMPS

Clamps are devices used to secure objects together tightly for woodworking, plumbing, and countless other tasks. Clamps are specialized, and there are many common varieties, including:

Image	Tool Variation	Description & Uses
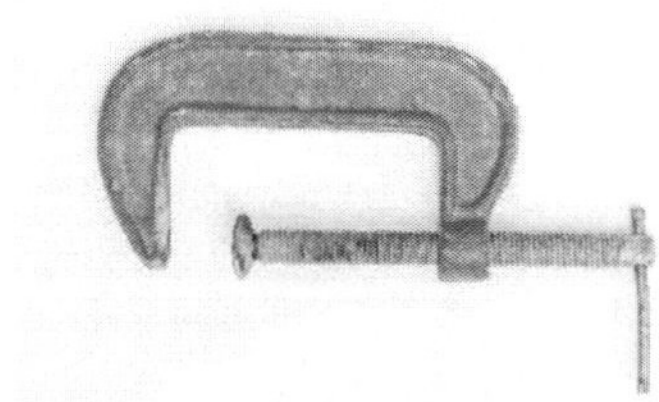	C-clamp or G-clamp	The screw section is used to increase and decrease jaw-width and applied pressure of this very common clamp.
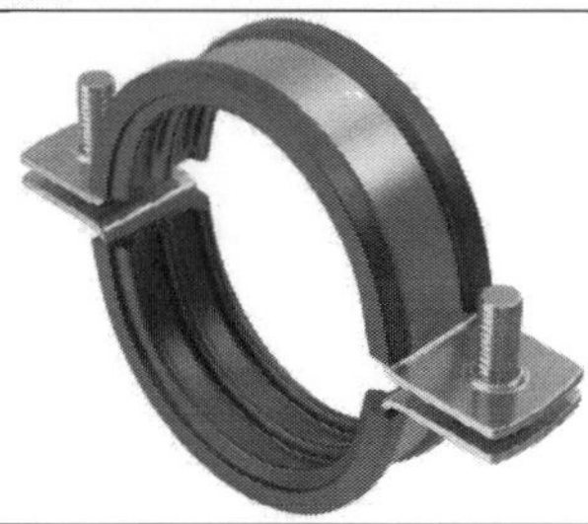	Pipe collar clamp	This clamp has jaws that form a circle so as to be fitted around a pipe.
	Hose clamp	An adjustable, circular band allows for tightening over a hose fitting to prevent leakage of fluid.
	F-Clamp, bar clamp	The upper jaw is attached to a long bar. The lower jaw can slide up and down and then uses a hand screw to tighten down on a workpiece.
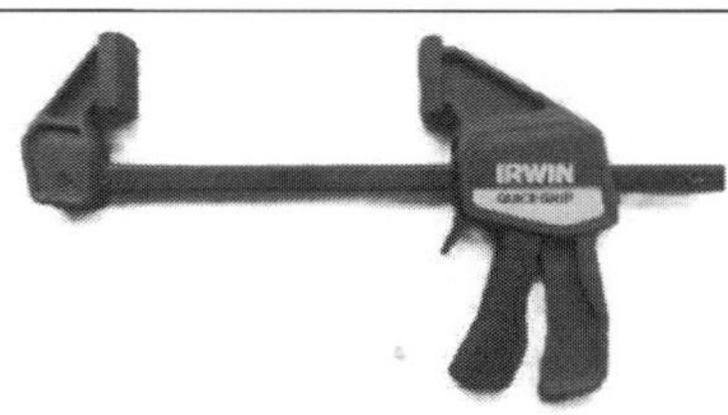	Squeeze Clamp, Quick-grip clamp	Similar in overall function to an F-clamp, but instead of a hand screw for the bottom jaw, this uses a trigger to tighten the bottom jaw. These are not as powerful, but tend to be faster to use.
	Spring clamp, pinch clamp, hand clamp	Spring clamps are extremely quick to use, but tend to be used for small, temporary workholding and do not exert a large amount of force.

Image	Tool Variation	Description & Uses
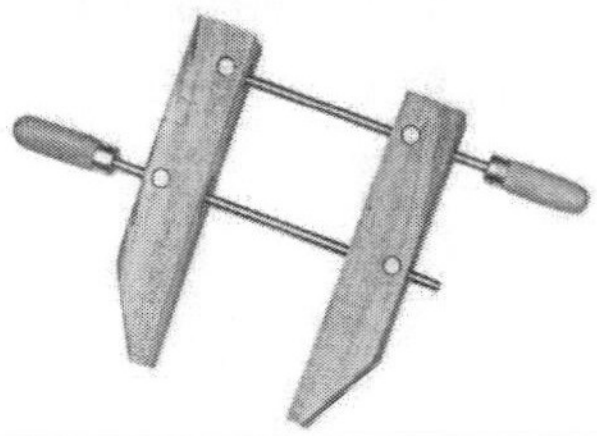	Wooden hand-screw clamp	Double screws hold the jaws at variable angles to grab workpieces with odd tapers. These can be used to hold workpieces on a bench and act as a third hand.
	Bench vise	Bench vises are bolted down to a bench and are commonly used for metalworking purposes.

Cutting Tools

Hand Saws

A **saw** is a tool used to cut wood, metal, pipe, or other materials with a serrated edge using a back-and-forth motion. Different saws have different types of blades and handles for different jobs. Most wood saws are classified into either a rip configuration or a crosscut configuration, but some try to meet in the middle and have characteristics of both. These are called combination blades. **Rip cuts** are when a cut happens along the grain fibers of a board, while crosscuts are cuts that go across the grain. **Crosscuts** require an alternating tooth geometry with knife-like teeth to sever the fibers cleanly. Rip cuts usually have teeth that act more like chisels, scooping out the material instead of slicing it. Blade selection makes a difference in tool longevity, safety, and cut quality.

Image	Tool Variation	Description & Uses
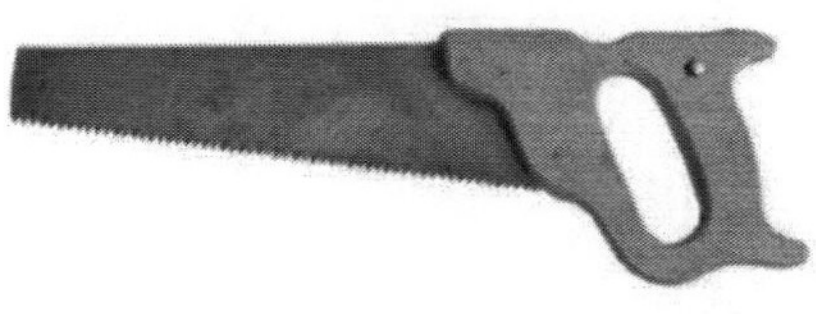	Hand saw or panel saw	With a long, flexible, slightly tapered and sharpened blade, hand saws are able to penetrate deeply through thick boards because they do not have a spine or back preventing cutting. These can come in rip or crosscut configurations.
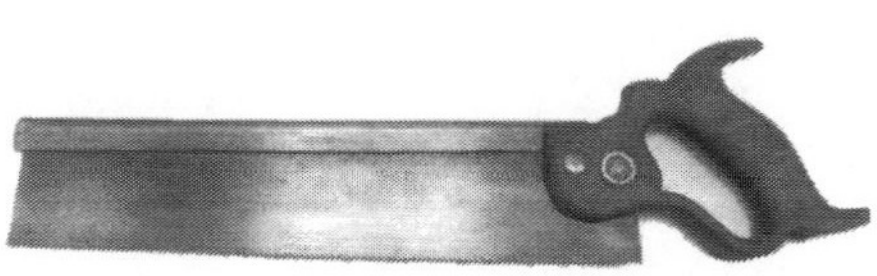	Back saw	A square, thin blade with a reinforced upper edge and small teeth that are set close together, making it ideal for straight, fine cuts. These can come in both rip and crosscut varieties.
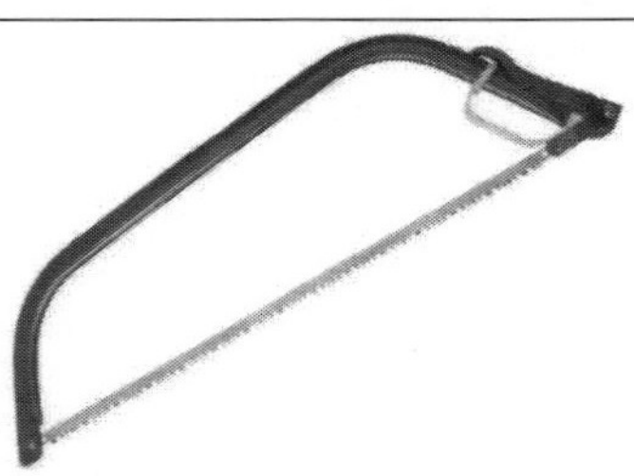	Bow saw or bucksaw	Shaped like a bow with a narrow blade. The blade typically has jagged teeth that can remove wet material without binding. These are commonly used to *buck* tree limbs while pruning or trimming trees. Bow saws are almost always used for crosscuts.

Image	Tool Variation	Description & Uses
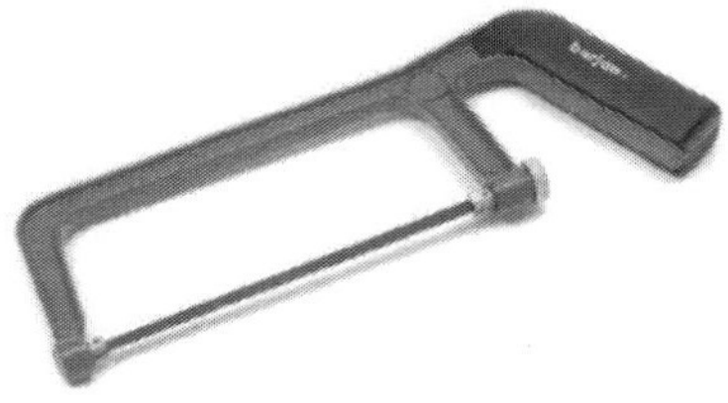	Hacksaw	Hacksaws are similar to buck saws in the tensioning mechanism, but they usually have teeth designed for metalworking. The teeth are hardened to allow for cutting metal, such as bolts that need to be trimmed.
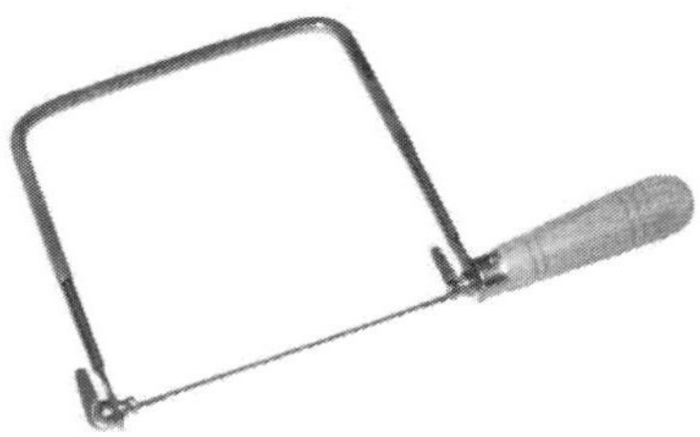	Coping saw	Good for precision and intricacy, the thin blade is held tight by the frame and is used commonly for cutting curves in wood. Coping saws usually have small teeth that work slowly but provide a clean result.
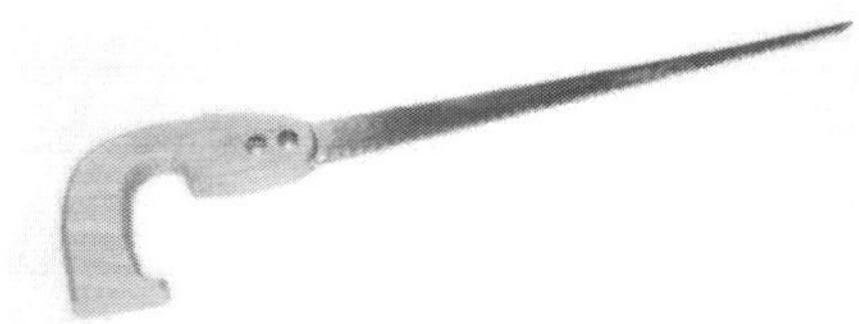	Keyhole saw, pad saw, jab saw, drywall saw	The blade is dagger shaped and most commonly used to cut small circles or odd shapes in drywall.

Powered Saws

Powered saws are specialized cutting tools that can be hand-held, stand-alone, or mounted on a work surface in order to cut various surfaces including wood, plastics, metal, and masonry.

Image	Tool Variation	Description & Uses
	Chainsaw	Used for felling or trimming trees, chainsaws have a continuous chain of specialized teeth that feeds around a metal bar. Polesaws can have small chainsaws mounted at the end for light pruning.
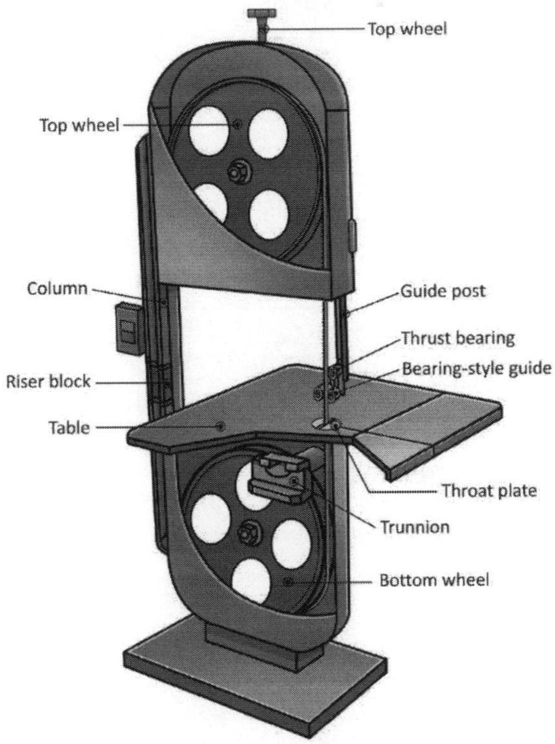	Band saw	Bandsaws have two wheels that a circular blade rides on like a belt. There are two types of bandsaws, wood-cutting and metal-cutting. Wood cutting bandsaws stand vertically and have a tooth configuration set for wood. Metal-cutting bandsaws can either be handheld or can be a plunge model that plunges into the cut like a miter saw. They have finer teeth for cutting through metal stock.
	Circular saw	Circular saws are a handheld tool with a spinning blade. They can be used for a variety of cuts, including both crosscuts and rip cuts, but they generally need to be guided with a straightedge or square to cut straight. These saws are extremely common, but they account for some of the highest proportion of accidents on jobsites.

Image	Tool Variation	Description & Uses
	Miter saw	A miter saw is a circular saw that plunges into a board that is held against a fence. They can typically be articulated to bevels and miters up to 45 degrees. Miter saws can only be used for crosscuts.
	Table saw	A table saw is a circular blade mounted in the middle of a table. Table saws use miter gauges or a fence, depending on what the user is making.
	Jigsaw	A narrow, easily maneuverable blade on a hand-held jigsaw allows for easy cutting of non-straight details and curves.
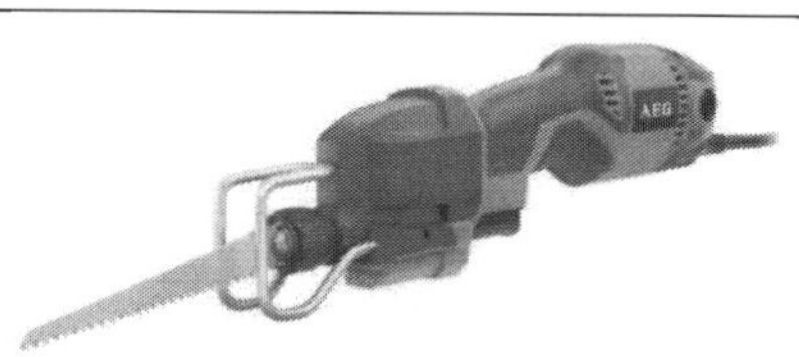	Reciprocating saw, Sawzall	Frequently used in construction and demolition, the reciprocating saw can cut both nails and wood, as well as plastics, bricks, and tiles.

Image	Tool Variation	Description & Uses
	Oscillating saw, oscillating multi-tool	Certain blade attachments change the functionality of the oscillating saw so that it can grind, scrape, or remove grout or caulk. Its saw form utilizes a serrated blade that oscillates side to side; this design allows for cuts that plunge straight into the work surface without requiring an approach from the side or drilling a starter hole first.

Drilling Tools

Drilling tools cut circular holes in wood, metal, plastic, or other materials using **bits**, which are specialized tips that both cut and remove material as they move. Common drill bits used for wood are characterized by a spiral-shaped blade with recessed flutes that make up the body of the bit and a shank, which feeds into and is held by the radially gripping **chuck** of the drill. Handheld drills are common, but when the user needs to make consistent depth or holes at particular angles and locations, a great tool for the job is a **drill press**.

Common Drill Bit Types

- **Spiral bit or twist bit**: These are the most typical type of drill bit. They can be made of various materials to drill into different media. Twist bits are usually small in diameter, typically maxing out at 0.5 inches. Twist bits have flutes along the sides to help remove the waste material as the hole is bored.
- **Brad-point bit**: These are similar to spiral bits, but they include a spike at the tip to help with accurate placement at the start of a cut.
- **Forstner bit**: These are woodworking bits designed to cut clean holes from one side. Forstner bits can be extremely large, but often require a drill press to safely operate.
- **Auger bit**: Auger bits often have a lead screw and a cutter at the front, with large flutes. These can be fairly large and long and are useful for drilling holes for cables or bolts.
- **Spade bit or paddle bit**: These are simple, flat bits that have a center spur and two cutters. These are generally cheap and cut fast, but they do not last long. They generally have a poor cut finish, so they are not good for finish work, but they are great for running cable through studs.
- **Hole Saw**: These are drill bits that have a cup-shaped saw attached. The center drill bit helps to aim the saw teeth and the hole saw attachment cuts out a perfect circle, leaving the waste intact. These tend to have clogging issues, but they require less effort than Forstner bits for large holes, such as doorknob holes.
- **Masonry bit**: Masonry bits are usually used in a hammer drill, which applies hammering force to masonry to break chunks out, while the flutes on the side draw out the waste. Unlike other drill bits, this is not primarily a cutting implement, but an impact tool.

Drill bit types

Boring Tools

Common in machining, a boring bar is used in conjunction with a lathe following the drilling process to **bore** a workpiece (enlarging an existing hole). A **lathe** is a machine tool that rotates a workpiece radially in order to sand, cut, drill, bore, and more. A **boring bar** is used in conjunction with a lathe to bore a pre-drilled hole into a workpiece to exact specifications. **Line boring** is when the boring bar is supported on both ends and the hole being enlarged must pass completely through the workpiece. With **back boring**, only one end of the boring bar fixed and supported. This can be used for blind holes, which do not pass completely through the workpiece, or holes that pass all the way through the workpiece.

Lathes

A **lathe** is a tool with a flat bed and two points that a workpiece is held between. One end spins freely while the other end drives the piece. While the workpiece is spinning, a cutter can work on the workpiece radially and make perfectly round objects. One common example that students learn on is a baseball bat. The blank starts as a long rectangular prism and is slowly shaped down into the tapered-cylindrical shape of a baseball bat. Lathes can be used for woodworking or metalworking for specialized parts, and they can even be used to thread cylindrical shapes to make specialized nuts and bolts.

Routers

Routers are cuttings tool that use high-speed cutters to plunge into and remove great quantities of material. One major difference between a **router** and a drill is that drills are only able to be plunged straight into a workpiece, while routers are able to work laterally, removing great quantities of material quickly for accurate joints. Router bits are made from either high-speed steel or carbide and are designed to handle lateral forces that drill bits are not designed to handle. Router bits frequently use bushings and bearings to ride along the edges of templates and workpieces to be accurately and safely guided. Routers can also use specialized cutters to apply profiles such as roundovers, roman ogees, beads, and more to the edges of workpieces. CNC machines frequently employ small routers for carving and shaping of parts.

Surface Preparing & Finishing Tools

Planing and Jointing

Jointers

In most woodworking processes, a board needs to be made flat, straight, and square before effectively and safely using it. The process of flattening and straightening one side of a board (either one face or one edge) is called **jointing** and generally requires the use of a machine called a jointer. The jointer has a precisely tuned body that allows for only high points to be touched. The jointer has a spinning cutter head that removes material from one side of a board, leaving a straight and flat surface. Jointers also have a fence that can be used with a flat face to joint the edge grain. A jointer is not designed to make parallel faces or edges; after a board is jointed on two sides, it can be taken to a planer to create a parallel face grain surface and a table saw can be used to cut a parallel edge.

Planers

A **planer** is a machine with a flat bottom and an opposing cutterhead with feed rollers that is used to remove thickness from a board. If a board has been jointed on one face, the jointed face can ride along the planer's flat bottom to make the other face parallel, making both surfaces true. A planer is not capable of flattening and straightening a board on its own, but will perpetuate any cup or twist that already exists in the board. The planer's other primary purpose is to remove thickness from a board to reach a desired final thickness. In the past, some have called planers "thicknessers" because of this function.

Handheld Power Planers

Handheld power planers are similar concepts to a jointer in that they have a rotating cutterhead and a fence. They are able to remove a lot of material quickly, but often leave a rough surface. They are unable to create perfectly flat and true surfaces, but they are useful for removing material quickly in tricky situations, such as trimming a door to fit an opening.

Files and Rasps

Files and rasps are manual, hand-held tools used for removing material from workpieces, most commonly of wood or metal. Rasps and files can come in a variety of shapes, including flat, convex, and rat-tail, which is the name for a long cylinder shape.

- **Files** produce a semi-fine finish but cut more slowly than rasps. They can be single cut, with parallel ridges, or double cut, with two sets of parallel ridges set at an angle to each other; double cut files are rougher on a workpiece than single cut. Files come in three grades from smoothest to coarsest: smooth, second cut, and bastard (coarse).
- **Mill files** are used to sharpen metal blades.
- **Rasps** have raised teeth instead of ridges like a file, and they have various levels of coarseness: wood (the roughest), cabinet, and patternmaker (the smoothest).

Grinders

Grinders are powered, hand-held tools used for cutting, rough and fine shaping, smoothing, brushing, and polishing many different types of materials including wood, metal, stone, and plastic.

They can sometimes be used for sanding jobs, whereas sanders cannot be typically be used for grinding jobs.

- **Angle grinders** are the most common form of grinder and are highly versatile. Angle grinders are handheld tools with a spinning wheel attachment near the handle. They can be used to clean metal (with the wire brush attachment), cut metal bolts (with the metal cutoff wheel attachment), cut masonry (with the diamond wheel attachment), and sharpen blades (with the grinding wheel).
- **Belt sanders** can be used to finish surfaces and sharpen metal blades, among other things, using an abrasive belt.
- **Bench grinders** can be mounted on a work bench and are used for grinding off large amounts of material or rust, sharpening metal blades, buffing and polishing surfaces, and cutting wood and other hard materials.

SANDERS

Sanding is the process of smoothing a surface using an abrasive material such as sandpaper. **Sandpaper** comes in varying grit levels; the higher the number, the finer the sandpaper grit. Fine-grit sandpaper should be used for more detailed jobs, such as the final sanding step before staining wood. Sandpaper is also a commonly used way to sharpen blades.

- **Sanding blocks** are hand-held, manual tools used to hold sandpaper securely and evenly while hand-sanding a surface. They are useful when a powered sander cannot fit or might damage to the project. Removable sandpaper is usually attached to one side of the block with Velcro.
- **Oscillating palm sanders** are handheld power tools that move a piece of sandpaper back and forth in the same way that a manual sanding block does. These have largely fallen out of favor with the popularization of the random orbit sander, which works more quickly and allows for simultaneous vacuuming. Palm sanders can also have a randomized effect that helps hide inconsistencies in sanding.
- **Orbital sanders** are handheld power tools that rotate a sandpaper disc. The spinning motion of an orbital sander allows for higher sanding speed than an oscillating sander, while holes in the sandpaper allow for a vacuum to remove dust that would otherwise clog up the sandpaper. **Random orbit sanders** are an improved version of an orbital sander that uses randomized motion to remove obvious circular scratch marks from a surface.
- **Belt sanders** use a spinning belt to quickly remove material from a surface, but are too aggressive for most projects and can leave obvious damage behind. Belt sanders are commonly used in flooring refinishing procedures.

Chapter Quiz

Ready to see how well you retained what you just read? Scan the QR code to go directly to the chapter quiz interface for this study guide. If you're using a computer, simply visit the online resources page at **mometrix.com/resources719/afct** and click the Chapter Quizzes link.

Mechanical Comprehension

Kinematics

To begin, we will look at the basics of physics. At its heart, physics is just a set of explanations for the ways in which matter and energy behave. There are three key concepts used to describe how matter moves:

1. Displacement
2. Velocity
3. Acceleration

Displacement

Concept: Where and how far an object has gone

Calculation: Final position – initial position

When something changes its location from one place to another, it is said to have undergone displacement. If a golf ball is hit across a sloped green into the hole, the displacement only takes into account the final and initial locations, not the path of the ball.

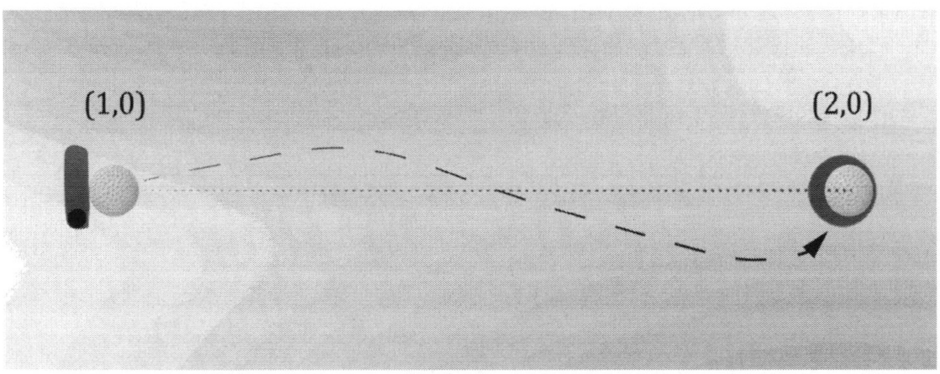

Displacement along a straight line is a very simple example of a vector quantity; it has both a magnitude and a direction. Direction is as important as magnitude in many measurements. If we can determine the original and final position of the object, then we can determine the total displacement with this simple equation:

$$\text{Displacement} = \text{final position} - \text{original position}$$

The hole (final position) is at the Cartesian coordinate location (2,0) and the ball is hit from the location (1,0). The displacement is:

$$\text{Displacement} = (2,0) - (1,0)$$

$$\text{Displacement} = (1,0)$$

The displacement has a magnitude of 1 and a direction of the positive x-direction.

VELOCITY

Concept: The rate of moving from one position to another

Calculation: Change in position / change in time

Velocity answers the question, "How quickly is an object moving?" For example, if a car and a plane travel between two cities that are a hundred miles apart, but the car takes two hours and the plane takes one hour, the car has the same displacement as the plane but a smaller velocity.

In order to solve some of the problems on the exam, you may need to assess the velocity of an object. If we want to calculate the average velocity of an object, we must know two things. First, we must know its displacement. Second, we must know the time it took to cover this distance. The formula for average velocity is quite simple:

$$\textbf{average velocity} = \frac{\textbf{displacement}}{\textbf{change in time}}$$

Or

$$\textbf{average velocity} = \frac{\textbf{final position} - \textbf{original position}}{\textbf{final time} - \textbf{original time}}$$

To complete the example, the velocity of the plane is calculated to be:

$$\text{plane average velocity} = \frac{100 \text{ miles}}{1 \text{ hour}} = 100 \text{ miles per hour}$$

The velocity of the car is less:

$$\text{car average velocity} = \frac{100 \text{ miles}}{2 \text{ hours}} = 50 \text{ miles per hour}$$

Often, people confuse the words *speed* and *velocity*. There is a significant difference. The average velocity is based on the amount of displacement, a vector. Alternately, the average speed is based on the distance covered or the path length. The equation for speed is:

$$\textbf{average speed} = \frac{\textbf{total distance traveled}}{\textbf{change in time}}$$

Notice that we used total distance and *not* change in position, because speed is path-dependent.

If the plane traveling between cities had needed to fly around a storm on its way, making the distance traveled 50 miles greater than the distance the car traveled, the plane would still have the same total displacement as the car.

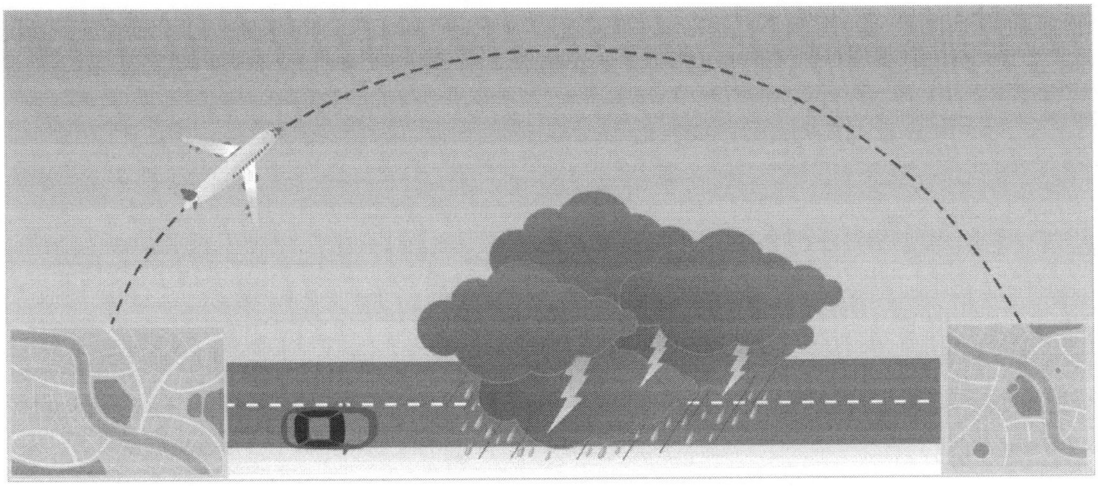

For this reason, the average speed can be calculated:

$$\text{plane average speed} = \frac{150 \text{ miles}}{1 \text{ hour}} = 150 \text{ miles per hour}$$

$$\text{car average speed} = \frac{100 \text{ miles}}{2 \text{ hours}} = 50 \text{ miles per hour}$$

ACCELERATION

Concept: How quickly something changes from one velocity to another

Calculation: Change in velocity / change in time

Acceleration is the rate of change of the velocity of an object. If a car accelerates from zero velocity to 60 miles per hour (88 feet per second) in two seconds, the car has an impressive acceleration. But if a car performs the same change in velocity in eight seconds, the acceleration is much lower and not as impressive.

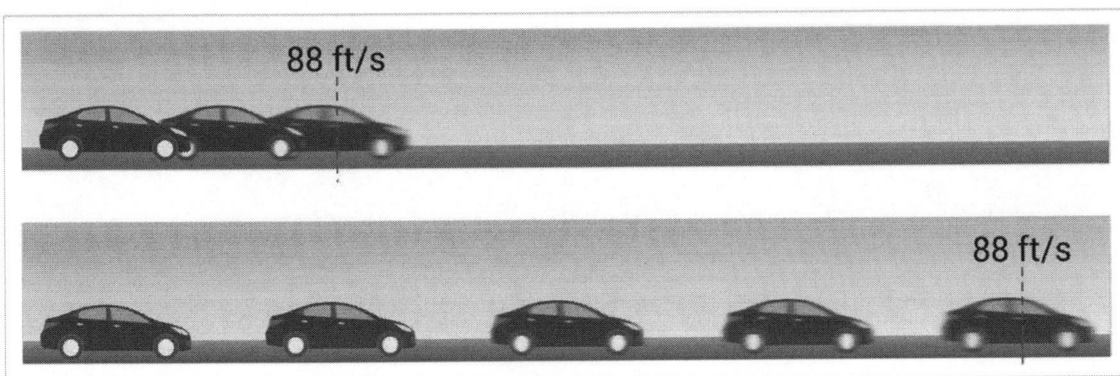

To calculate average acceleration, we may use the equation:

$$\textbf{average acceleration} = \frac{\textbf{change in velocity}}{\textbf{change in time}}$$

The acceleration of the cars is found to be:

$$\text{Car \#1 average acceleration} = \frac{\text{88 feet per second}}{\text{2 seconds}} = 44\ \frac{\text{feet}}{\text{second}^2}$$

$$\text{Car \#2 average acceleration} = \frac{\text{88 feet per second}}{\text{8 seconds}} = 11\ \frac{\text{feet}}{\text{second}^2}$$

Acceleration will be expressed in units of distance divided by time squared; for instance, meters per second squared or feet per second squared.

Review Video: Velocity and Acceleration
Visit mometrix.com/academy and enter code: 671849

Projectile Motion

A specific application of the study of motion is projectile motion. Simple projectile motion occurs when an object is in the air and experiencing only the force of gravity. We will disregard drag for this topic. Some common examples of projectile motion are thrown balls, flying bullets, and falling rocks. The characteristics of projectile motion are:

1. The horizontal component of velocity doesn't change
2. The vertical acceleration due to gravity affects the vertical component of velocity

Because gravity only acts downwards, objects in projectile motion only experience acceleration in the y-direction (vertical). The horizontal component of the object's velocity does not change in flight. This means that if a rock is thrown out off a cliff, the horizontal velocity (think of the shadow if the sun is directly overhead) will not change until the ball hits the ground.

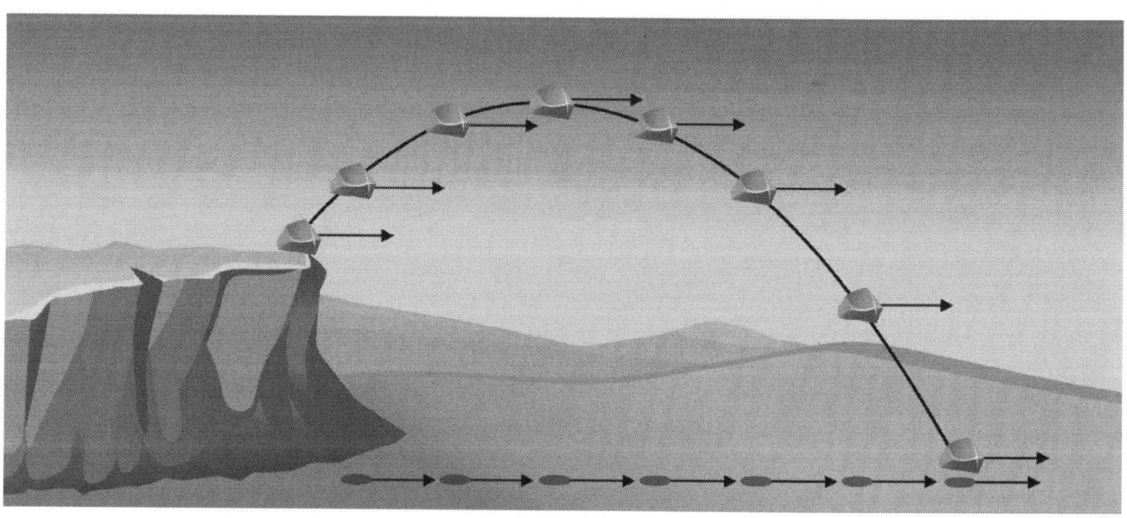

The velocity in the vertical direction is affected by gravity. Gravity imposes an acceleration of $g = 9.8\frac{\text{m}}{\text{s}^2}$ or $32\frac{\text{ft}}{\text{s}^2}$ downward on projectiles. The vertical component of velocity at any point is equal to:

vertical velocity = original vertical velocity − g × time

When these characteristics are combined, there are three points of particular interest in a projectile's flight. At the beginning of a flight, the object has a horizontal component and a vertical component giving it a large speed. At the top of a projectile's flight, the vertical velocity equals zero, making the top the slowest part of travel. When the object passes the same height as the launch, the vertical velocity is opposite of the initial vertical velocity, making the speed equal to the initial speed.

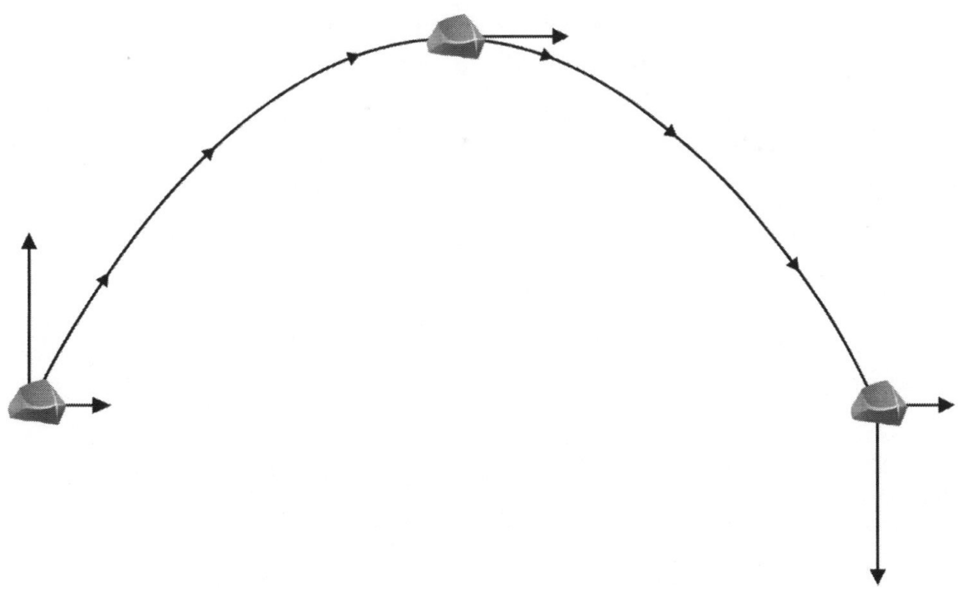

If the object continues falling below the initial height from which it was launched (e.g., it was launched from the edge of a cliff), it will have an even greater velocity than it did initially from that point until it hits the ground.

Review Video: Projectile Motion
Visit mometrix.com/academy and enter code: 719700

Rotational Kinematics

Concept: Increasing the radius increases the linear speed

Calculation: Linear speed = radius × rotational speed

Another interesting application of the study of motion is rotation. In practice, simple rotation is when an object rotates around a point at a constant speed. Most questions covering rotational kinematics will provide the distance from a rotating object to the center of rotation (radius) and ask about the linear speed of the object. A point will have a greater linear speed when it is farther from the center of rotation.

If a potter is spinning his wheel at a constant speed of one revolution per second, the clay six inches away from the center will be going faster than the clay three inches from the center. The clay directly in the center of the wheel will not have any linear velocity.

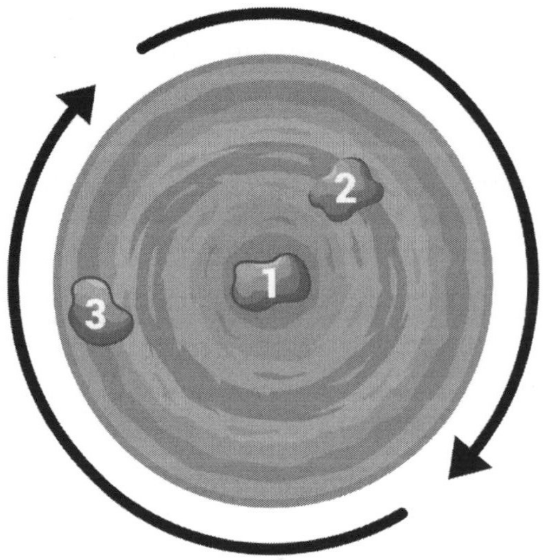

To find the linear speed of rotating objects using radians, we use the equation:

$$\textbf{linear speed} = (\textbf{rotational speed [in radians]}) \times (\textbf{radius})$$

Using degrees, the equation is:

$$\textbf{linear speed} = (\textbf{rotational speed [in degrees]}) \times \frac{\boldsymbol{\pi}\ \textbf{radians}}{\textbf{180 degrees}} \times (\textbf{radius})$$

To find the speed of the pieces of clay, we use the known values (rotational speed of 1 revolution per second, radii of 0 inches, 3 inches, and 6 inches) and the knowledge that one revolution = 2π.

$$\text{clay \#1 speed} = \left(2\pi\frac{\text{rad}}{\text{s}}\right) \times (0 \text{ inches}) = 0\frac{\text{inches}}{\text{second}}$$

$$\text{clay \#2 speed} = \left(2\pi\frac{\text{rad}}{\text{s}}\right) \times (3 \text{ inches}) = 18.8\frac{\text{inches}}{\text{second}}$$

$$\text{clay \#3 speed} = \left(2\pi\frac{\text{rad}}{\text{s}}\right) \times (6 \text{ inches}) = 37.7\frac{\text{inches}}{\text{second}}$$

Review Video: Linear Speed
Visit mometrix.com/academy and enter code: 327101

Cams

In the study of motion, a final application often tested is the cam. A cam and follower system allows mechanical systems to have timed, specified, and repeating motion. Although cams come in varied forms, tests focus on rotary cams. In engines, a cam shaft coordinates the valves for intake and exhaust. Cams are often used to convert rotational motion into repeating linear motion.

Cams rotate around one point. The follower sits on the edge of the cam and moves along with the edge. To understand simple cams, count the number of bumps on the cam. Each bump will cause the follower to move outwards.

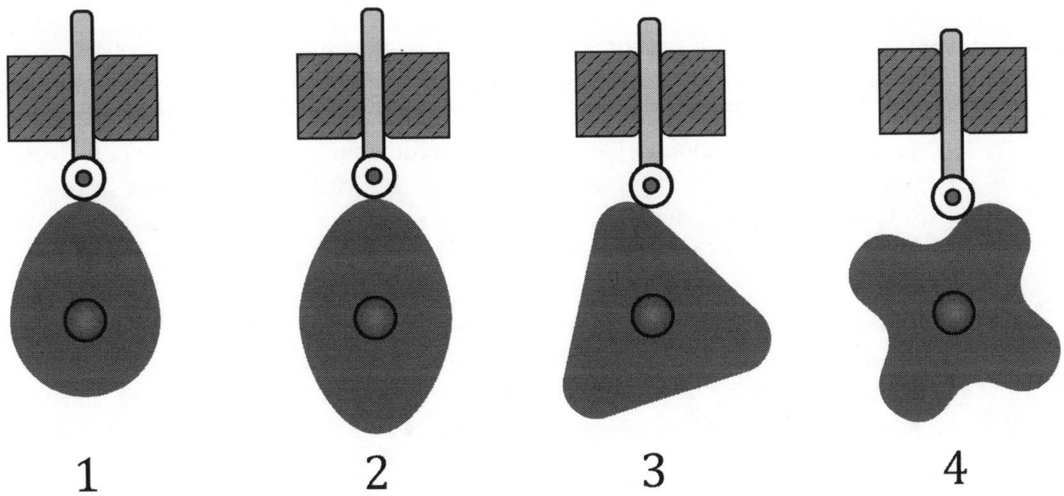

Another way to consider cams is to unravel the cam profile into a straight object. The follower will then follow the top of the profile.

Kinetics

Newton's Three Laws of Mechanics

The questions on the exam may require you to demonstrate familiarity with the concepts expressed in Newton's three laws of motion which relate to the concept of force.

Newton's first law – A body at rest tends to remain at rest, while a body in motion tends to remain in motion, unless acted upon by an external force.

Newton's second law – The acceleration of an object is directly proportional to the force being exerted on it and inversely proportional to its mass.

Newton's third law – For every force, there is an equal and opposite force.

FIRST LAW

Concept: Unless something interferes, an object won't start or stop moving

Although intuition supports the idea that objects do not start moving until a force acts on them, the idea of an object continuing forever without any forces can seem odd. Before Newton formulated his laws of mechanics, general thought held that some force had to act on an object continuously in order for it to move at a constant velocity. This seems to make sense; when an object is briefly pushed, it will eventually come to a stop. Newton, however, determined that unless some other force acted on the object (most notably friction or air resistance), it would continue in the direction it was pushed at the same velocity forever.

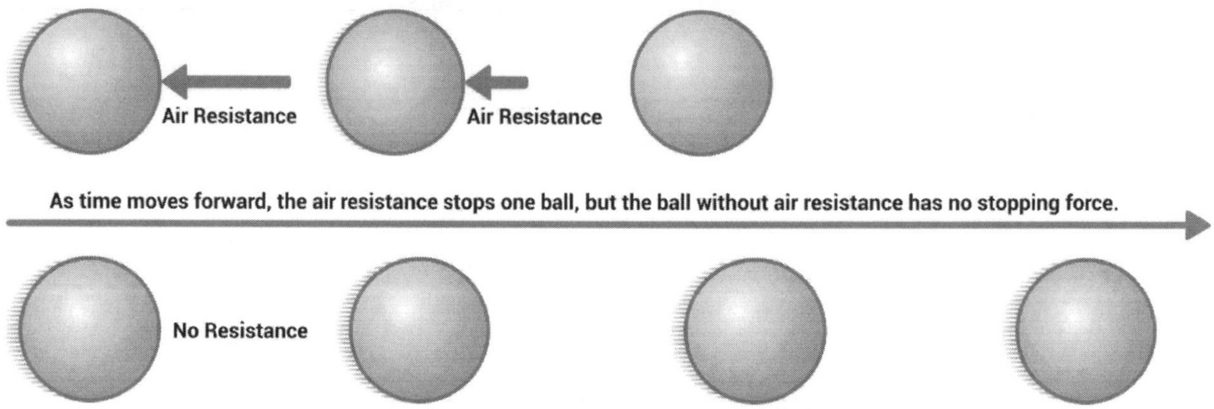

Review Video: Newton's First law of motion
Visit mometrix.com/academy and enter code: 590367

SECOND LAW

Concept: Acceleration increases linearly with force.

Although Newton's second law can be conceptually understood as a series of relationships describing how an increase in one factor will decrease another factor, the law can be understood best in equation format:

$$\textbf{Force} = \textbf{mass} \times \textbf{acceleration}$$

Or

$$\textbf{Acceleration} = \frac{\textbf{force}}{\textbf{mass}}$$

Or

$$\textbf{Mass} = \frac{\textbf{force}}{\textbf{acceleration}}$$

Each of the forms of this equation allows for a different look at the same relationships. To examine the relationships, change one factor and observe the result. If a steel ball with a diameter of 6.3 cm has a mass of 1 kg and an acceleration of 1 m/s^2, then the net force on the ball will be 1 Newton.

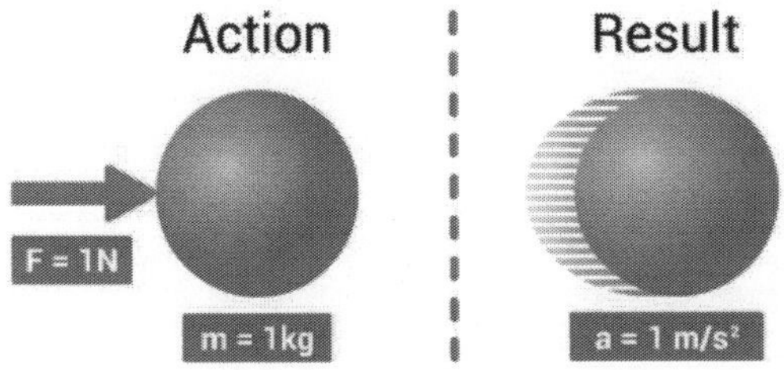

Review Video: Newton's Second law of motion
Visit mometrix.com/academy and enter code: 737975

THIRD LAW

Concept: Nothing can push or pull without being pushed or pulled in return.

When any object exerts a force on another object, the other object exerts the opposite force back on the original object. To observe this, consider two spring-based fruit scales, both tipped on their sides as shown with the weighing surfaces facing each other. If fruit scale #1 is pressing fruit scale #2 into the wall, it exerts a force on fruit scale #2, measurable by the reading on scale #2. However, because fruit scale #1 is exerting a force on scale #2, scale #2 is exerting a force on scale #1 with an opposite direction, but the same magnitude.

FORCE

Concept: A push or pull on an object

Calculation: Force = mass × acceleration

A force is a vector that causes acceleration of a body. Force has both magnitude and direction. Furthermore, multiple forces acting on one object combine in vector addition. This can be demonstrated by considering an object placed at the origin of the coordinate plane. If it is pushed along the positive direction of the *x*-axis, it will move in this direction. If the force acting on it is in the positive direction of the *y*-axis, it will move in that direction.

However, if both forces are applied at the same time, then the object will move at an angle to both the *x*- and *y*-axes, an angle determined by the relative amount of force exerted in each direction. In this way, we may see that the resulting force is a vector sum; a net force that has both magnitude and direction.

Resultant vectors from applied forces:

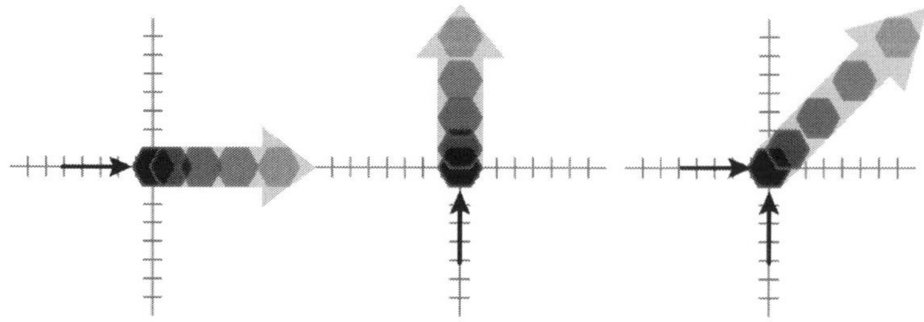

Review Video: Push and Pull Forces
Visit mometrix.com/academy and enter code: 104731

MASS

Concept: The amount of matter

Mass can be defined as the quantity of matter in an object. If we apply the same force to two objects of different mass, we will find that the resulting acceleration is different. In other words, the acceleration of an object is directly proportional to the force being exerted on it and inversely proportional to its mass.

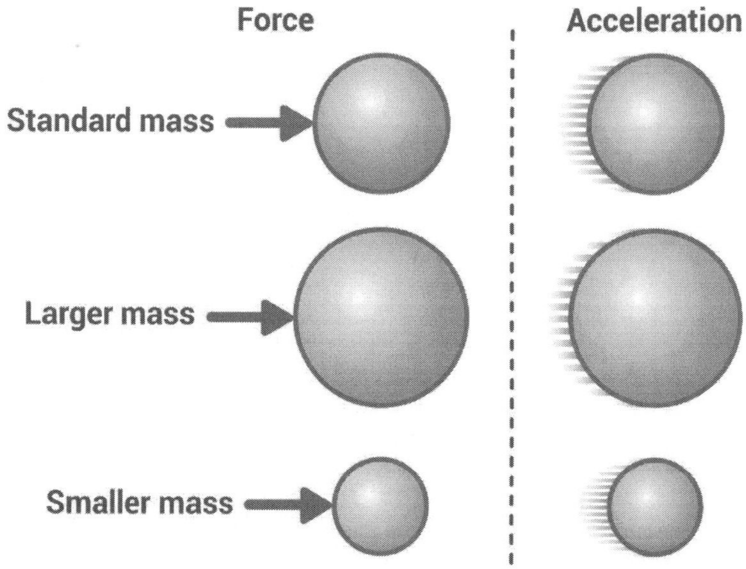

GRAVITY

Gravity is a force that exists between all objects with matter. Gravity is a pulling force between objects, meaning that the forces on the objects point toward the opposite object. When Newton's third law is applied to gravity, the force pairs from gravity are shown to be equal in magnitude and opposite in direction.

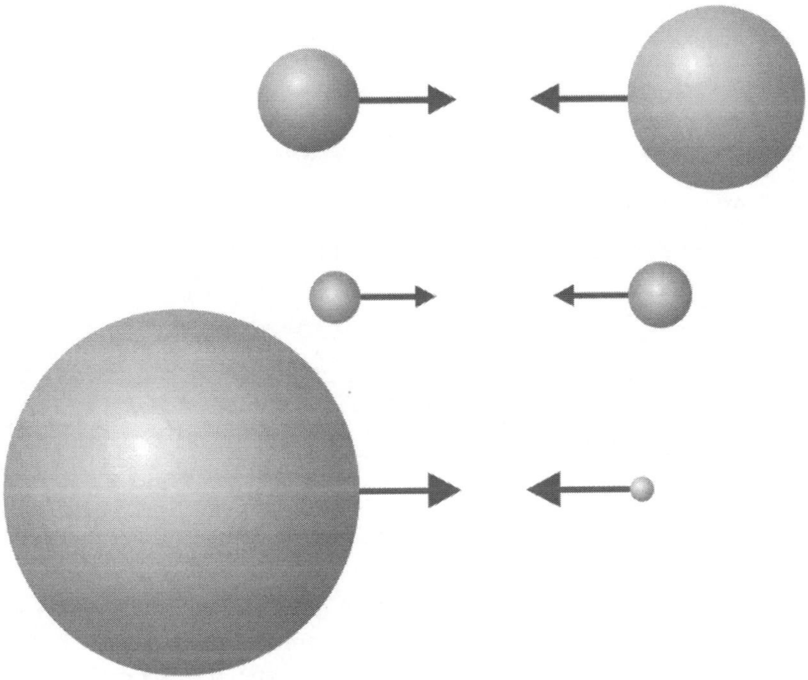

WEIGHT

Weight is sometimes confused with mass. While mass is the amount of matter, weight is the force exerted by the earth on an object with matter by gravity. The earth pulls every object of mass toward its center while every object of mass pulls the earth toward its center. The object's pull on the earth is equal in magnitude to the pull which the earth exerts, but, because the mass of the earth is very large in comparison (5.97×10^{24} kg), only the object appears to be affected by the force.

The gravity of the earth causes a constant acceleration due to gravity (g) at a specific altitude. For most earthbound applications, the acceleration due to gravity is 32.2 ft/s^2 or 9.8 m/s^2 in a downward direction. The equation for the force of gravity (weight) on an object is the equation from Newton's Second Law with the constant acceleration due to gravity (g).

$$\textbf{Weight} = \textbf{mass} \times \textbf{acceleration due to gravity}$$

$$\mathbf{W} = \mathbf{m} \times \mathbf{g}$$

The SI (International Standard of Units) unit for weight is the Newton $\left(\frac{\text{kg}\times\text{m}}{\text{s}^2}\right)$. The English Engineering unit system uses the pound, or lb, as the unit for weight and force $\left(\frac{\text{slug}\times\text{ft}}{\text{s}^2}\right)$. Thus, a 2 kg object under the influence of gravity would have a weight of:

$$\text{W} = 2\text{ kg} \times 9.8\frac{\text{m}}{\text{s}^2} = 19.6\text{ N downward}$$

Review Video: Mass, Weight, Volume, Density, and Specific Gravity
Visit mometrix.com/academy and enter code: 920570

Normal Force

Concept: The force perpendicular to a contact surface

The word *normal* is used in mathematics to mean perpendicular, and so the force known as normal force should be remembered as the perpendicular force exerted on an object that is resting on some other surface. For instance, if a box is resting on a horizontal surface, we may say that the normal force is directed upwards through the box (the opposite, downward force is the weight of the box). If the box is resting on a wedge, the normal force from the wedge is not vertical but is perpendicular to the wedge edge.

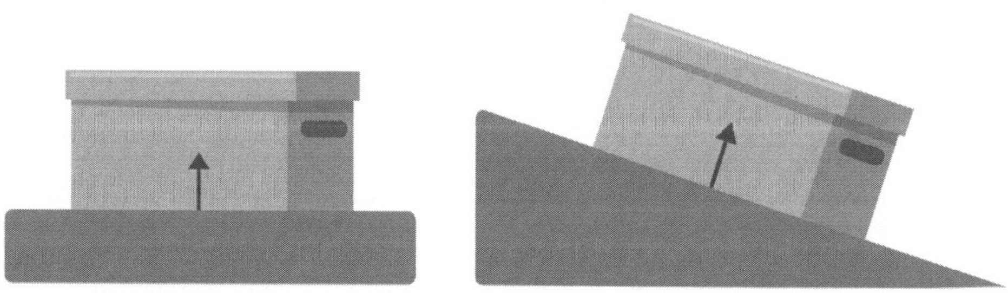

Tension

Concept: A pulling force like that from a cord or rope.

Another force that may come into play on the exam is called tension. Anytime a cord is attached to a body and pulled so that it is taut, we may say that the cord is under tension. The cord in tension applies a pulling tension force on the connected objects. This force is pointed away from the body and along the cord at the point of attachment. In simple considerations of tension, the cord is assumed to be both without mass and incapable of stretching. In other words, its only role is as the connector between two bodies. The cord is also assumed to pull on both ends with the same magnitude of tension force.

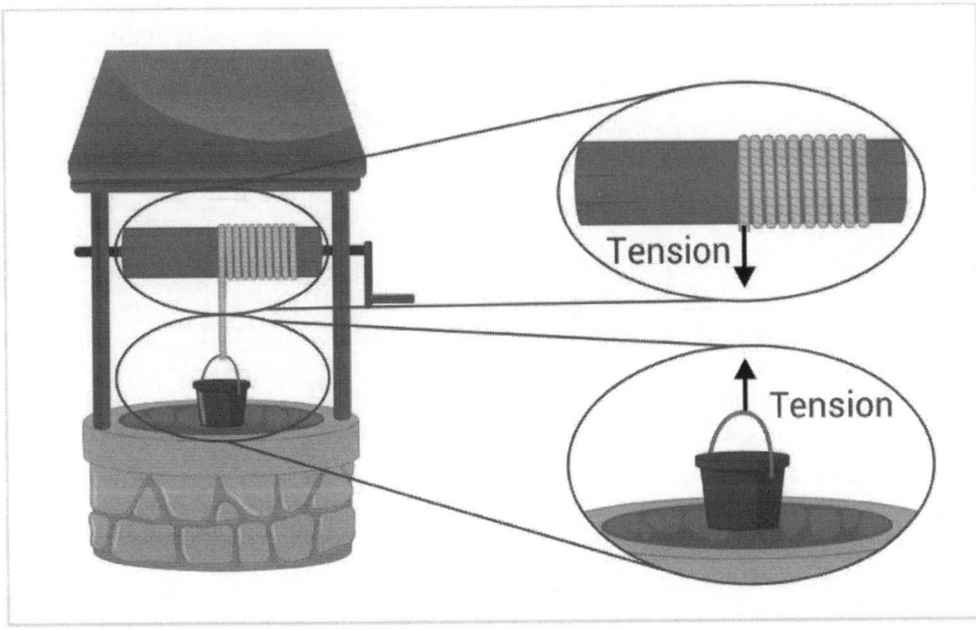

Friction

Concept: Friction is a resistance to motion between contacting surfaces

In order to illustrate the concept of friction, let us imagine a book resting on a table. As it sits, the force of its weight is equal to and opposite of the normal force. If, however, we were to exert a force on the book, attempting to push it to one side, a frictional force would arise, equal and opposite to our force. This kind of frictional force is known as static frictional force.

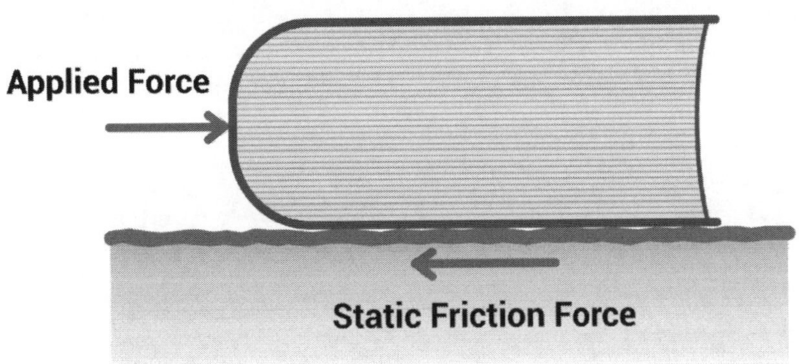

As we increase our force on the book, however, we will eventually cause it to accelerate in the direction of our force. At this point, the frictional force opposing us will be known as kinetic friction. For many combinations of surfaces, the magnitude of the kinetic frictional force is lower than that of the static frictional force, and consequently, the amount of force needed to maintain the movement of the book will be less than that needed to initiate the movement.

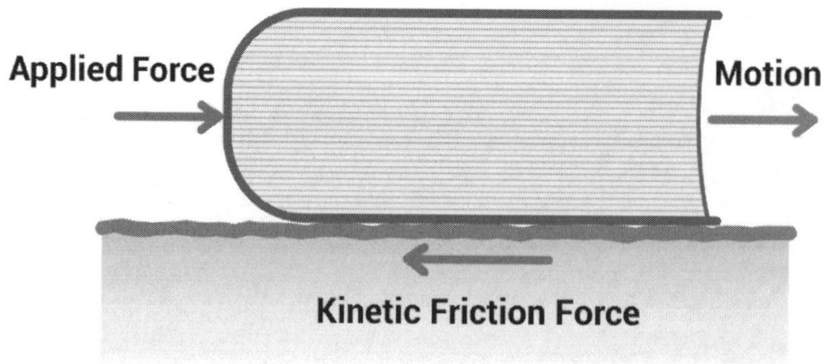

Review Video: Friction
Visit mometrix.com/academy and enter code: 716782

Rolling Friction

Occasionally, a question will ask you to consider the amount of friction generated by an object that is rolling. If a wheel is rolling at a constant speed, then the point at which it touches the ground will not slide, and there will be no friction between the ground and the wheel inhibiting movement. In fact, the friction at the point of contact between the wheel and the ground is static friction necessary to propel with wheels. When a vehicle accelerates, the static friction between the wheels and the ground allows the vehicle to achieve acceleration. Without this friction, the vehicle would spin its wheels and go nowhere.

Although the static friction does not impede movement for the wheels, a combination of frictional forces can resist rolling motion. One such frictional force is bearing friction. Bearing friction is the kinetic friction between the wheel and an object it rotates around, such as a stationary axle.

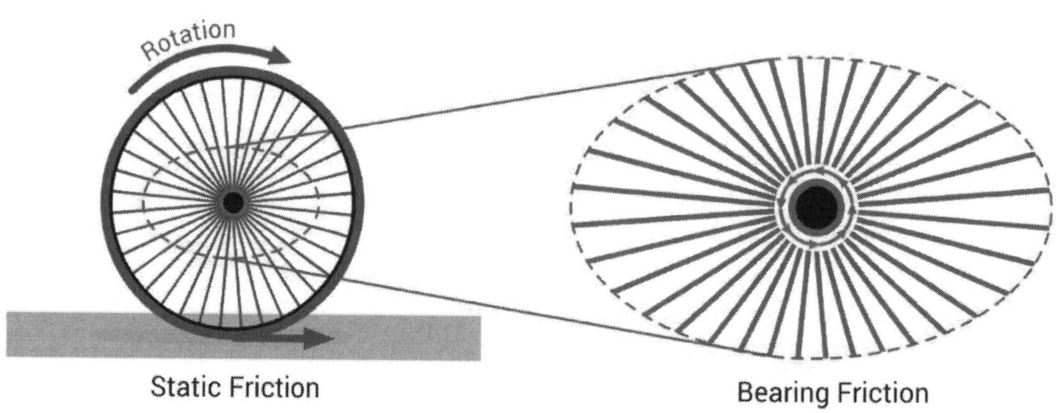

Drag Force

Friction can also be generated when an object is moving through air or liquid. A drag force occurs when a body moves through some fluid (either liquid or gas) and experiences a force that opposes the motion of the body. The drag force is greater if the air or fluid is thicker or is moving in the direction opposite to the object. Obviously, the higher the drag force, the greater amount of positive force required to keep the object moving forward.

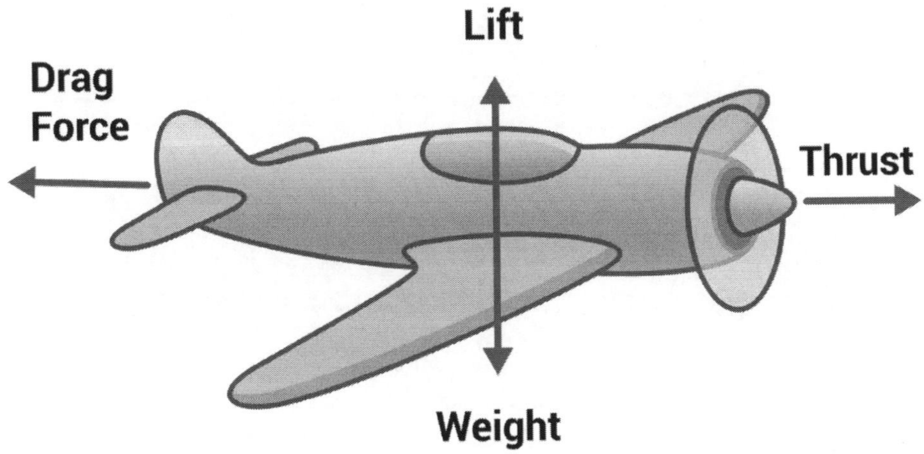

Balanced Forces

An object is in equilibrium when the sum of all forces acting on the object is zero. When the forces on an object sum to zero, the object does not accelerate. Equilibrium can be obtained when forces in the y-direction sum to zero, forces in the x-direction sum to zero, or forces in both directions sum to zero.

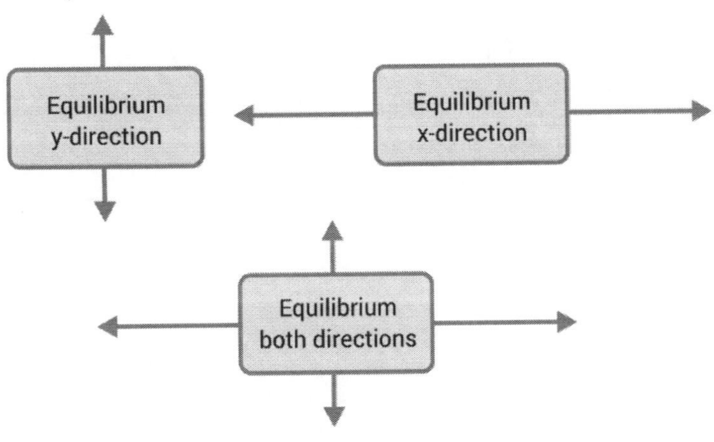

In most cases, a problem will provide one or more forces acting on an object and ask for a force to balance the system. The force will be the opposite of the current force or sum of current forces.

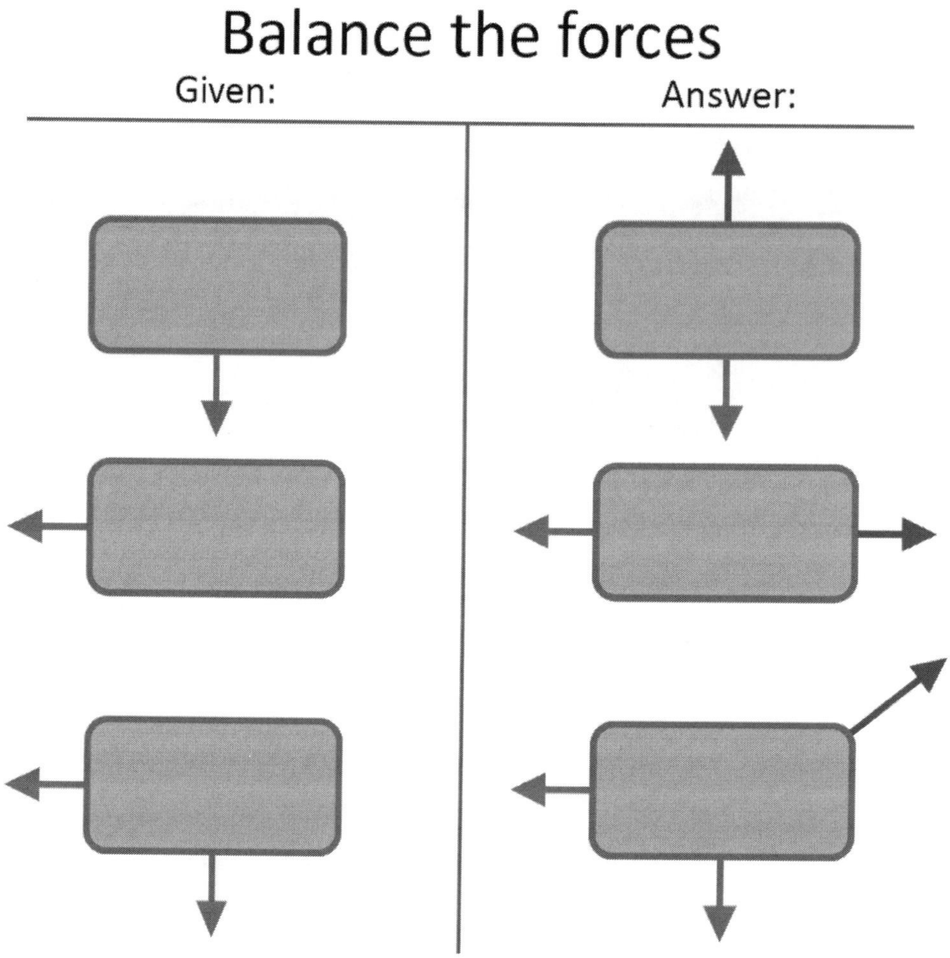

ROTATIONAL KINETICS

Many equations and concepts in linear kinematics and kinetics transfer to rotation. For example, angular position is an angle. Angular velocity, like linear velocity, is the change in the position (angle) divided by the time. Angular acceleration is the change in angular velocity divided by time. Although most tests will not require you to perform angular calculations, they will expect you to understand the angular version of force: torque.

Concept: Torque is a twisting force on an object

Calculation: Torque = radius × force

Torque, like force, is a vector and has magnitude and direction. As with force, the sum of torques on an object will affect the angular acceleration of that object. The key to solving problems with torque is understanding the lever arm. A better description of the torque equation is:

Torque = force × the distance perpedicular to the force from the center of rotation

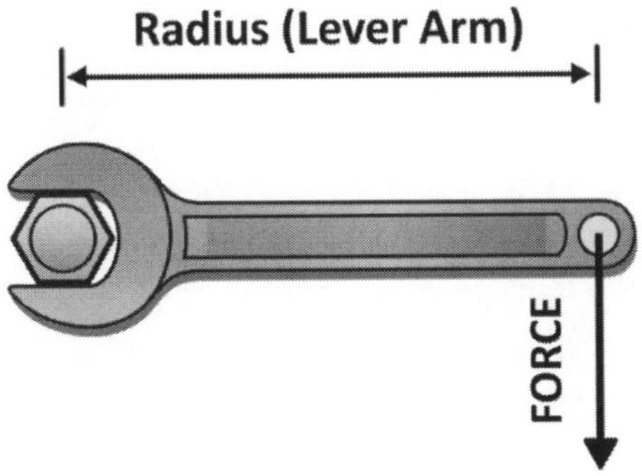

Because torque is directly proportional to the radius, or lever arm, a greater lever arm will result in a greater torque with the same amount of force. The wrench on the right has twice the radius and, as a result, twice the torque.

Alternatively, a greater force also increases torque. The wrench on the right has twice the force and twice the torque.

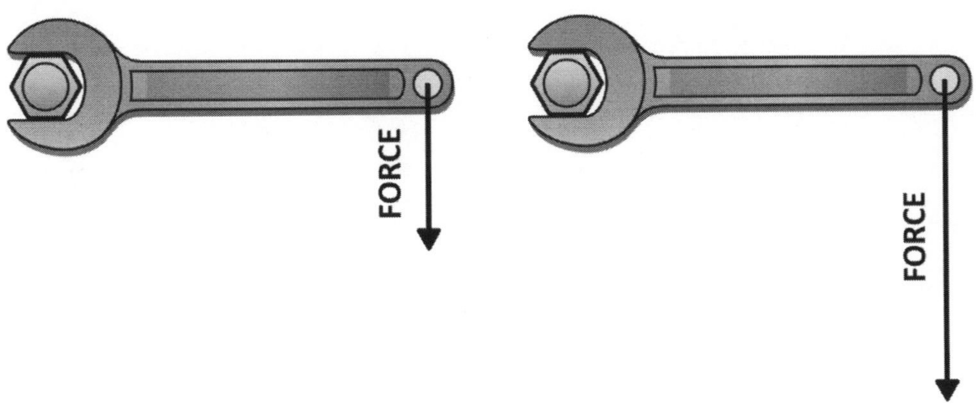

Work/Energy

Work

Concept: Work is the transfer of energy from one object to another

Calculation: Work = force × displacement

The equation for work in one dimension is fairly simple: W = F × d In the equation, the force and the displacement are the magnitude of the force exerted and the total change in position of the object on which the force is exerted, respectively. If force and displacement have the same direction, then the work is positive. If they are in opposite directions, however, the work is negative.

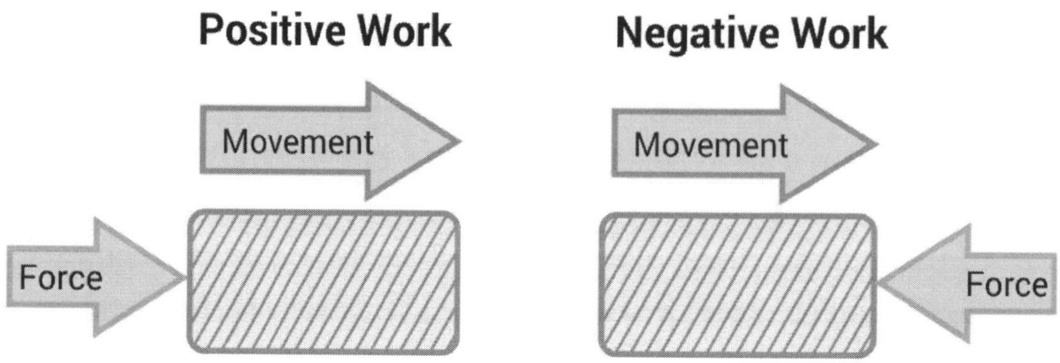

For two-dimensional work, the equation is a bit more complex:

$$\textbf{Work} = \textbf{Force} \times \textbf{displacement} \times \textbf{cos}(\boldsymbol{\theta}\ \textbf{between displacement and force})$$

$$\mathbf{W = F \times d \times cos(\boldsymbol{\theta})}$$

The angle in the equation is the angle between the direction of the force and the direction of the displacement. Thus, the work done when a box is pulled at a 20 degree angle with a force of 100 lb for 20 ft will be less than the work done when a differently weighted box is pulled horizontally with a force of 100 lb for 20 ft.

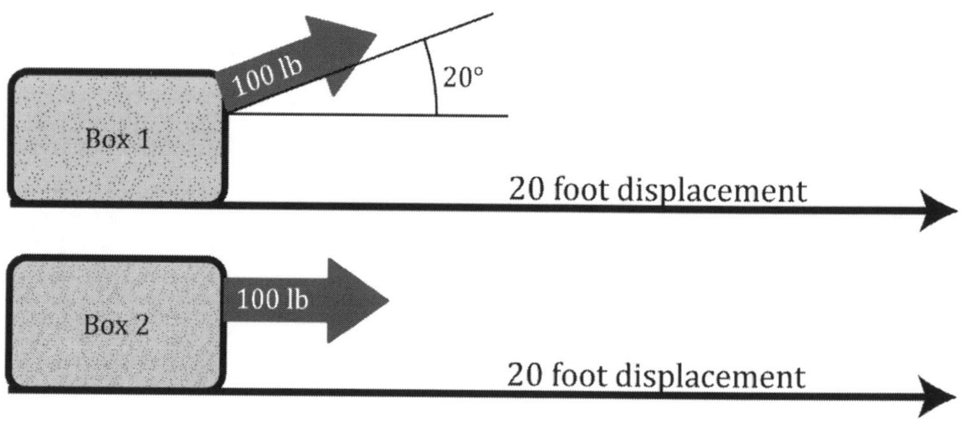

$$W_1 = 100\text{lb} \times 20\text{ft} \times \cos(20°) = 1880\ \text{ft} \cdot \text{lb}$$

$$W_2 = 100\text{lb} \times 20\text{ft} \times \cos(0°) = 2000\ \text{ft} \cdot \text{lb}$$

The unit ft · lb is the unit for both work and energy.

Review Video: Work
Visit mometrix.com/academy and enter code: 681834

ENERGY

Concept: The ability of a body to do work on another object

Energy is a word that has developed several different meanings in the English language, but in physics, it refers to the measure of a body's ability to do work. In physics, energy may not have a million meanings, but it does have many forms. Each of these forms, such as chemical, electric, and nuclear, is the capability of an object to perform work. However, for the purpose of most tests, mechanical energy and mechanical work are the only forms of energy worth understanding in depth. Mechanical energy is the sum of an object's kinetic and potential energies. Although they will be introduced in greater detail, these are the forms of mechanical energy:

Kinetic Energy – energy an object has by virtue of its motion

Gravitational Potential Energy – energy by virtue of an object's height

Elastic Potential Energy – energy stored in compression or tension

Neglecting frictional forces, mechanical energy is conserved.

As an example, imagine a ball moving perpendicular to the surface of the earth, in other words straight up and down, with its weight being the only force acting on it. As the ball rises, the weight will be doing work on the ball, decreasing its speed and its kinetic energy and slowing it down until it momentarily stops. During this ascent, the potential energy of the ball will be rising. Once the ball begins to fall back down, it will lose potential energy as it gains kinetic energy. Mechanical energy is conserved throughout; the potential energy of the ball at its highest point is equal to the kinetic energy of the ball at its lowest point prior to impact.

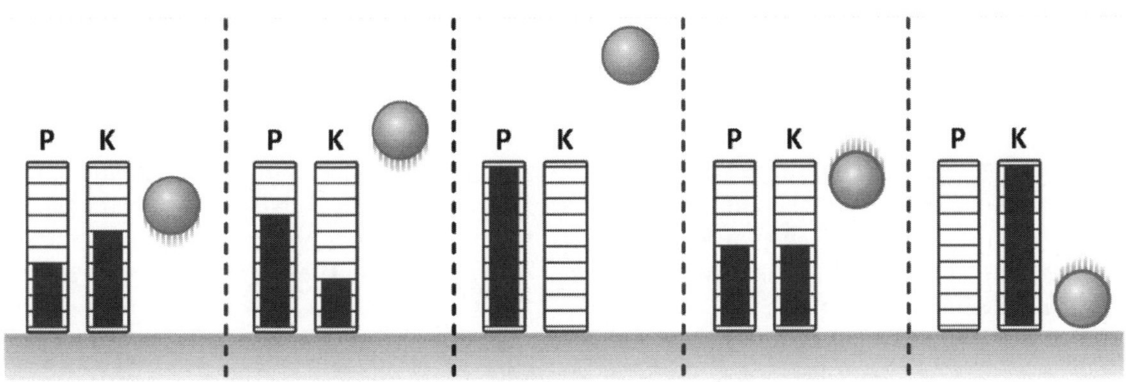

In systems where friction and air resistance are not negligible, we observe a different sort of result. For example, imagine a block sliding across the floor until it comes to a stop due to friction. Unlike a compressed spring or a ball flung into the air, there is no way for this block to regain its energy with a return trip. Therefore, we cannot say that the lost kinetic energy is being stored as potential energy. Instead, it has been dissipated and cannot be recovered. The total mechanical energy of the block-floor system has been not conserved in this case but rather reduced. The total energy of the system has not decreased, since the kinetic energy has been converted into thermal energy, but that energy is no longer useful for work.

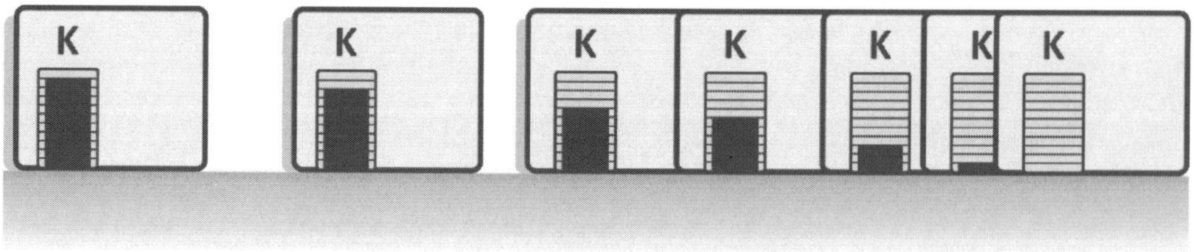

Energy, though it may change form, will be neither created nor destroyed during physical processes. However, if we construct a system and some external force performs work on it, the result may be slightly different. If the work is positive, then the overall store of energy is increased; if it is negative, however, we can say that the overall energy of the system has decreased.

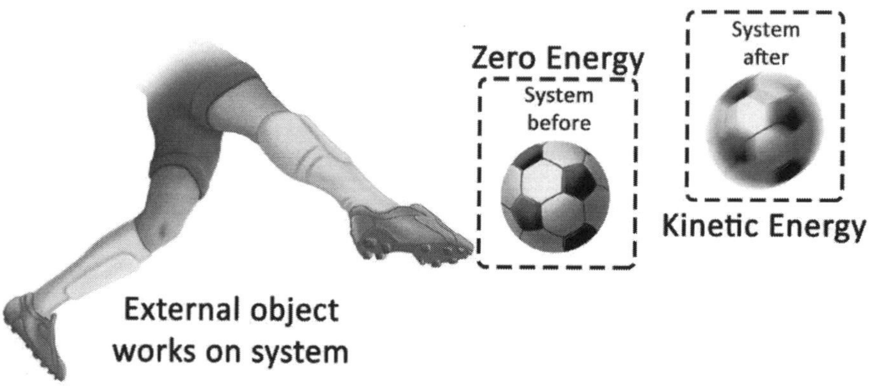

Kinetic Energy

The kinetic energy of an object is the amount of energy it possesses by reason of being in motion. Kinetic energy cannot be negative. Changes in kinetic energy will occur when a force does work on an object, such that the motion of the object is altered. This change in kinetic energy is equal to the amount of work that is done. This relationship is commonly referred to as the work-energy theorem.

One interesting application of the work-energy theorem is that of objects in a free fall. To begin with, let us assert that the force acting on such an object is its weight, which is equal to its mass times g (the force of gravity). The work done by this force will be positive, as the force is exerted in the direction in which the object is traveling. Kinetic energy will, therefore, increase, according to the work-kinetic energy theorem.

If the object is dropped from a great enough height, it eventually reaches its terminal velocity, where the drag force is equal to the weight, so the object is no longer accelerating and its kinetic energy remains constant.

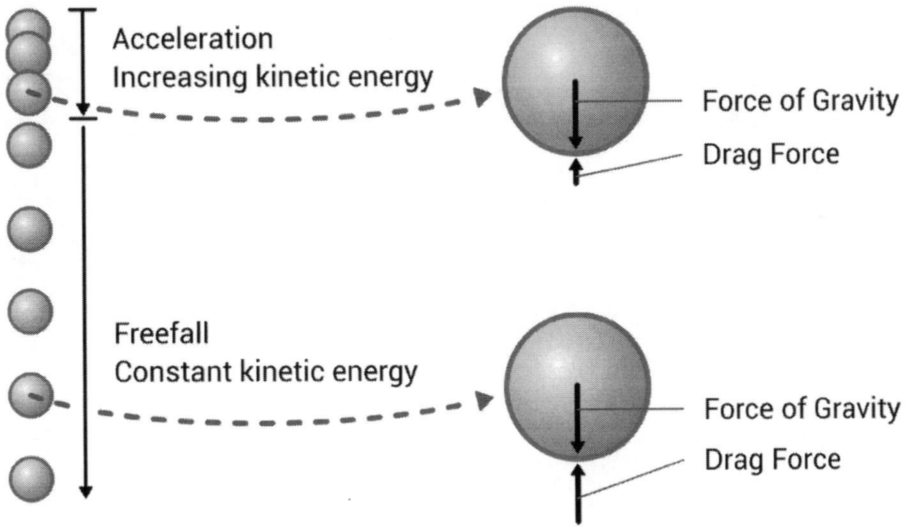

GRAVITATIONAL POTENTIAL ENERGY

Gravitational potential energy is simply the potential for a certain amount of work to be done by one object on another using gravity. For objects on earth, the gravitational potential energy is equal to the amount of work which the earth can act on the object. The work which gravity performs on objects moving entirely or partially in the vertical direction is equal to the force exerted by the earth (weight) times the distance traveled in the direction of the force (height above the ground or reference point): Work from gravity = weight × height above the ground. Thus, the gravitational potential energy is the same as the potential work.

Gravitational Potential Energy = weight × height

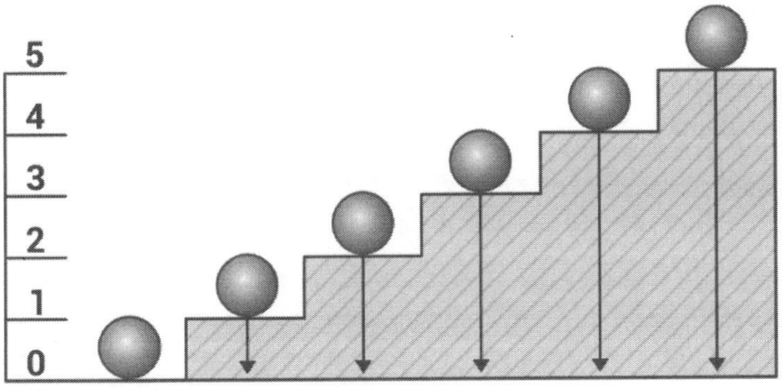

ELASTIC POTENTIAL ENERGY

Elastic potential energy is the potential for a certain amount of work to be done by one object on another using elastic compression or tension. The most common example is the spring. A spring will resist any compression or tension away from its equilibrium position (natural position). A small buggy is pressed into a large spring. The spring contains a large amount of elastic potential energy. If the buggy and spring are released, the spring will exert a force on the buggy, pushing it for a distance. This work will put kinetic energy into the buggy. The energy can be imagined as a liquid poured from one container into another. The spring pours its elastic energy into the buggy, which receives the energy as kinetic energy.

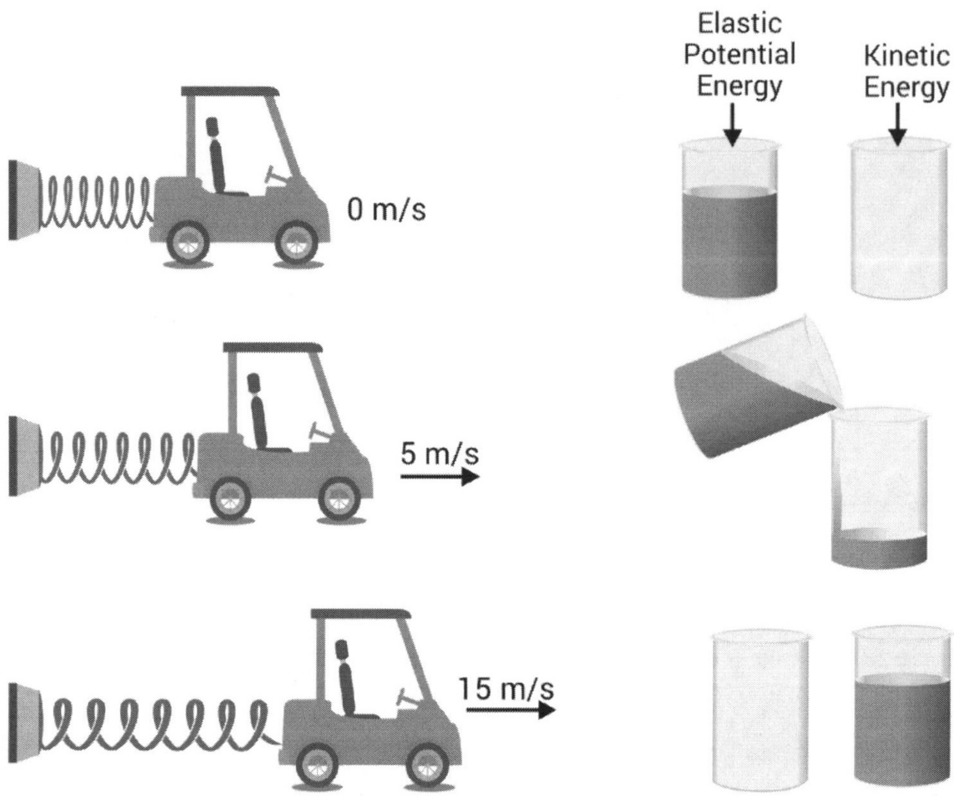

POWER

Concept: The rate of work

Calculation: Work/time

On occasion, you may need to demonstrate an understanding of power as it is defined in applied physics. Power is the rate at which work is done. Power, like work and energy, is a scalar quantity. Power can be calculated by dividing the amount of work performed by the amount of time in which the work was performed: $\textbf{Power} = \frac{\textbf{work}}{\textbf{time}}$. If more work is performed in a shorter amount of time, more power has been exerted. Power can be expressed in a variety of units. The preferred metric expression is one of watts or joules per seconds. Engine power is often expressed in horsepower.

Machines

SIMPLE MACHINES

Concept: Tools which transform forces to make tasks easier.

As their job is to transform forces, simple machines have an input force and an output force or forces. Simple machines transform forces in two ways: direction and magnitude. A machine can change the direction of a force, with respect to the input force, like a single stationary pulley which only changes the direction of the output force. A machine can also change the magnitude of the force like a lever.

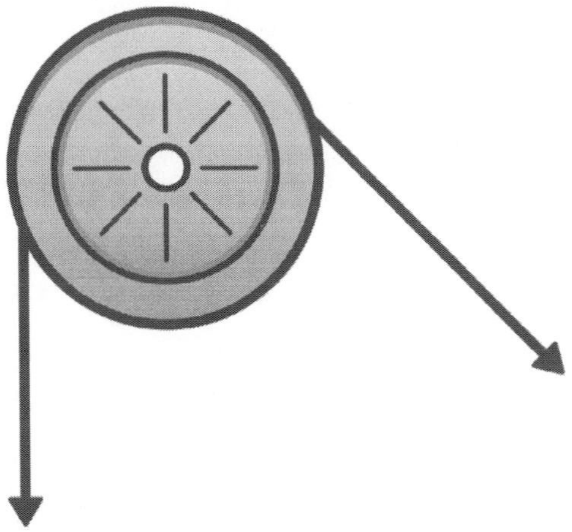

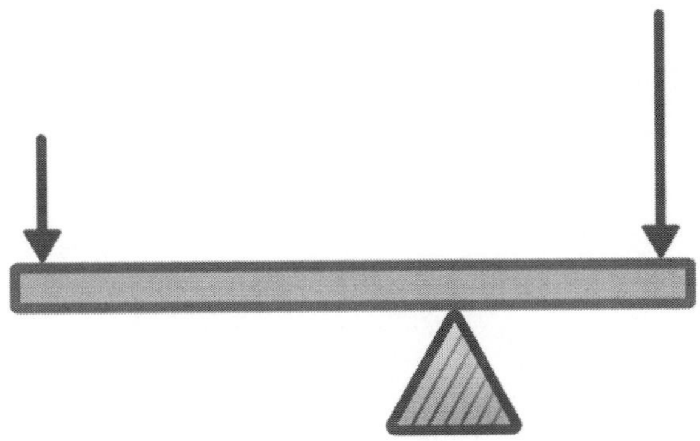

Simple machines include the inclined plane, the wedge, the screw, the pulley, the lever, and the wheel.

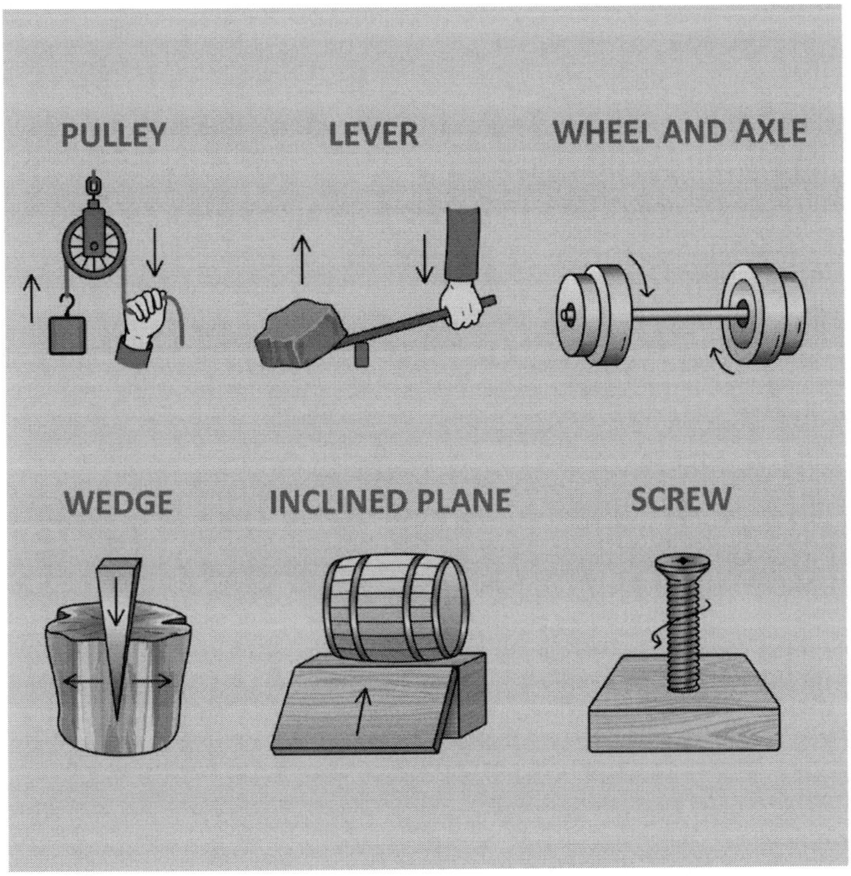

Mechanical Advantage

Concept: The amount of change a simple machine provides to the magnitude of a force

Calculation: Output force/input force

Mechanical advantage is the measure of the output force divided by the input force. Thus, mechanical advantage measures the change performed by a machine. Machines cannot create energy, only transform it. Thus, in frictionless, ideal machines, the input work equals the output work.

$$\mathbf{Work_{input} = Work_{output}}$$

$$\mathbf{force_{input} \times distance_{input} = force_{output} \times distance_{output}}$$

This means that a simple machine can increase the force of the output by decreasing the distance which the output travels or it can increase the distance of the output by decreasing the force at the output.

By moving parts of the equation for work, we can arrive at the equation for mechanical advantage.

$$\mathbf{Mechanical\ Advantage = \frac{force_{output}}{force_{input}} = \frac{distance_{input}}{distance_{output}}}$$

If the mechanical advantage is greater than one, the output force is greater than the input force and the input distance is greater than the output distance. Conversely, if the mechanical advantage is less than one, the input force is greater than the output force and the output distance is greater than the input distance. In equation form this is:

If Mechanical Advantage > 1:

$$\mathbf{force_{input} < force_{output}\ and\ distance_{output} < distance_{input}}$$

If Mechanical Advantage < 1:

$$\mathbf{force_{input} > force_{output}\ and\ distance_{output} > distance_{input}}$$

Inclined Plane

The inclined plane is perhaps the most common of the simple machines. It is simply a flat surface that elevates as you move from one end to the other; a ramp is an easy example of an inclined plane. Consider how much easier it is for an elderly person to walk up a long ramp than to climb a shorter but steeper flight of stairs; this is because the force required is diminished as the distance increases. Indeed, the longer the ramp, the easier it is to ascend.

On the exam, this simple fact will most often be applied to moving heavy objects. For instance, if you have to move a heavy box onto the back of a truck, it is much easier to push it up a ramp than to lift it directly onto the truck bed. The longer the ramp, the greater the mechanical advantage, and the easier it will be to move the box. The mechanical advantage of an inclined plane is equal to the slant length divided by the rise of the plane.

$$\textbf{Mechanical Advantage} = \frac{\textbf{slant length}}{\textbf{rise}}$$

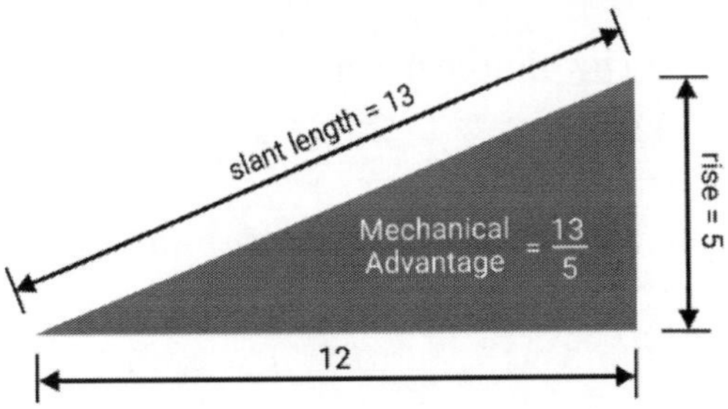

As you solve this kind of problem, however, remember that the same amount of work is being performed whether the box is lifted directly or pushed up a twenty-foot ramp; a simple machine only changes the force and the distance.

WEDGE

A wedge is a variation on the inclined plane, in which the wedge moves between objects or parts and forces them apart. The unique characteristic of a wedge is that, unlike an inclined plane, it is designed to move. Perhaps the most familiar use of the wedge is in splitting wood. A wedge is driven into the wood by hitting the flat back end. The thin end of a wedge is easier to drive into the wood since it has less surface area and, therefore, transmits more force per area. As the wedge is driven in, the increased width helps to split the wood.

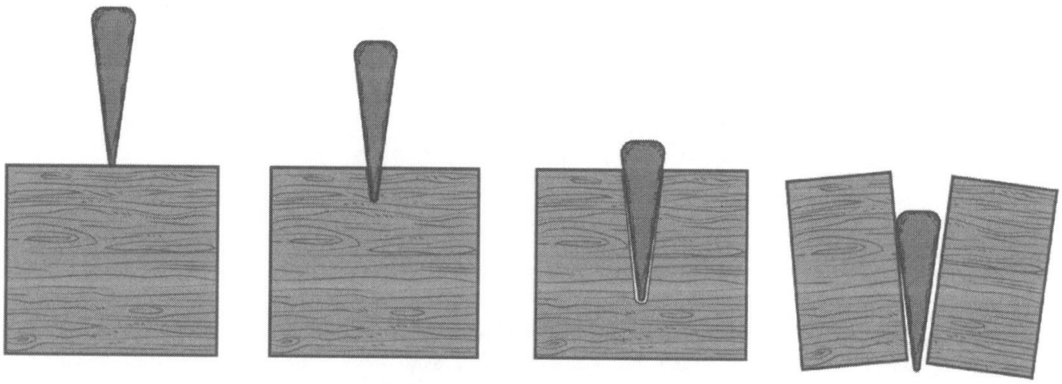

The exam may require you to select the wedge that has the highest mechanical advantage. This should be easy: the longer and thinner the wedge, the greater the mechanical advantage. The equation for mechanical advantage is:

$$\textbf{Mechanical Advantage} = \frac{\textbf{Length}}{\textbf{Width}}$$

Screw

A screw is simply an inclined plane that has been wound around a cylinder so that it forms a sort of spiral.

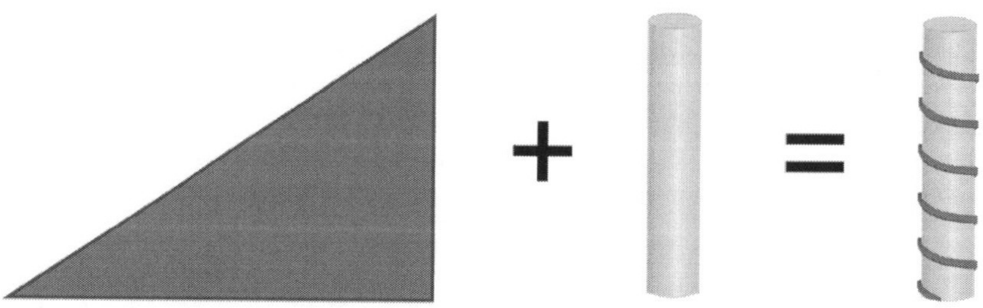

When it is placed into some medium, as for instance wood, the screw will move either forward or backward when it is rotated. The principle of the screw is used in a number of different objects, from jar lids to flashlights. On the exam, you are unlikely to see many questions regarding screws, though you may be presented with a given screw rotation and asked in which direction the screw will move. However, for consistency's sake, the equation for the mechanical advantage is a modification of the inclined plane's equation. Again, the formula for an inclined plane is:

$$\textbf{Mechanical Advantage} = \frac{\textbf{slant length}}{\textbf{rise}}$$

Because the rise of the inclined plane is the length along a screw, length between rotations = rise. Also, the slant length will equal the circumference of one rotation = 2πr.

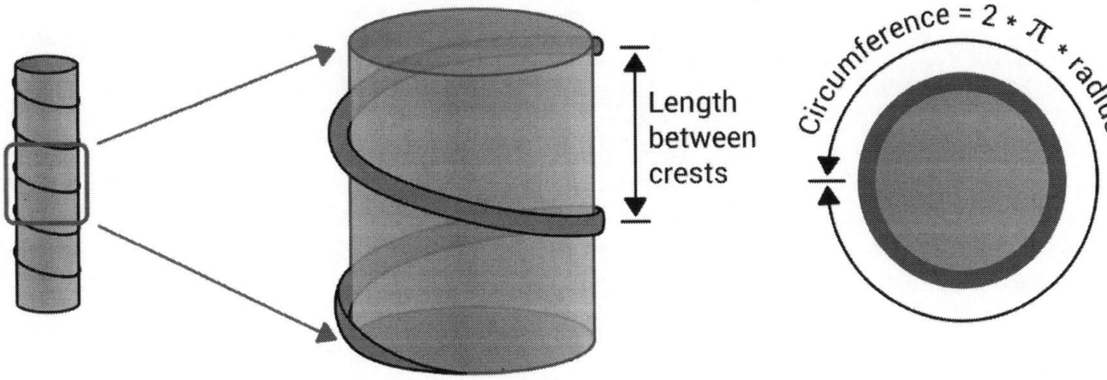

$$\textbf{Mechanical Advantage} = \frac{\textbf{2} \times \boldsymbol{\pi} \times \textbf{radius}}{\textbf{length between crests}}$$

LEVER

The lever is the most common kind of simple machine. See-saws, shovels, and baseball bats are all examples of levers. There are three classes of levers which are differentiated by the relative orientations of the fulcrum, resistance, and effort. The fulcrum is the point at which the lever rotates, the effort is the point on the lever where force is applied, and the resistance is the part of the lever that acts in response to the effort.

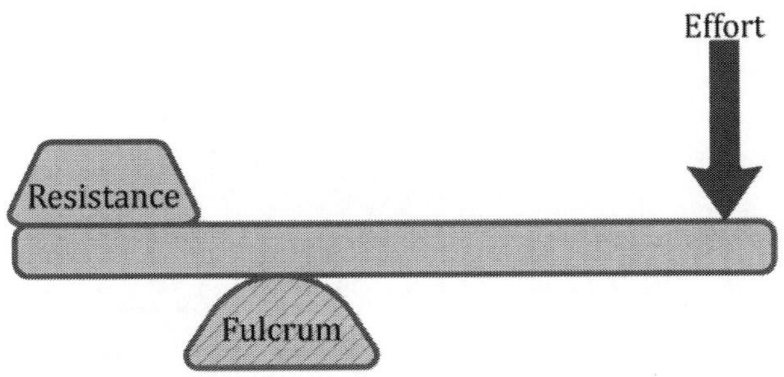

The mechanical advantage of a lever depends on the distances of the effort and resistance from the fulcrum.

$$\textbf{Mechanical Advantage} = \frac{\textbf{effort distance}}{\textbf{resistance distance}}$$

Each class of lever has a different arrangement of effort, fulcrum, and resistance:

First-Class Lever

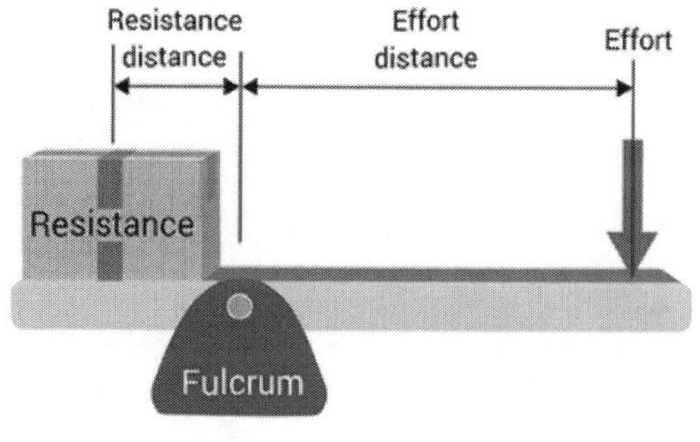

First-Class Lever

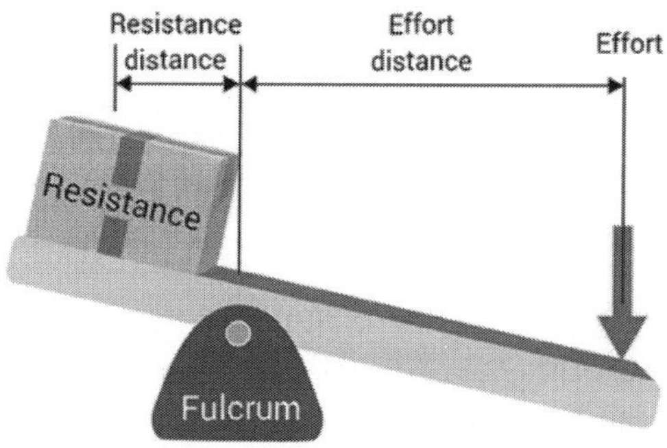

Second-Class Lever

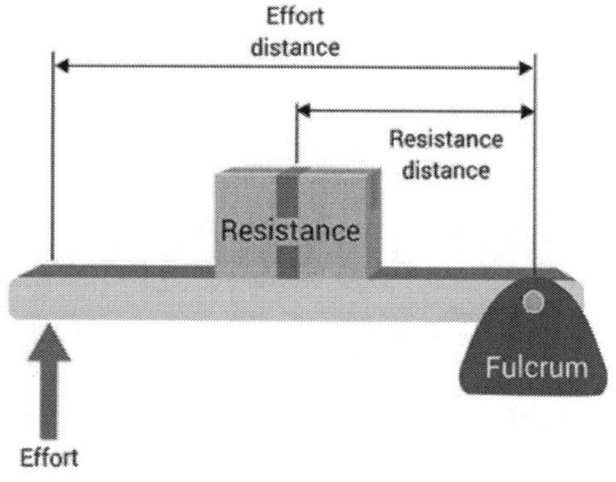

Second-Class Lever

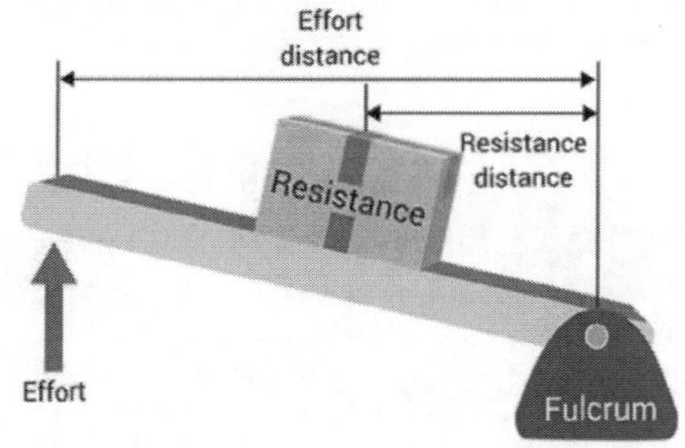

Third-Class Lever

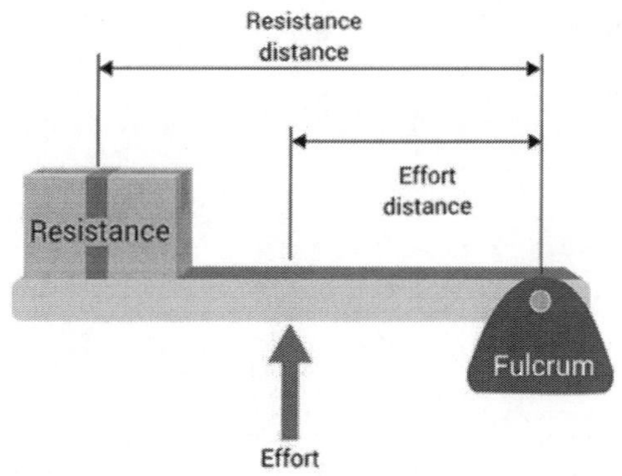

Third-Class Lever

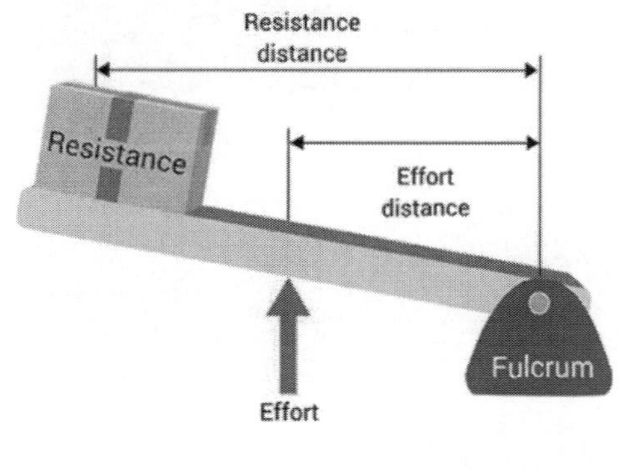

In a first-class lever, the fulcrum is between the effort and the resistance. A seesaw is a good example of a first-class lever when effort is applied to force one end up, the other end goes down, and vice versa. The shorter the distance between the fulcrum and the resistance, the easier it will be to move the resistance. As an example, consider whether it is easier to lift another person on a see-saw when they are sitting close to the middle or all the way at the end. A little practice will show you that it is much more difficult to lift a person the farther away he or she is on the see-saw.

In a second-class lever, the resistance is in between the fulcrum and the effort. While a first-class lever is able to increase force and distance through mechanical advantage, a second-class lever is only able to increase force. A common example of a second-class lever is the wheelbarrow; the force exerted by your hand at one end of the wheelbarrow is magnified at the load. Basically, with a second-class lever, you are trading distance for force; by moving your end of the wheelbarrow a bit farther, you produce greater force at the load.

Third-class levers are used to produce greater distance. In a third-class lever, the force is applied in between the fulcrum and the resistance. A baseball bat is a classic example of a third-class lever; the bottom of the bat, below where you grip it, is considered the fulcrum. The end of the bat, where the ball is struck, is the resistance. By exerting effort at the base of the bat, close to the fulcrum, you are able to make the end of the bat fly quickly through the air. The closer your hands are to the base of the bat, the faster you will be able to make the other end of the bat travel.

Review Video: Levers
Visit mometrix.com/academy and enter code: 103910

PULLEY

The pulley is a simple machine in which a rope is carried by the rotation of a wheel. Another name for a pulley is a block. Pulleys are typically used to allow the force to be directed from a convenient location. For instance, imagine you are given the task of lifting a heavy and tall bookcase. Rather than tying a rope to the bookcase and trying to lift it, it would make sense to tie a pulley system to a rafter above the bookcase and run the rope through it, so that you could pull down on the rope and lift the bookcase. Pulling down allows you to incorporate your weight (normal force) into the act of lifting, thereby making it easier.

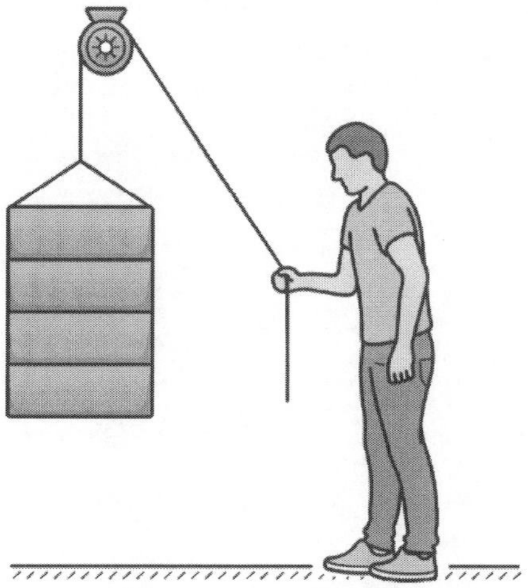

If there is just one pulley above the bookcase, you have created a first-class lever that will not diminish the amount of force that needs to be applied to lift the bookcase. There is another way to use a pulley, however, that can make the job of lifting a heavy object considerably easier. First, tie the rope directly to the rafter. Then, attach a pulley to the top of the bookcase and run the rope through it. If you can then stand so that you are above the bookcase, you will have a much easier time lifting this heavy object. Why? Because the weight of the bookcase is now being distributed: half of it is acting on the rafter, and half of it is acting on you. In other words, this arrangement allows you to lift an object with half the force. This simple pulley system, therefore, has a mechanical advantage of 2. Note that in this arrangement, the unfixed pulley is acting like a second-class lever. The price you pay for your mechanical advantage is that whatever distance you raise your end of the rope, the bookcase will only be lifted half as much.

Of course, it might be difficult for you to find a place high enough to enact this system. If this is the case, you can always tie another pulley to the rafter and run the rope through it and back down to the floor. Since this second pulley is fixed, the mechanical advantage will remain the same.

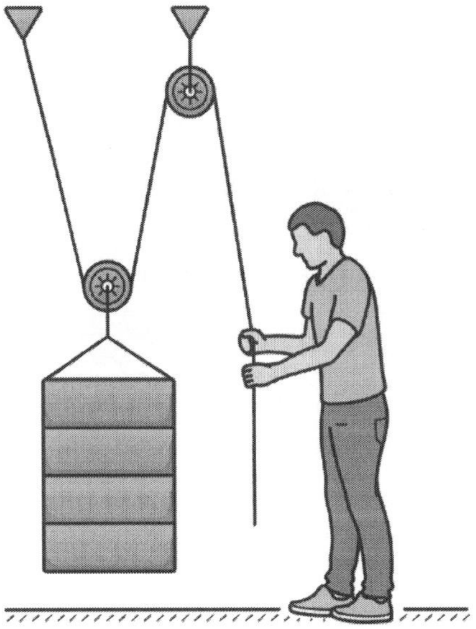

There are other, slightly more complex ways to obtain an even greater mechanical advantage with a system of pulleys. On the exam, you may be required to determine the pulley and tackle (rope) arrangement that creates the greatest mechanical advantage. The easiest way to determine the answer is to count the number of ropes that are going to and from the unfixed pulley; the more ropes coming and going, the greater the mechanical advantage.

Wheel and Axle

Another basic arrangement that makes use of simple machines is called the wheel and axle. When most people think of a wheel and axle, they immediately envision an automobile tire. The steering wheel of the car, however, operates on the same mechanical principle, namely that the force required to move the center of a circle is much greater than the force required to move the outer rim of a circle. When you turn the steering wheel, you are essentially using a second-class lever by increasing the output force by increasing the input distance. The force required to turn the wheel from the outer rim is much less than would be required to turn the wheel from its center. Just imagine how difficult it would be to drive a car if the steering wheel was the size of a saucer!

Conceptually, the mechanical advantage of a wheel is easy to understand. For instance, all other things being equal, the mechanical advantage created by a system will increase along with the radius. In other words, a steering wheel with a radius of 12 inches has a greater mechanical advantage than a steering wheel with a radius of ten inches; the same amount of force exerted on the rim of each wheel will produce greater force at the axis of the larger wheel.

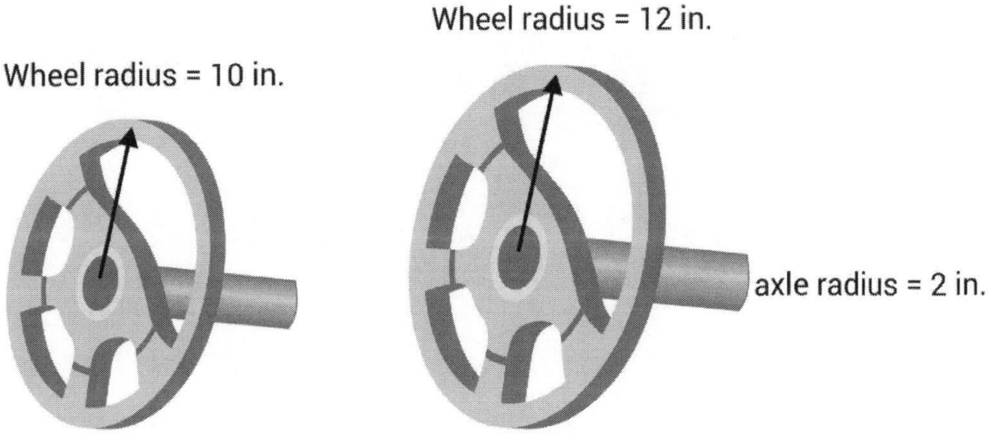

The equation for the mechanical advantage of a wheel and axle is:

$$\textbf{Mechanical Advantage} = \frac{\textbf{radius}_{\textbf{wheel}}}{\textbf{radius}_{\textbf{axle}}}$$

Thus, the mechanical advantage of the steering wheel with a larger radius will be:

$$\textbf{Mechanical Advantage} = \frac{\textbf{12 inches}}{\textbf{2 inches}} = \textbf{6}$$

Review Video: Simple Machines – Wheel and Axle
Visit mometrix.com/academy and enter code: 574045

GEARS

The exam may ask you questions involving some slightly more complex mechanisms. It is very common, for instance, for there to be a couple of questions concerning gears. Gears are a system of interlocking wheels that can create immense mechanical advantages. The amount of mechanical advantage, however, will depend on the gear ratio; that is, on the relation in size between the gears.

When a small gear is driving a big gear, the speed of the big gear is relatively slow; when a big gear is driving a small gear, the speed of the small gear is relatively fast.

The equation for the mechanical advantage is:

$$\textbf{Mechanical Advantage} = \frac{\textbf{Torque}_{\textbf{output}}}{\textbf{Torque}_{\textbf{input}}} = \frac{\textbf{r}_{\textbf{output}}}{\textbf{r}_{\textbf{input}}} = \frac{\textbf{\# of teeth}_{\textbf{output}}}{\textbf{\# of teeth}_{\textbf{input}}}$$

Note that mechanical advantage is greater than 1 when the output gear is larger. In these cases, the output velocity (ω) will be lower. The equation for the relative speed of a gear system is:

$$\frac{\omega_{\text{input}}}{\omega_{\text{output}}} = \frac{r_{\text{output}}}{r_{\text{input}}}$$

$$\textit{Mechanical Advantage} = \frac{\textit{teeth}_{\textit{output}}}{\textit{teeth}_{\textit{input}}} = \frac{20}{10} = 2$$

$$\textit{Mechanical Advantage} = \frac{\textit{teeth}_{\textit{output}}}{\textit{teeth}_{\textit{input}}} = \frac{16}{8} = 2$$

USES OF GEARS

Gears are used to change the direction, location, and amount of output torque, as well as change the angular velocity of output.

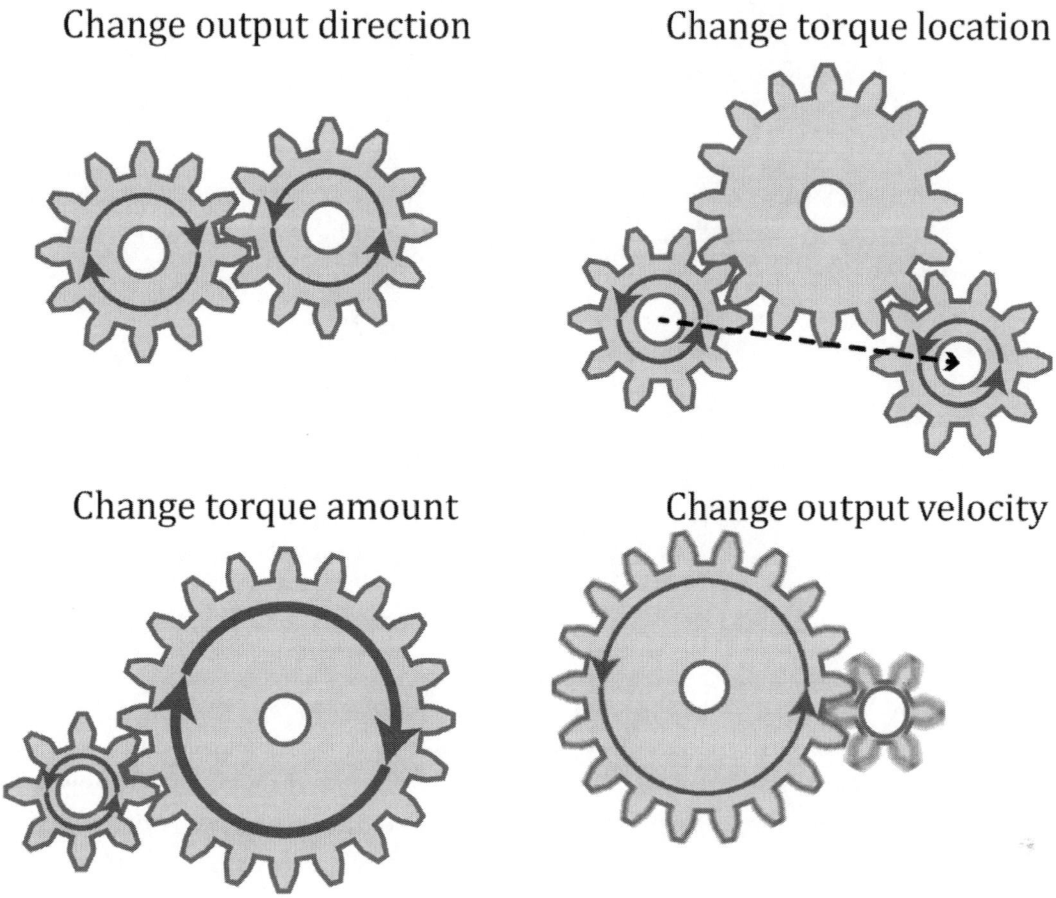

GEAR RATIOS

A gear ratio is a measure of how much the speed and torque are changing in a gear system. It is the ratio of output speed to input speed. Because the number of teeth is directly proportional to the speed in meshing gears, a gear ratio can also be calculated using the number of teeth on the gears. When the driving gear has 30 teeth and the driven gear has 10 teeth, the gear ratio is 3:1.

$$\text{Gear Ratio} = \frac{\#\text{ of teeth}_{\text{driving}}}{\#\text{ of teeth}_{\text{driven}}} = \frac{30}{10} = \frac{3}{1} = 3:1$$

This means that the smaller, driven gear rotates 3 times for every 1 rotation of the driving gear.

The Hydraulic Jack

The hydraulic jack is a simple machine using two tanks and two pistons to change the amount of an output force.

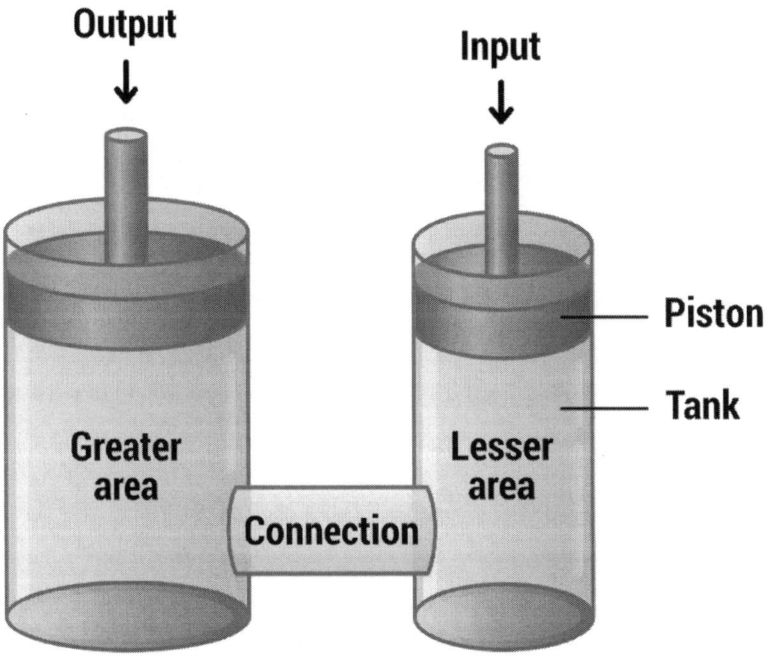

Since fluids are effectively incompressible, when you apply pressure to one part of a contained fluid, that pressure will have to be relieved in equal measure elsewhere in the container. Suppose the input piston has half the surface area of the output piston (10 in^2 compared to 20 in^2), and it is being pushed downward with 50 pounds of force. The pressure being applied to the fluid is $50 \text{ lb} \div 10 \text{ in}^2 = 5 \frac{\text{lb}}{\text{in}^2}$ or 5 psi. When that 5 psi of pressure is applied to the output piston, it pushes that piston upward with a force of $5 \frac{\text{lb}}{\text{in}^2} \times 20 \text{ in}^2 = 100 \text{ lb}$.

The hydraulic jack functions similarly to a first-class lever, but with the important factor being the area of the pistons rather than the length of the lever arms. Note that the mechanical advantage is based on the relative areas, not the relative radii, of the pistons. The radii must be squared to compute the relative areas.

$$\textbf{Mechanical Advantage} = \frac{\textbf{Force}_{\textbf{output}}}{\textbf{Force}_{\textbf{input}}} = \frac{\textbf{area}_{\textbf{output}}}{\textbf{area}_{\textbf{input}}} = \frac{{\textbf{radius}_{\textbf{output}}}^2}{{\textbf{radius}_{\textbf{input}}}^2}$$

Pulleys and Belts

Another system involves two pulleys connected by a drive belt (a looped band that goes around both pulleys). The operation of this system is similar to that of gears, with the exception that the pulleys will rotate in the same direction, while interlocking gears will rotate in opposite directions.

A smaller pulley will always spin faster than a larger pulley, though the larger pulley will generate more torque.

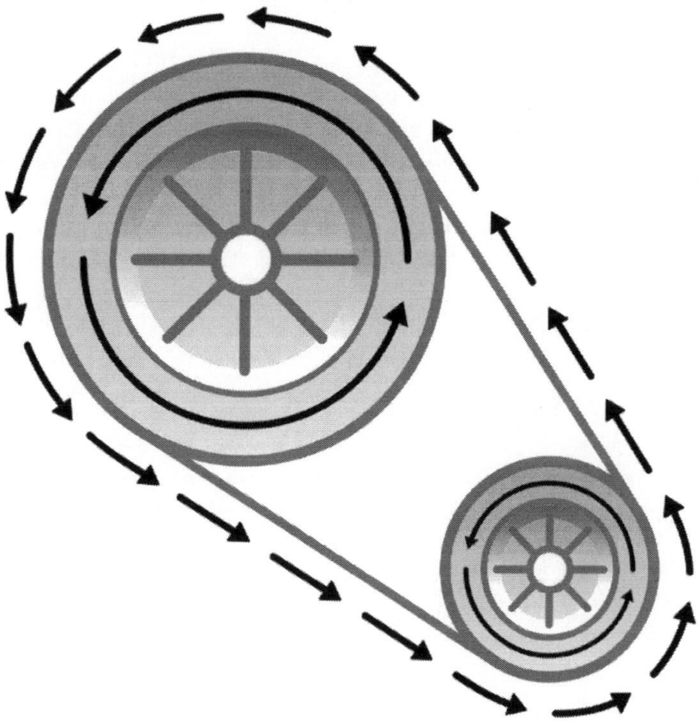

The speed ratio between the pulleys can be determined by comparing their radii; for instance, a 4-inch pulley and a 12-inch pulley will have a speed ratio of 3:1.

Momentum/Impulse

Linear Momentum

Concept: How much a body will resist stopping

Calculation: Momentum = mass × velocity

In physics, linear momentum can be found by multiplying the mass and velocity of an object. Momentum and velocity will always be in the same direction. Newton's second law describes momentum, stating that the rate of change of momentum is proportional to the force exerted and is in the direction of the force. If we assume a closed and isolated system (one in which no objects leave or enter, and upon which the sum of external forces is zero), then we can assume that the momentum of the system will neither increase nor decrease. That is, we will find that the momentum is a constant. The law of conservation of linear momentum applies universally in physics, even in situations of extremely high velocity or with subatomic particles.

Collisions

This concept of momentum takes on new importance when we consider collisions. A collision is an isolated event in which a strong force acts between each of two or more colliding bodies for a brief period of time. However, a collision is more intuitively defined as one or more objects hitting each other.

When two bodies collide, each object exerts a force on the opposite member. These equal and opposite forces change the linear momentum of the objects. However, when both bodies are considered, the net momentum in collisions is conserved.

There are two types of collisions: elastic and inelastic. The difference between the two lies in whether kinetic energy is conserved. If the total kinetic energy of the system is conserved, the collision is elastic. Visually, elastic collisions are collisions in which objects bounce perfectly. If some of the kinetic energy is transformed into heat or another form of energy, the collision is inelastic. Visually, inelastic collisions are collisions in which the objects stick to each other or bounce but do not return to their original height.

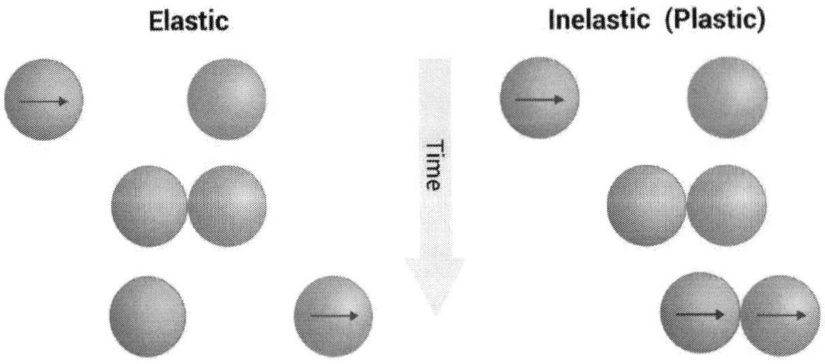

If the two bodies involved in an elastic collision have the same mass, then the body that was moving will stop completely, and the body that was at rest will begin moving at the same velocity as the projectile was moving before the collision.

Fluids

FLUIDS

Concept: Liquids and gasses

A few of the questions on the exam will probably require you to consider the behavior of fluids. It sounds obvious, perhaps, but fluids can best be defined as substances that flow. A fluid will conform, slowly or quickly, to any container in which it is placed. Both liquids and gasses are considered to be fluids. Fluids are essentially those substances in which the atoms are not arranged in any permanent, rigid way. In ice, for instance, atoms are all lined up in what is known as a crystalline lattice, while in water and steam, the only intermolecular arrangements are haphazard connections between neighboring molecules.

Flow Rates

When liquids flow in and out of containers at certain rates, the change in volume is the volumetric flow in minus the volumetric flow out. Volumetric flow is essentially the amount of volume moved past some point divided by the time it took for the volume to pass.

$$\textbf{Volumetric flow rate} = \frac{\textbf{volume moved}}{\textbf{time for the movement}}$$

If the flow into a container is greater than the flow out, the container will fill with the fluid. However, if the flow out of a container is greater than the flow into a container, the container will drain of the fluid.

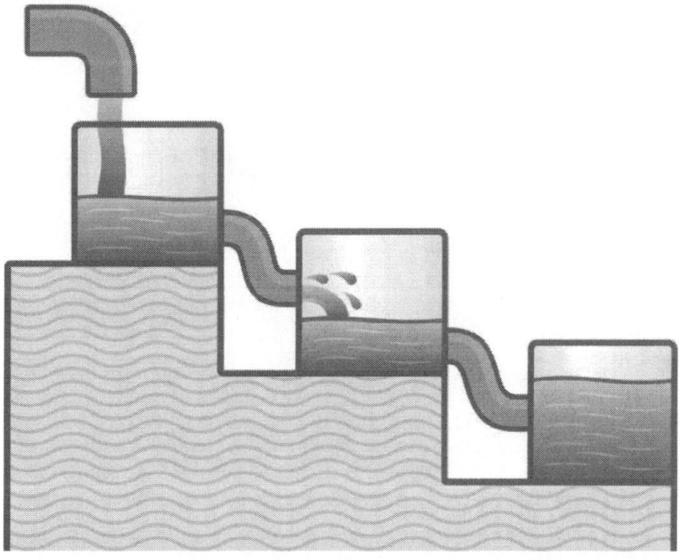

DENSITY

Concept: How much mass is in a specific volume of a substance

Calculation: Density $= \rho = \frac{\text{mass}}{\text{volume}}$

Density is essentially how much stuff there is in a volume or space. The density of a fluid is generally expressed with the symbol ρ (the Greek letter *rho*). Density is a scalar property, meaning that it has no direction component.

PRESSURE

Concept: The amount of force applied per area

Calculation: Pressure $= \frac{\text{force}}{\text{area}}$

Pressure, like fluid density, is a scalar and does not have a direction. The equation for pressure is concerned only with the magnitude of that force, not with the direction in which it is pointing. The SI unit of pressure is the Newton per square meter, or Pascal.

As every deep-sea diver knows, the pressure of water becomes greater the deeper you go below the surface; conversely, experienced mountain climbers know that air pressure decreases as they gain a higher altitude. These pressures are typically referred to as hydrostatic pressures because they involve fluids at rest.

Pascal's Principle

The exam may also require you to demonstrate some knowledge of how fluids move. Anytime you squeeze a tube of toothpaste, you are demonstrating the idea known as Pascal's principle. This principle states that a change in the pressure applied to an enclosed fluid is transmitted undiminished to every portion of the fluid as well as to the walls of the containing vessel.

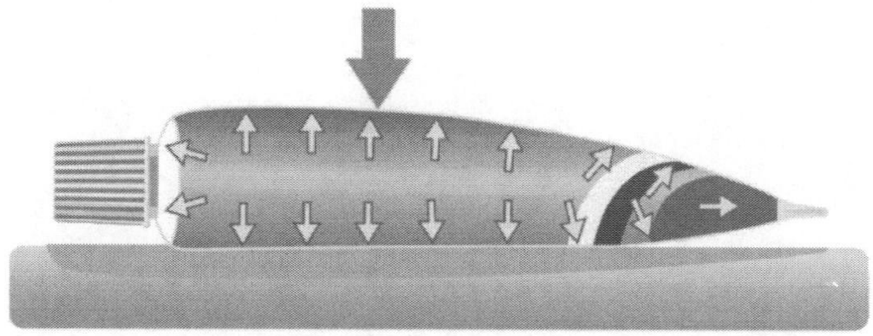

Buoyant Force

If an object is submerged in water, it will have a buoyant force exerted on it in the upward direction. Often, of course, this buoyant force is much too small to keep an object from sinking to the bottom. Buoyancy is summarized in Archimedes' principle; a body wholly or partially submerged in a fluid will be buoyed up by a force equal to the weight of the fluid that the body displaces.

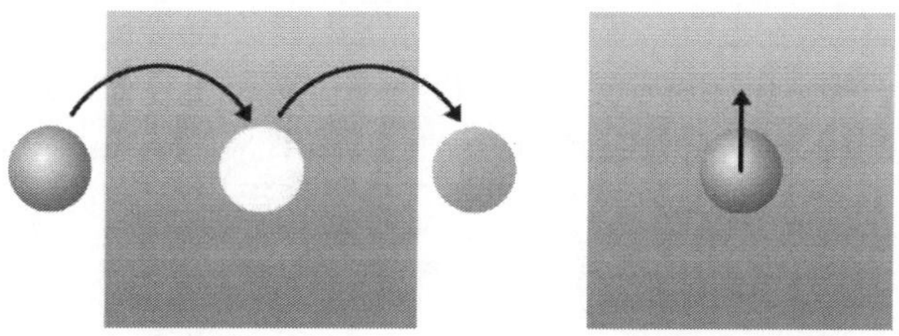

If the buoyant force is greater than the weight of an object, the object will go upward. If the weight of the object is greater than the buoyant force, the object will sink. When an object is floating on the surface, the buoyant force has the same magnitude as the weight.

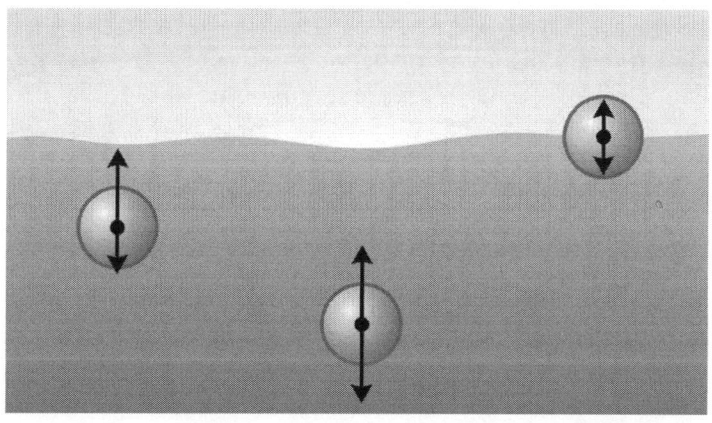

Even though the weight of a floating object is precisely balanced by a buoyant force, these forces will not necessarily act at the same point. The weight will act from the center of mass of the object, while the buoyancy will act from the center of mass of the hole in the water made by the object (known as the center of buoyancy). If the floating object is tilted, then the center of buoyancy will shift and the object may be unstable. In order to remain in equilibrium, the center of buoyancy must always shift in such a way that the buoyant force and weight provide a restoring torque, one that will restore the body to its upright position. This concept is, of course, crucial to the construction of boats which must always be made to encourage restoring torque.

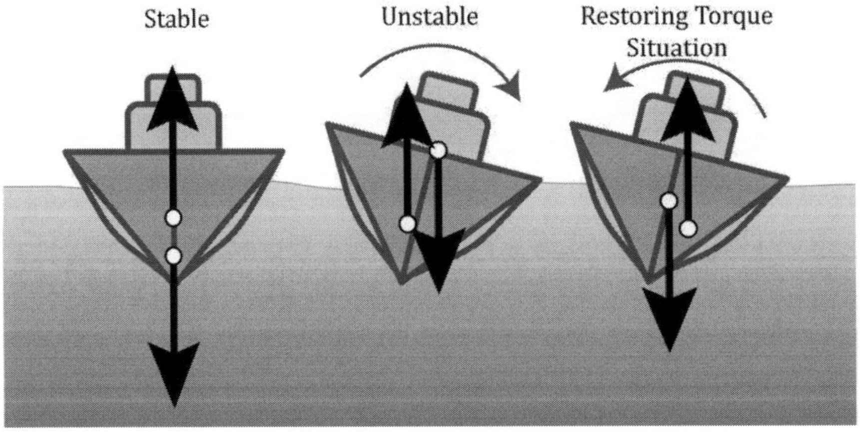

Ideal Fluids

Because the motion of actual fluids is extremely complex, the exam usually assumes ideal fluids when they set up their problems. Using ideal fluids in fluid dynamics problems is like discounting friction in other problems. Therefore, when we deal with ideal fluids, we are making four assumptions. It is important to keep these in mind when considering the behavior of fluids on the exam. First, we are assuming that the flow is steady; in other words, the velocity of every part of the fluid is the same. Second, we assume that fluids are incompressible and therefore have a consistent density. Third, we assume that fluids are nonviscous, meaning that they flow easily and without resistance. Fourth, we assume that the flow of ideal fluids is irrotational: that is, particles in the fluid will not rotate around a center of mass.

Bernoulli's Principle

When fluids move, they do not create or destroy energy; this modification of Newton's second law for fluid behavior is called Bernoulli's principle. It is essentially just a reformulation of the law of conservation of mechanical energy for fluid mechanics.

The most common application of Bernoulli's principle is that pressure and speed are inversely related, assuming constant altitude. Thus, if the elevation of the fluid remains constant and the speed of a fluid particle increases as it travels along a streamline, the pressure will decrease. If the fluid slows down, the pressure will increase.

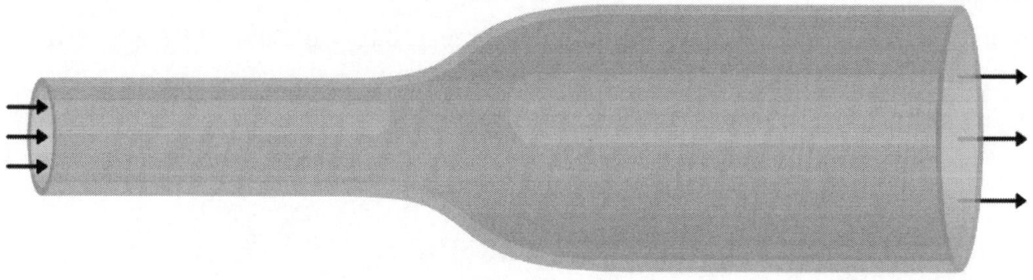

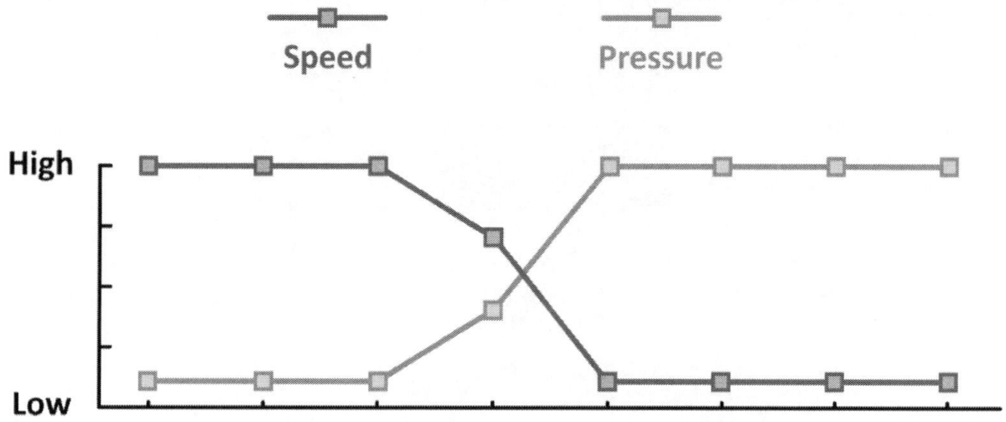

Heat Transfer

HEAT TRANSFER

Heat is a type of energy. Heat transfers from the hot object to the cold object through the three forms of heat transfer: conduction, convection, and radiation.

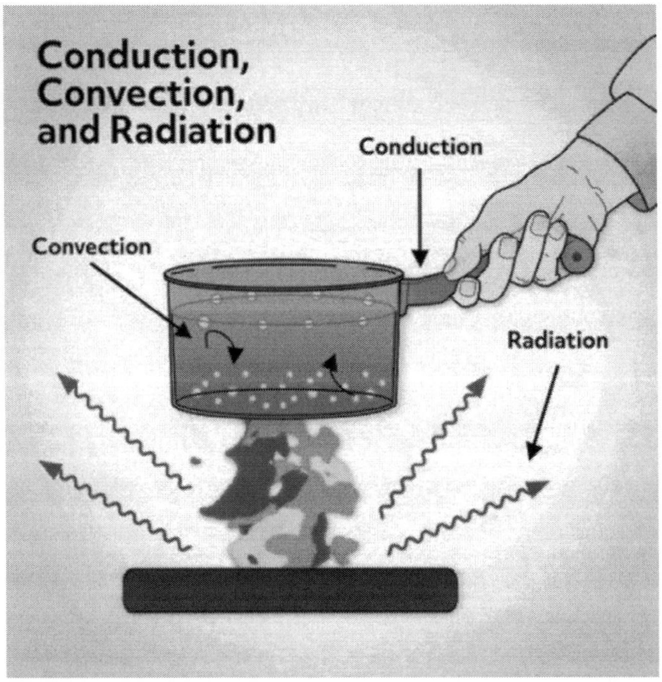

Conduction is the transfer of heat by physical contact. When you touch a hot pot, the pot transfers heat to your hand by conduction.

Convection is the transfer of heat by the movement of fluids. When you put your hand in steam, the steam transfers heat to your hand by convection.

Radiation is the transfer of heat by electromagnetic waves. When you put your hand near a campfire, the fire heats your hand by radiation.

Review Video: Heat Transfer
Visit mometrix.com/academy and enter code: 451646

PHASE CHANGES

Materials exist in four phases or states: solid, liquid, gas, and plasma. However, as most tests will not cover plasma, we will focus on solids, liquids, and gases. The solid state is the densest in almost all cases (water is the most notable exception), followed by liquid, and then gas.

The catalyst for phase change (changing from one phase to another) is heat. When a solid is heated, it will change into a liquid. The same process of heating will change a liquid into a gas.

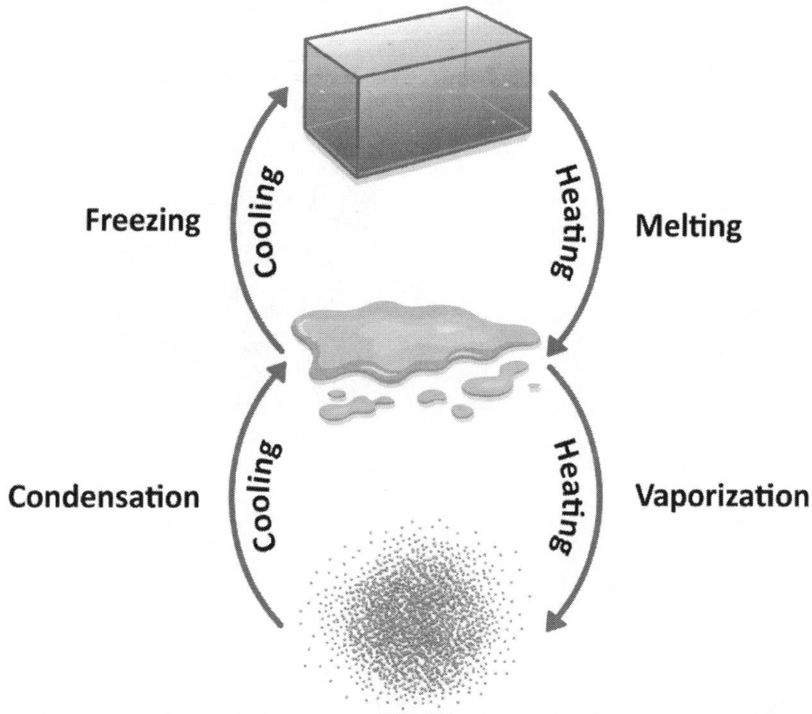

Review Video: States of Matter
Visit mometrix.com/academy and enter code: 742449

Optics

OPTICS

Lenses change the way light travels. Lenses are able to achieve this by the way in which light travels at different speeds in different mediums. The essentials to optics with lenses deal with concave and convex lenses. Concave lenses make objects appear smaller, while convex lenses make objects appear larger.

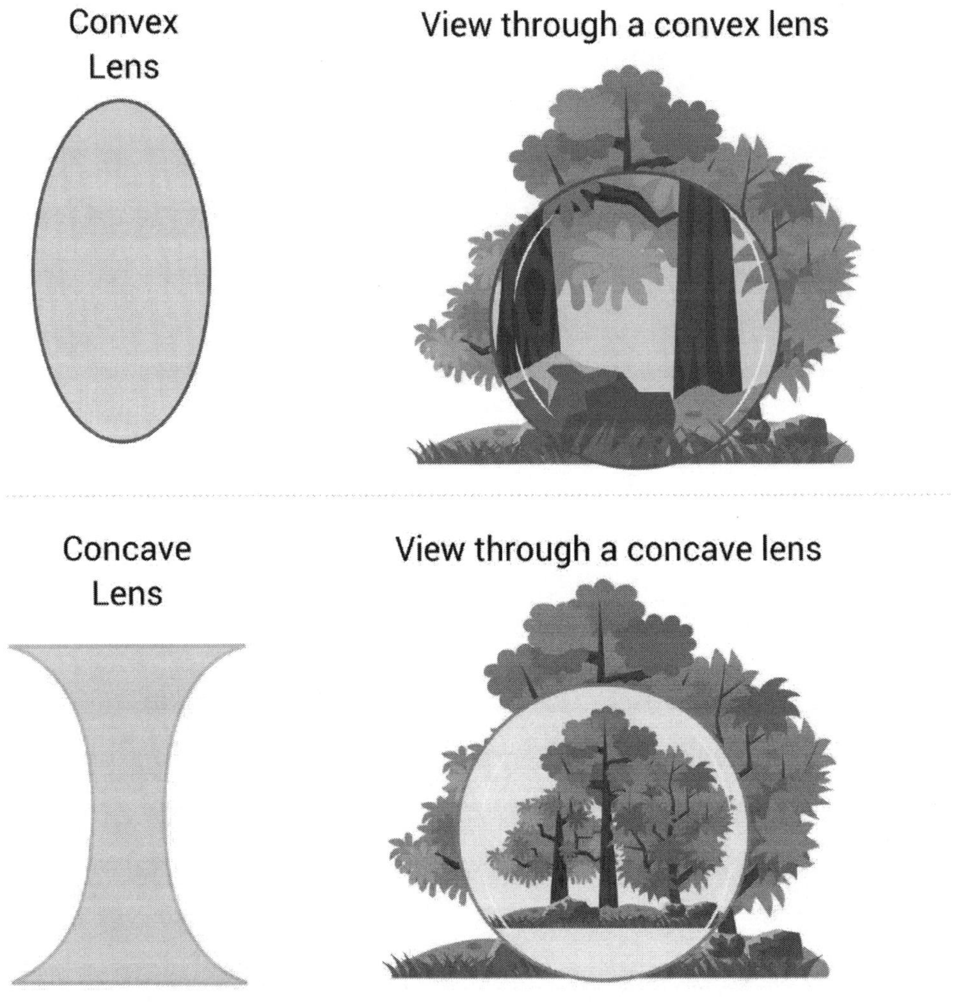

Electricity

ELECTRIC CHARGE

Much like gravity, electricity is an everyday observable phenomenon which is very complex, but may be understood as a set of behaviors. As the gravitational force exists between objects with mass, the electric force exists between objects with electrical charge. In all atoms, the protons have a positive charge, the electrons have a negative charge, and the neutrons have no charge. An imbalance of electrons and protons in an object results in a net charge. Unlike gravity, which only pulls, electrical forces can push objects apart as well as pull them together.

Similar electric charges repel each other. Opposite charges attract each other.

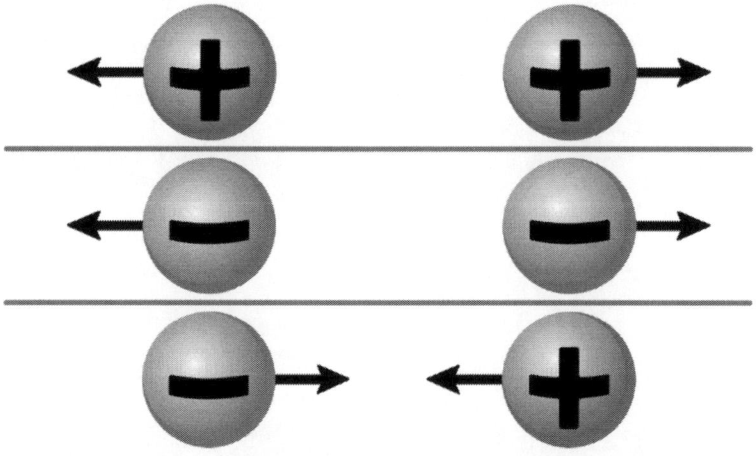

Review Video: Electric Charge
Visit mometrix.com/academy and enter code: 323587

CURRENT

Electrons (and electrical charge with it) move through conductive materials by switching quickly from one atom to another. This electrical flow can manipulate energy like mechanical systems.

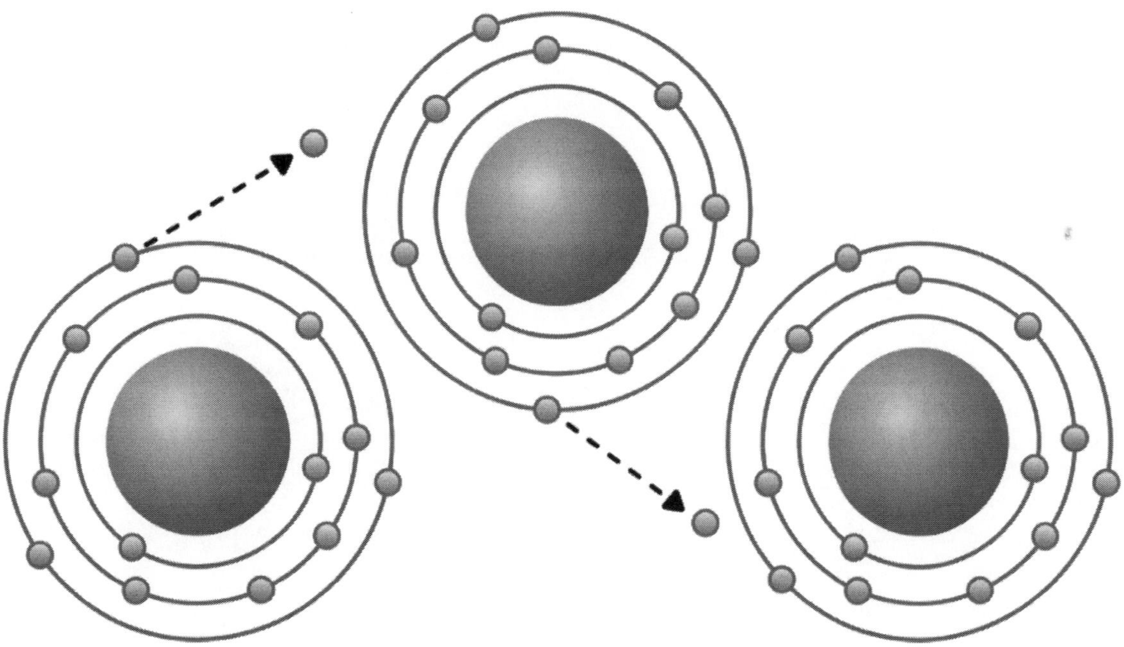

The term for the rate at which the charge flows through a conductive material is *current*. Because each electron carries a specific charge, current can be thought of as the number of electrons passing a point in a length of time. Current is measured in Amperes (A), each unit of which is approximately 6.24×10^{18} electrons per second.

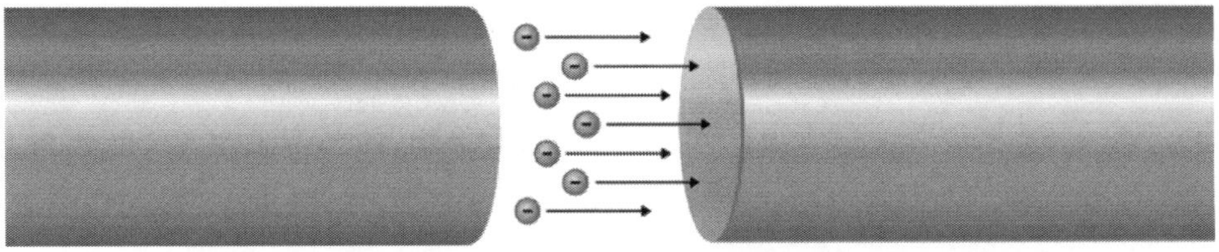

Electric current carries energy much like moving balls carry energy.

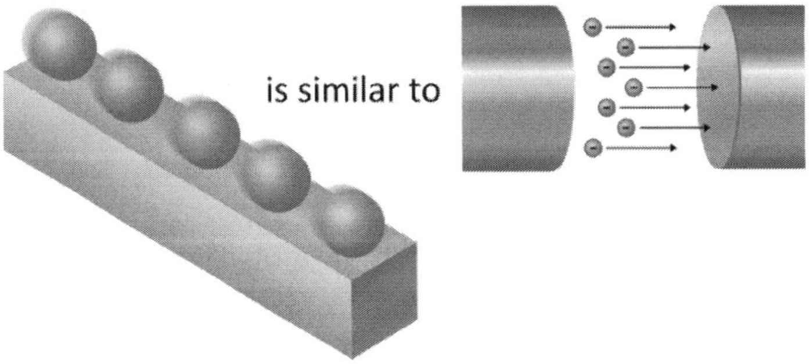

Voltage

Voltage is the potential for electric work. It can also be thought of as the *push* behind electrical work. Voltage is similar to gravitational potential energy.

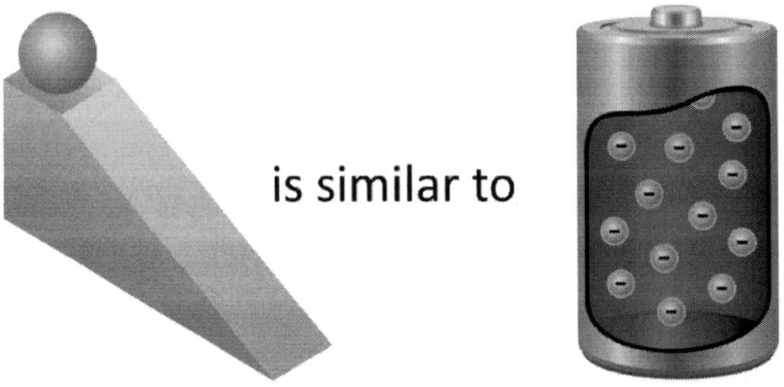

Anything used to generate a voltage, such as a battery or a generator, is called a voltage source. Voltage is conveniently measured in Volts (V).

Resistance

Resistance is the amount something hinders the flow of electrical current. Electrical resistance is much like friction, resisting flow and dissipating energy.

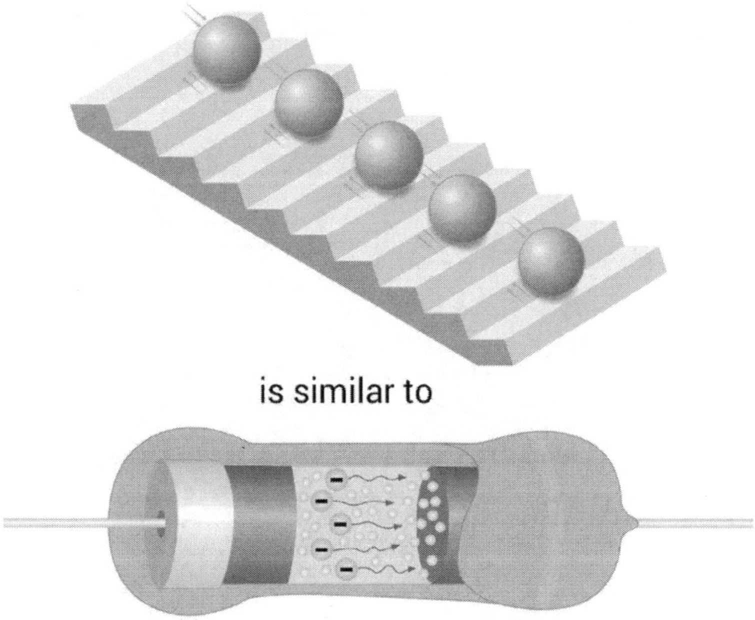

Different objects have different resistances. A resistor is an electrical component designed to have a specific resistance, measured in Ohms (Ω).

Review Video: Resistance of Electric Currents
Visit mometrix.com/academy and enter code: 668423

Basic Circuits

A circuit is a closed loop through which current can flow. A simple circuit contains a voltage source and a resistor. The current flows from the positive side of the voltage source through the resistor to the negative side of the voltage source.

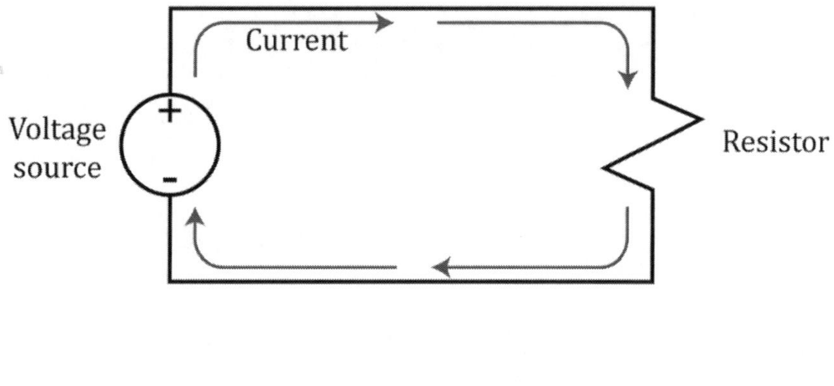

If we plot the voltage of a simple circuit, the similarities to gravitational potential energy appear.

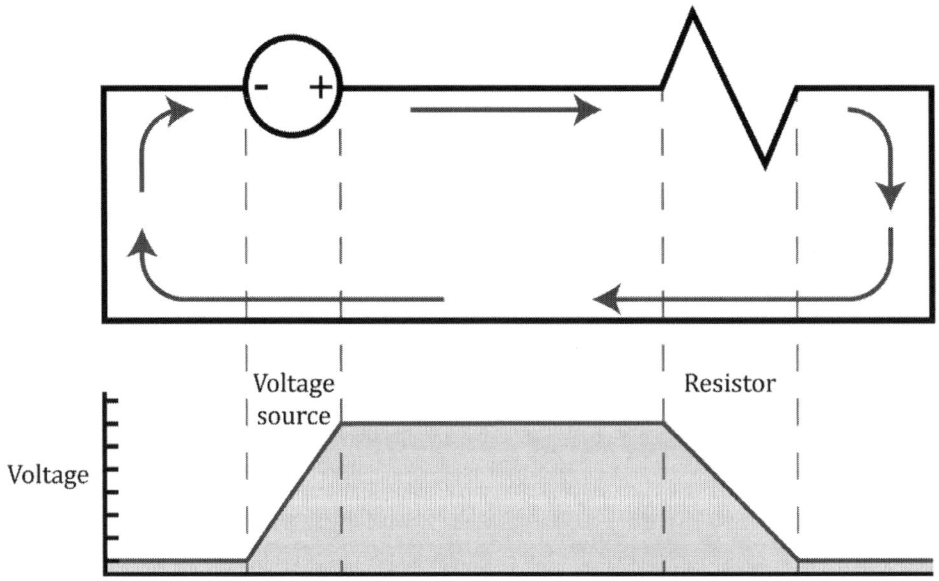

If we consider the circuit to be a track, the electrons would be balls, the voltage source would be a powered lift, and the resistor would be a sticky section of the track. The lift raises the balls, increasing their potential energy. This potential energy is expended as the balls roll down the sticky section of the track.

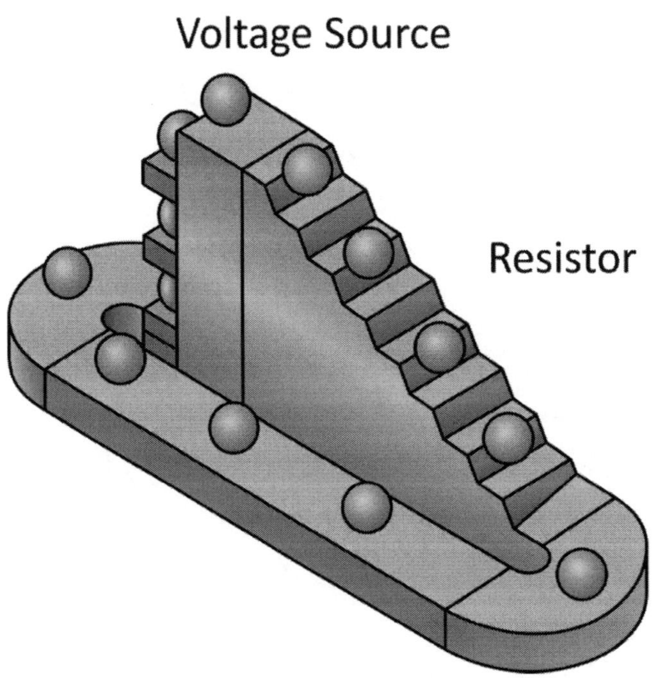

Ohm's Law

A principle called Ohm's Law explains the relationship between the voltage, current, and resistance. The voltage drop over a resistance is equal to the amount of current times the resistance:

$$\textbf{Voltage (V)} = \textbf{current (I)} \times \textbf{resistance (R)}$$

We can gain a better understanding of this equation by looking at a reference simple circuit and then changing one variable at a time to examine the results.

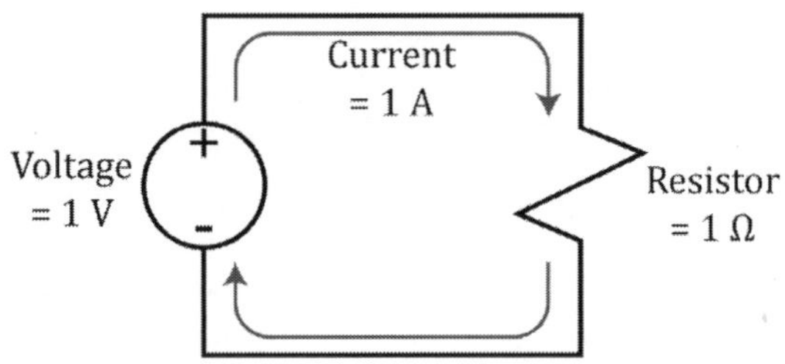

Voltage = Current * Resistance
1V = 1A * 1Ω

Increased Resistance

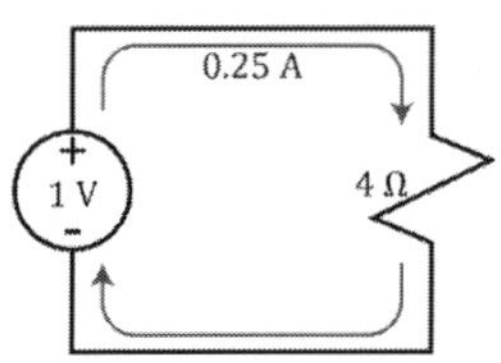

Voltage = Current * Resistance
1V = 0.25A * 4Ω

Increased Current

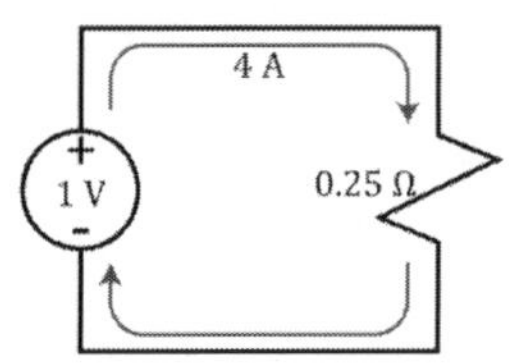

Voltage = Current * Resistance
1V = 4A * 0.25Ω

Increased Voltage

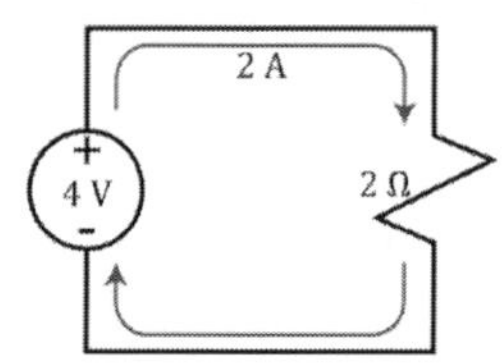

Voltage = Current * Resistance
4V = 2A * 2Ω

Series Circuits

A series circuit is a circuit with two or more resistors on the same path. The same current runs through both resistors. However, the total voltage drop splits between the resistors. The resistors in series can be added together to make an equivalent basic circuit.

$$\mathbf{R_{equiv} = R_1 + R_2}$$

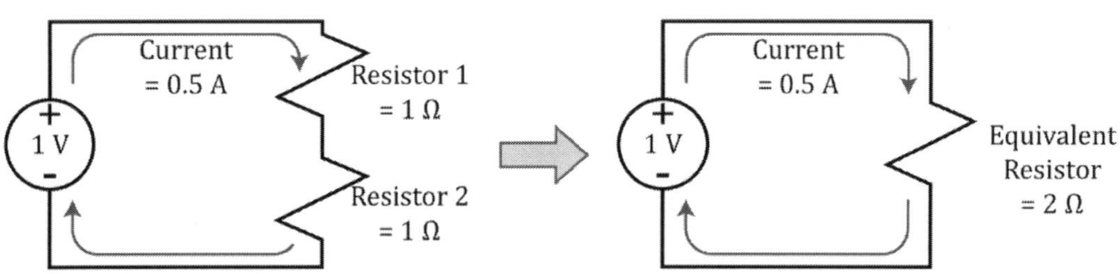

Voltage = Current * Resistance
1V = 0.5A * 2Ω

Voltage = Current * Resistance
1V = 0.5A * 2Ω

Parallel Circuits

A parallel circuit is a circuit with two or more resistors on different, parallel paths. Unlike the series circuit, the current splits between the different paths in a parallel circuit. Resistors in parallel can be reduced to an equivalent circuit, but not by simply adding the resistances. The inverse of the equivalent resistance of parallel resistors is equal to the sum of the inverses of the resistance of each leg of the parallel circuit. In equation form that means:

$$\frac{1}{R_{equiv}} = \frac{1}{R_1} + \frac{1}{R_2}$$

Or when solved for equivalent resistance:

$$R_{equiv} = \frac{1}{\frac{1}{R_1} + \frac{1}{R_2}}$$

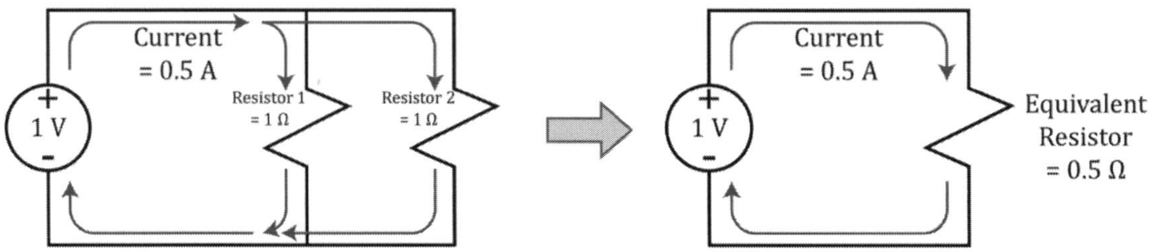

$$R_{equiv} = \frac{1}{\frac{1}{1\ \Omega} + \frac{1}{1\ \Omega}} = 0.5\ \Omega$$

Electrical Power

Electrical power, or the energy output over time, is equal to the current resulting from a voltage source times the voltage of that source:

$$\textbf{Power(P)} = \textbf{current (I)} \times \textbf{voltage (V)}$$

Thanks to Ohm's Law, we can write this relation in two other ways:

$$P = I^2R$$

$$P = \frac{V^2}{R}$$

For instance, if a circuit is composed of a 9 Volt battery and a 3 Ohm resistor, the power output of the battery will be:

$$\text{Power} = \frac{V^2}{R} = \frac{9^2}{3} = 27 \text{ Watts}$$

AC vs. DC

Up until this point, current has been assumed to flow in one direction. One directional flow is called Direct Current (DC). However, there is another type of electric current: Alternating Current (AC).

Many circuits use AC power sources, in which the current flips back and forth rapidly between directions.

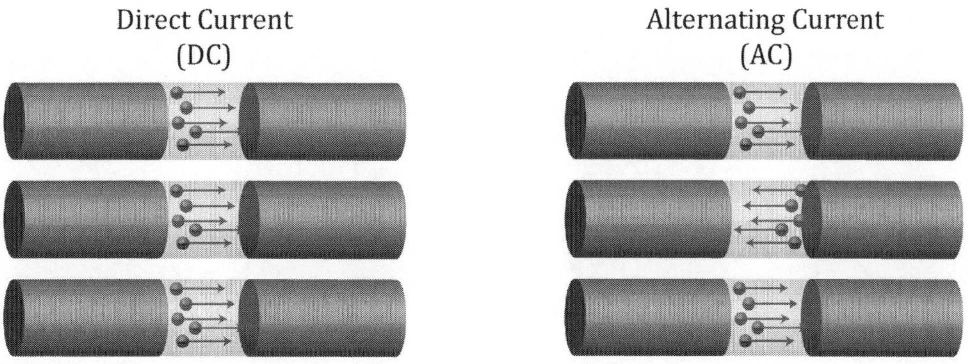

Capacitors

Capacitors are electrical components which store voltage. Capacitors are made from two conductive surfaces separated from each other by a space and/or insulation. Capacitors resist changes to voltage. Capacitors don't stop AC circuits (although they do affect the current flow), but they do stop DC circuits, acting as open circuits.

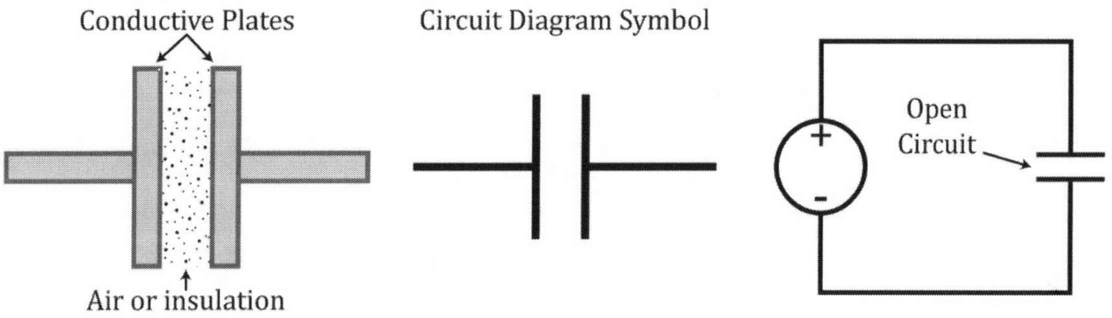

Inductors

Inductors are electrical components which effectively store current. Inductors use the relationship between electricity and magnetism to resist changes in current by running the current through coils of wire. Inductors don't stop DC circuits, but they do resist AC circuits as AC circuits utilize changing currents.

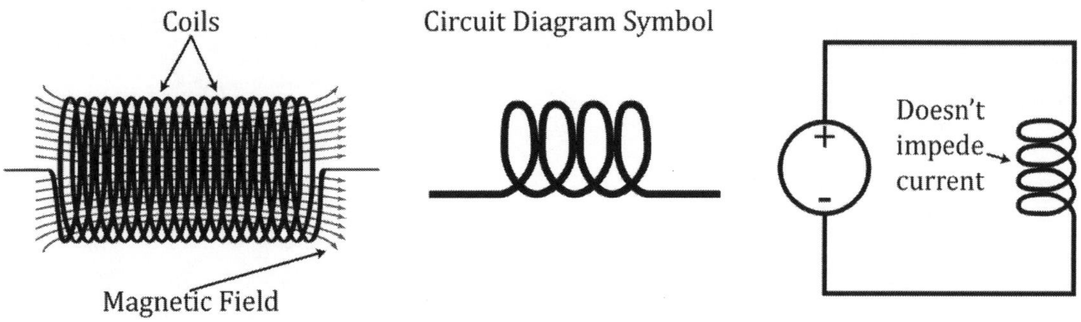

Diodes

Diodes are electrical components which limit the flow of electricity to one direction. If current flows through a diode in the intended direction, the diode will allow the flow. However, a diode will stop current if it runs the wrong way.

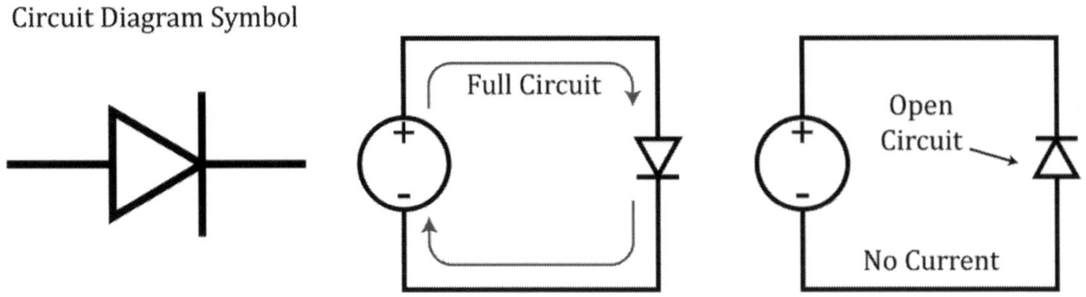

Magnetism

Magnetism

Magnetism is an attraction between opposite poles of magnetic materials and a repulsion between similar poles of magnetic materials. Magnetism can be natural or induced with the use of electric currents. Magnets almost always exist with two polar sides: north and south. A magnetic force exists between two poles on objects. Different poles attract each other. Like poles repel each other.

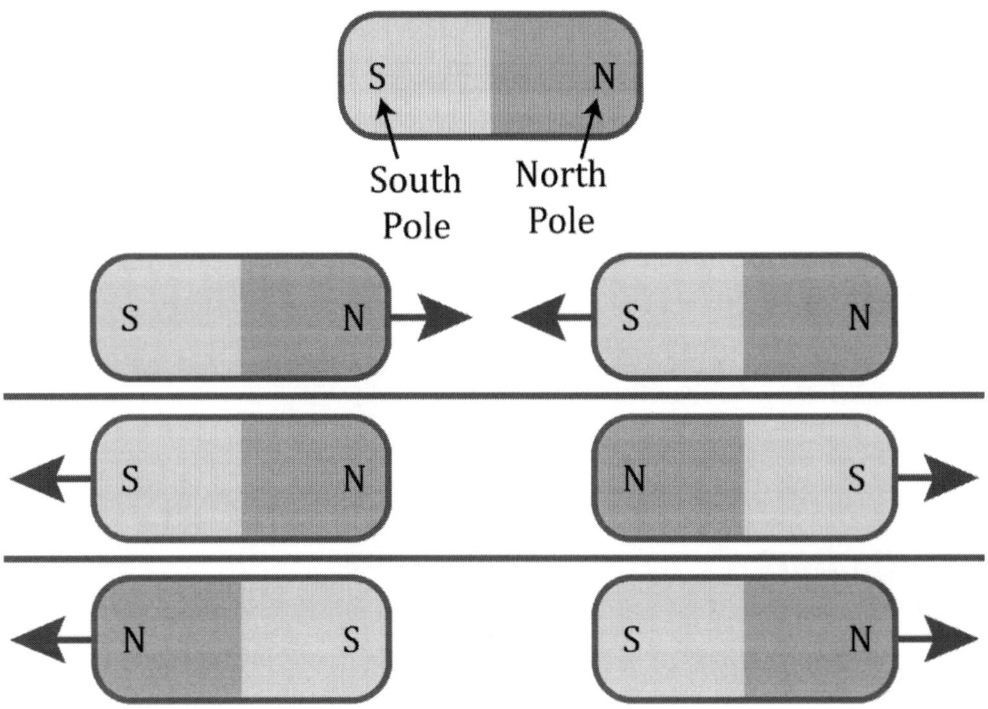

Chapter Quiz

Ready to see how well you retained what you just read? Scan the QR code to go directly to the chapter quiz interface for this study guide. If you're using a computer, simply visit the online resources page at **mometrix.com/resources719/afct** and click the Chapter Quizzes link.

Assembling Objects

This section of the test measures your ability to imagine the way an object will look when its pieces are joined together properly. The questions that make up this section will begin with a subdivided image that may have joined or disconnected sections. Some images may be marked with one or more points that may each be labelled with a letter. If there is a dotted line drawn from the letter to the object, this means that the letter corresponds to a place on the side of the object that cannot be seen.

Your task will be to imagine how the object will look when rearranged according to the question by assembling, rearranging, connecting, stacking, and reflecting the images.

Subdivided Objects

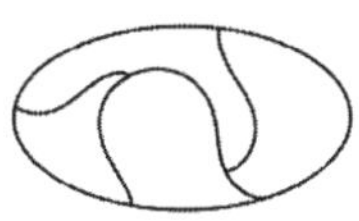

Joined Sections

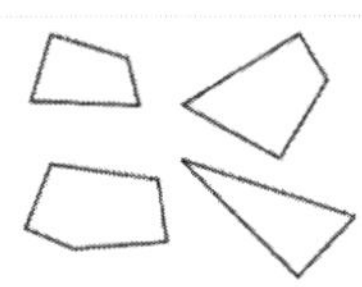

Disconnected Sections

Connecting and Stacking Points on Objects

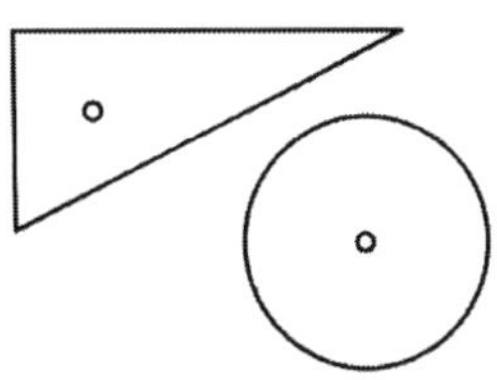

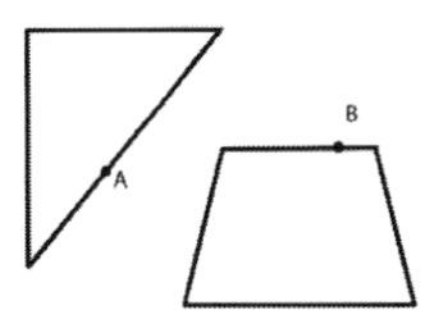

Assembling

When assembling disconnected sections of a shape, process of elimination can be used to quickly reduce the number of possible answers. Start by counting the number of sides on each section and noting if any edges are rounded.

Section A

Section B

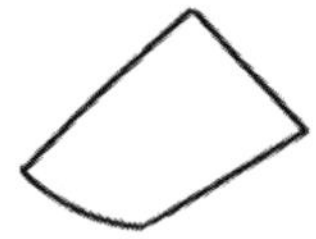

Section C

Section D

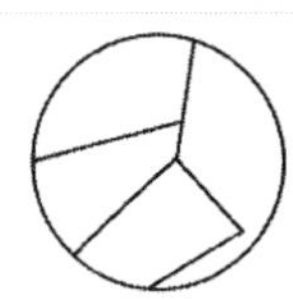

Whole Shape

For example, each subsection of the image above has a rounded edge. The section A has two straight edges, section B has three straight edges, section C has three straight edges, and section D has three straight edges. Then examine each assembled shape in the answer choices, eliminating choices with more or less than four total sections and those that have no rounded edges. Count the number of straight edges of each section or each shape, and quickly mark the number of sides on each. Eliminate answer choices with subsections with just one or four or more straight edges, as all of the sections above have two or three. If further answer choice elimination is still needed, match the specific subsections to those in the assembled shapes, starting with the most unique first (section D in this example).

There are a few things to keep in mind when considering possible solutions to an assembly problem. To begin with, remember that the pieces can be turned in any way. They may be rotated, spun, and flipped. They may not, however, be folded, bent, or twisted. Furthermore, they may not change in size; each piece should be the same size in the answer as it is in the original picture. Occasionally, the makers of the exam will place the pieces in the correct configuration but will drastically alter the sizes of one or more pieces. This automatically invalidates the answer. It is best to imagine the pieces as solid three-dimensional objects, which can be manipulated in all directions but cannot have their fundamental size and shape altered.

Similarly, make sure that the answer you select has the appropriate number of pieces. If there are five different components in the original drawing, there must be five connected parts in the answer. It is common for the exam to leave out a piece or include an extra piece in one or more of the possible answers; even if these answers are right in all other respects, they cannot be correct if they include more or fewer pieces than the original drawing.

If further elimination is needed, comparison of the types of angles in each shape may be necessary. Roughly assess which angles appear to be right, acute, and obtuse, and compare those findings to the answer choices.

It may also be necessary to compare relative side lengths, as with the example. The short ends of the four non-triangular sections of the shape on the left do not all appear to be equal as they do in the shape on the right.

Note that rulers and protractors are not allowed, so differences between segment lengths and angles should be obvious.

Rearranging

If you are asked to rearrange an assembled object, keep in mind that the process of elimination is also helpful. When approaching the following object, note that there are two smaller elongated rectangles, two larger right triangles, one larger equilateral triangle, and four small squares. Quickly eliminate any answer choices that don't contain only and all of those shapes before moving on to more detailed examination.

Note that the overall shape below is a square, but the rearranged object may form a rectangle or more unusual shape. Don't eliminate any answer choices because they don't re-form the original silhouette.

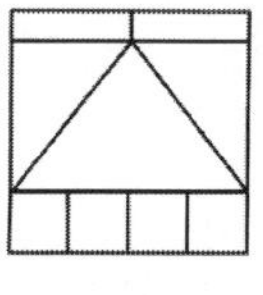

Connecting

When connecting points on an object, note that objects may be rotated unless the question states otherwise. If point A is on the corner of a triangle and point B is roughly halfway between the corners of a square and a question asks for the resulting image if a line connected the two points, answer choices with point A on a line or point B on a corner can quickly be eliminated. If further answer choice elimination is needed, check for more specific markers. For example, if a point is on the side of a shape with edges of different lengths, note which side it is on and eliminate any answer choices that don't match. If a point is on a corner of a shape with corners of varying angles, eliminate any answer choices that don't match.

As this is a pattern-recognition exercise and not geometry, side lengths and angles will be visibly different to allow for selection and elimination of shapes.

STACKING

When stacking objects, first note which one should be on top and eliminate all answer choices that are not stacked in the correct order. Then note relative size of the objects and if they can be rotated or not. If they are stacked so that specific points match up, note how that positioning will impact the final image. If the circle below is stacked on top of the triangle at the indicated points, the long end of the triangle will project out from underneath the circle.

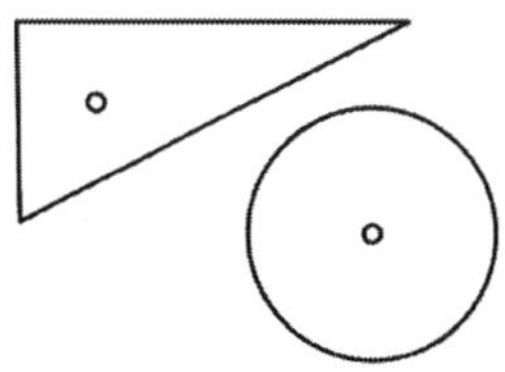

REFLECTING

To reflect an object vertically, flip it on its horizontal axis. To reflect an object horizontally, flip it on its vertical axis.

Vertical Reflection

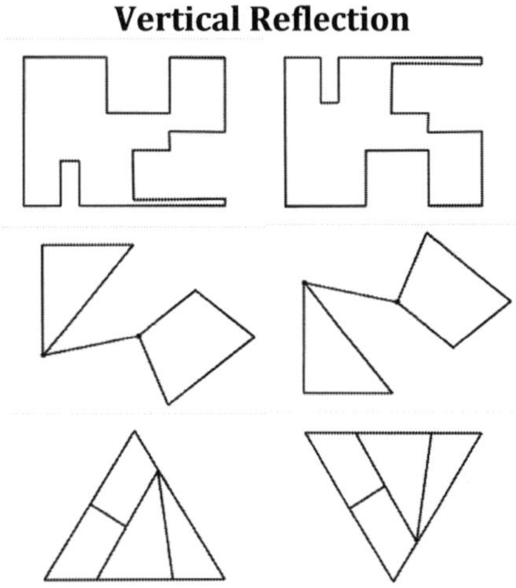

Horizontal Reflection

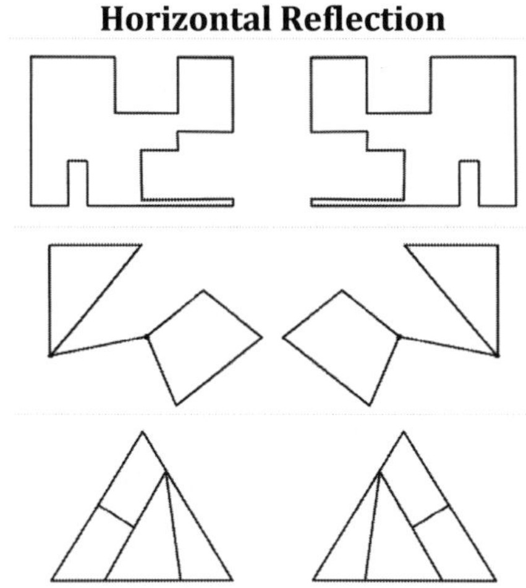

CHECK YOUR WORK

Once you have worked through the problem in this systematic manner and have selected your answer, go back and double-check your work. To begin with, make sure that all of the letters are joined properly in the answer you have chosen. Then, make sure that your answer has the right number of pieces. Finally, make sure that the pieces in the assembled object are similar in size to the pieces in the original drawing. If all of these factors check out, you can be comfortable that you have selected the right answer.

This methodical way of working through assembly problems may seem too time-consuming given the limits of the exam, but with a little bit of practice you can speed through the process within the time given. In fact, by adhering to this organized way of solving assembly problems, you will actually save time, since you will never get confused or lost in a problem and have to go back to the beginning. All it takes to master these problems is a little strategic knowledge and a little preparation.

Further Practice

There are a few common activities you can use to prepare for the assembly section of the exam. For instance, even though jigsaw puzzles do not offer an exact replication of the items you will encounter on the exam, they still exercise your spatial reasoning skills. Envisioning which pieces of the puzzle will fit together, and how the resulting arrangement will look, is a great way to hone your assembly skills. For an even greater challenge, try turning all the pieces of the puzzle face down, so that you cannot use the picture to guide your work: this will force you to rely more on your sense of orientation and arrangement.

Another way to prepare for this section of the exam is to take apart a small piece of machinery and study its configuration. Yard sales and junk bins are great places to find old appliances and electronics equipment. With the help of a screwdriver, wrench, and pair of pliers, you should be able to take apart most any appliance with ease. Once you have broken the item down into a pile of parts, see if you can put those parts back together into a functional whole. Even better, have someone else take apart the item and then see if you can put it back together. Of course, it is not recommended that you try this with valuable or expensive pieces of hardware. Also, some electronic appliances contain small batteries which should not be handled by non-professionals; always obey any warnings listed on the equipment. Nevertheless, taking apart and putting together small machines can be a fantastic way to improve your assembly skills.

Finally, there is a wealth of spatial intelligence exercises to be found on the internet. Just by entering "spatial intelligence" into a search engine, you should receive listings for dozens of simple, free puzzles and games that strengthen your ability to visualize and perform basic assemblies. Some of these programs are so sophisticated that they allow you to manipulate three-dimensional objects on your computer screen! While for many people working on a computer is no substitute for direct contact with an object, these online exercises are a clean, fast way to stretch your mental muscles.

Whatever method you choose, be sure to prepare for at least a few hours before sitting for the examination. For most students, the most difficult thing about the assembly questions is getting comfortable with the format and learning how to approach the problem. By remembering the strategies discussed above, and utilizing some of the suggested practice exercises, you can make sure that you will be ready to attack assembly problems immediately.

AFCT Practice Test

Want to take this practice test in an online interactive format?
Check out the online resources page, which includes interactive practice questions and much more: **mometrix.com/resources719/afct**

General Science

1. What is the name for any substance that stimulates the production of antibodies?

a. Collagen
b. Hemoglobin
c. Lymph
d. Antigen

2. Which of the following correctly lists the cellular hierarchy from the simplest to the most complex structure?

a. Tissue, cell, organ, organ system, organism
b. Organism, organ system, organ, tissue, cell
c. Organ system, organism, organ, tissue, cell
d. Cell, tissue, organ, organ system, organism

3. If a cell is placed in a hypertonic solution, what will happen to the cell?

a. It will swell.
b. It will shrink.
c. It will stay the same.
d. Its membrane permeability will increase.

4. Which group of major parts and organs make up the immune system?

a. Lymphatic system, spleen, tonsils, thymus, and bone marrow
b. Brain, spinal cord, and nerve cells
c. Heart, veins, arteries, and capillaries
d. Nose, trachea, bronchial tubes, lungs, alveolus, and diaphragm

5. The rate of a chemical reaction depends on all of the following EXCEPT:

a. Temperature
b. Surface area
c. Presence of catalysts
d. Amount of mass lost

6. Which of the answer choices provided best defines the following statement?

For a given mass and constant temperature, an inverse relationship exists between the volume and pressure of a gas.

a. The ideal gas law
b. Boyle's law
c. Charles's law
d. The Stefan-Boltzmann law

7. Which of the following statements correctly compares prokaryotic and eukaryotic cells?

a. Prokaryotic cells have a true nucleus, eukaryotic cells do not.
b. Both prokaryotic and eukaryotic cells have membrane-bound organelles.
c. Prokaryotic cells do not contain membrane-bound organelles, eukaryotic cells do.
d. Prokaryotic cells are more complex than eukaryotic cells.

8. What is the role of ribosomes?

a. Protein production
b. Waste removal
c. Transport
d. Storage

9. If an organism is AaBb, which of the following combinations in the gametes is NOT possible?

a. AB
b. aa
c. aB
d. Ab

10. Which of the following represents a chemical change?

a. Water sublimating
b. An apple turning brown
c. Salt dissolving in water
d. Rock being pulverized

11. What happens to the temperature of a substance as it is changing phase from a liquid to a solid?

a. Its temperature increases due to the absorption of latent heat.
b. Its temperature decreases due to the heat of vaporization.
c. Its temperature decreases due to the latent heat of fusion.
d. Its temperature remains the same due to the latent heat of fusion.

12. What is the typical result of mitosis in humans?

a. Two diploid cells
b. Two haploid cells
c. Four diploid cells
d. Four haploid cells

13. Which of the following does NOT exist as a diatomic molecule?

a. Boron
b. Fluorine
c. Oxygen
d. Nitrogen

14. How does the freezing point of sea water compare to that of fresh water?

a. Sea water has a higher freezing point.
b. Sea water has a lower freezing point.
c. They are the same.
d. Sea water does not freeze.

15. Which of the following best describes how the water inside an organism affects its temperature?

a. Water increases body temperature by rapidly absorbing heat due to its low heat capacity.
b. Water keeps body temperature stable by absorbing large amounts of heat with only small changes in temperature due to its high specific heat capacity.
c. Water decreases body temperature by using heat energy to evaporate from the surface of the skin.
d. Water does not affect body temperature.

Arithmetic Reasoning

1. Mrs. Patterson's classroom has sixteen empty chairs. All the chairs are occupied when every student is present. If $\frac{2}{5}$ of the students are absent, how many students make up her entire class?

a. 16 students
b. 24 students
c. 32 students
d. 40 students

2. A man earns $15.23 per hour and gets a raise of $2.34 per hour. What is his new hourly rate of pay?

a. $12.89
b. $15.46
c. $17.57
d. $35.64

3. A man buys two shirts. One is $7.50 and the other is $3.00. A 6% tax is added to his total. How much does he pay in all?

a. $10.50
b. $11.13
c. $14.58
d. $16.80

4. How many people can travel on 6 planes if each plane carries 300 passengers?

a. 1,800
b. 1,200
c. 600
d. 350

5. A company employing 540 individuals plans to increase its workforce by 13%. How many people will the company employ after the expansion? Round to the nearest whole number.

a. 527
b. 547
c. 553
d. 610

6. A woman must earn $250 in the next four days to pay a traffic ticket. How much will she have to earn each day?

a. $50.00
b. $62.50
c. $83.33
d. $1,000.00

7. A mountain climber climbs through rough terrain. She climbs 480 feet, 610 feet, 295 feet, and 303 feet over a period of 4 days. Estimate the distance she climbs over the four-day period to the nearest hundred feet.

a. 1,500 feet
b. 1,600 feet
c. 1,700 feet
d. 1,800 feet

8. Two women have credit cards. One earns 3 points for every dollar she spends. The other earns 6 points for every dollar she spends. If they each spend $5.00, how many combined total points will they earn?

a. 15
b. 30
c. 45
d. 60

9. If a chef can make 25 pastries in a day, how many can he make in a week?

a. 32
b. 74
c. 126
d. 175

10. A 13-story building has 65 apartments. If each floor has an equal number of apartments, how many apartments are on each floor?

a. 2
b. 3
c. 4
d. 5

11. A fruit vendor has 52 mangoes, 88 kiwis, 48 pineapples, and 45 papayas. How many pieces of fruit does the vendor have?

a. 221
b. 231
c. 233
d. 243

12. Three children decide to buy a gift for their father. The gift costs $78. One child contributes $24. The second contributes $15 less than the first. How much will the third child have to contribute?

a. $15
b. $39
c. $45
d. $62

13. In a town, the ratio of men to women is 2 : 1. If the number of women in the town is doubled, what will be the new ratio of men to women?

a. 1 : 2
b. 1 : 1
c. 2 : 1
d. 3 : 1

14. A woman has $450 in a bank account. She earns 5% interest on her end-of-month balance. How much interest will she earn for the month?

a. $5.00
b. $22.50
c. $427.50
d. $472.50

15. A car lot has an inventory of 476 cars. If 36 people bought cars in the week after the inventory was taken, how many cars will remain in inventory at the end of that week?

a. 440
b. 476
c. 484
d. 512

Word Knowledge

Refer to the following for questions 1–7:

Select the answer that is closest in meaning to the underlined portion.

1. The math test was quite <u>challenging.</u>

a. reasonable
b. lengthy
c. difficult
d. simple

2. The audience applauded after the woman <u>concluded</u> her presentation.

a. delivered
b. prepared
c. attended
d. finished

3. The company <u>instantly</u> agreed to the terms of the contract.

a. reluctantly
b. eventually
c. immediately
d. definitely

4. The new car was very <u>costly</u>.

a. expensive
b. cheap
c. attractive
d. rare

5. The woman's <u>response</u> to the question was correct.

a. hesitation
b. answer
c. decision
d. concern

6. He <u>observed</u> the eagles with binoculars.

a. watched
b. hunted
c. scared
d. sold

7. She is having <u>difficulties</u> with her new computer.

a. experiences
b. solutions
c. pleasures
d. problems

8. Generous most nearly means:

a. Giving
b. Truthful
c. Selfish
d. Harsh

9. Instructor most nearly means:

a. Pupil
b. Teacher
c. Survivor
d. Dictator

10. Residence most nearly means:

a. Home
b. Area
c. Plan
d. Resist

11. Gigantic most nearly means:

a. Small
b. Great
c. Huge
d. Scary

12. Opportunity most nearly means.

a. Event
b. Plan
c. Direction
d. Chance

13. Frequently most nearly means:

a. Difficulty
b. Freely
c. Often
d. Easy

14. Purchased most nearly means:

a. Sold
b. Bargained
c. Complained
d. Bought

15. Entire most nearly means:

a. Whole
b. Divide
c. Tired
d. Basic

Paragraph Comprehension

1. Mitosis refers to the process of cell division that occurs in most higher life forms. During interphase, all of the genetic material within the cell is replicated. Then, the strands that contain the genetic material, which are known as chromatin, become compacted and condensed. Centrosomes then move to opposite ends of the cells, after which the nucleus contained in the original single cell disintegrates.

Immediately before the chromatin becomes compacted:

a. The genetic material in the cell is copied.
b. The centrosomes move to opposite ends of the cell.
c. The nucleus inside of the cell disintegrates.
d. The process of mitosis takes place.

2. Obesity in the Western world has reached epidemic levels. While exercise is important to maintaining a healthy weight, healthy eating is even more important. Even the most active people cannot burn off hundreds of excess calories if they are consumed on a daily basis.

It can be concluded that:

a. Most people need to exercise more.
b. Many people do not practice healthy eating.
c. Obesity would not be a problem if people were active.
d. Most people do not know how to choose healthy foods.

3. Racism is still a widespread problem in North America. For example, one man of Arab descent was held at an airport for hours for no apparent reason. The man said he was later told that officials thought he was carrying a bomb. An African-American woman was passed over for a promotion. She says the job went to a less qualified applicant.

The author is constructing her argument by:

a. Relying on studies conducted by others.
b. Relying on the self-reported experiences of others.
c. Relying on events that she personally witnessed.
d. Relying on accepted facts and proven statistics.

4. *Beowulf* is an epic poem that is important because it is often viewed as the first significant work of English literature. Although it was first written in AD 700, it is thought to be even hundreds of years older than that. It is believed that the story of *Beowulf* was told for centuries before it ever made its way on to paper. It is still taught today in various schools and universities.

***Beowulf* is a significant poem because:**

a. It was first written down in AD 700.
b. It was told for centuries before it was written down.
c. It is still taught today in academic settings.
d. It is the first important work of English literature.

5. Cats are by far superior pets compared to dogs. They are perfect for the working person, as they don't mind being left alone during the day. In addition, they are very easy to litter train. They require little care or effort, and are much cheaper to feed compared to dogs.

The author's purpose in writing this passage is:

a. To compare cats and dogs.
b. To convince the reader that cats are better pets.
c. To show why cats are cheaper to feed.
d. To explain why cats are preferred to dogs.

6. Malaria is a dangerous disease that is still common in many countries. It is carried and transmitted to humans by female mosquitoes. When infected mosquitos bite humans or animals, the malaria parasite is introduced into the human's or animal's bloodstream. The parasites travel to the liver. There, they multiply, and soon they infect red blood cells. Malaria symptoms like fever will begin to be experienced at this point.

After the malaria parasites infect the red blood cells:

a. Symptoms like fever occur.
b. The parasites multiply.
c. The parasites travel to the liver.
d. Malaria is transmitted by mosquitoes.

7. Many people feel that summer water sports are dangerous. While accidents do occur, the vast majority are preventable. For example, boating is a relatively safe activity, provided that life vests are worn and a reasonable speed is maintained. When diving, it's important to know the area well and be certain that water is deep enough. Finally, alcohol should never be consumed while engaging in water sports or activities. Following these simple tips would prevent many accidents.

The main idea expressed in the passage is:

a. Summer sports are dangerous.
b. Many people who engage in water activities are careless.
c. Boating is a safe activity if precautions are followed.
d. Summer water activities aren't necessarily dangerous.

8. At one time, people who wanted to be writers had to write a query letter to a magazine and then wait weeks, sometimes months, for a response, which was usually a rejection. Today, with blogs, virtually anybody can put their work out there for others to view. It's as easy as setting up your blog, naming it, and posting anything you want: opinions, poems, short stories, news articles, etc. Of course, while people who have blogs may choose to call themselves writers or journalists, it's unlikely they are making a living by putting their random thoughts out there into cyberspace.

It can be concluded that:

a. It is easier to make a living as a writer now.
b. There are more people who want to be writers now.
c. Most people do not submit query letters to magazines anymore.
d. There is no approval process for getting a blog.

9. Organic food has become quite popular in the last number of years, but the price of organic foods still prevents many people from eating them on a regular basis. People choose to buy organic foods because they are becoming more concerned about what types of chemicals, fertilizers, and pesticides are in their food. Organic food can usually be easily obtained by visiting a grocery store or a farmer's market, and the selection of foods is also quite good.

People don't eat organic food because:

a. It's hard to find.
b. It contains chemicals.
c. The selection is poor.
d. It's too expensive.

10. Studies have shown again and again that birth order strongly influences the person one will eventually become. Oldest children have been shown to be more responsible and perform better in school. Younger children tend to do less well in school and be more free spirited. Cindy is a good example. She graduated on the Dean's list, and her parents report she always did her chores as a child.

It can be concluded that:

a. Cindy was an oldest child.
b. Cindy was a youngest child.
c. There have been no studies done on middle children.
d. Birth order only matters if there are exactly two children.

Mathematics Knowledge

1. If $x = -3$, calculate the value of the following expression.

$$3x^3 + (3x + 4) - 2x^2$$

a. -104
b. -58
c. 58
d. 104

2. Given the following system of equations, what is the value of y?

$$\begin{cases} 2x - 6y = 12 \\ -6x + 14y = 42 \end{cases}$$

a. -52.5
b. -19.5
c. -2.44
d. 6.56

3. In the following inequality, solve for x.

$$-4x + 8 \geq 48$$

a. $x \geq 10$
b. $x \geq -10$
c. $x \leq 10$
d. $x \leq -10$

4. Which of the following lines is perpendicular to the line $y = -5x + 27$?

a. $y = 5x + 27$
b. $y = -\frac{x}{5} + 27$
c. $y = \frac{x}{5} + 27$
d. $y = -\frac{x}{5} - 27$

5. Factor the following expression.

$$9x^2y - 18xy - 27y$$

a. $9(x^2y - 2xy - 3y)$
b. $9y(x + 3)(x + 1)$
c. $9y(x - 3)(x + 1)$
d. $9y(x + 3)(x - 1)$

6. If $x - 6 = 0$, then what is the value of x?

a. 0
b. 3
c. 6
d. 9

7. A line passes through the points $(-3, 18)$ and $(5, 2)$. What is the slope of the line?

a. -2
b. $-\frac{1}{2}$
c. $\frac{1}{2}$
d. 2

8. In the following inequality, solve for q.

$$-3q + 12 \geq 4q - 30$$

a. $q \geq 6$
b. $q = 6$
c. $q \neq 6$
d. $q \leq 6$

9. Chan receives a bonus from his job. He pays 30% in taxes, gives 30% to charity, and uses another 25% to pay off an old debt. He has $600 left. What was the total amount of Chan's bonus?

a. $4,000
b. $3,600
c. $3,200
d. $3,000

10. If one side of a square has a length of 56 cm, what is its perimeter?

a. 112 cm
b. 224 cm
c. 448 cm
d. 3,136 cm

11. Which of the following expressions is equivalent to $(3x^{-2})^3$?

a. $9x^{-6}$
b. $9x^6$
c. $27x^{-4}$
d. $27x^{-6}$

12. A rectangle has a width of 7 cm and a length of 9 cm. What is its perimeter?

a. 16 cm
b. 32 cm
c. 48 cm
d. 62 cm

13. A rectangular lot is three yards wide and four yards long. What is the area of the lot in square feet?

a. 4 ft^2
b. 12 ft^2
c. 36 ft^2
d. 108 ft^2

14. What is the midpoint of the points $(-20, 8)$ and $(5, 3)$?

a. (5.5,7.5)
b. (7.5,5.5)
c. (5.5, −7.5)
d. (−7.5,5.5)

15. If 5 people buy 3 pens each and 3 people buy 7 pencils each, what is the ratio of the total number of pens to the total number of pencils?

a. 5 : 7
b. 3 : 7
c. 5 : 3
d. 1 : 1

Electronics Information

1. Which of the following is true regarding current and voltage?

a. Current is potential energy.
b. Voltage is kinetic energy.
c. Current is the buildup of charge.
d. Voltage is the potential energy difference between two charged terminals.

2. What is the voltage across a 3 Ω resistor if the ammeter reads 4 A?

a. 0.75 V
b. 7 V
c. 12 V
d. 1.33 V

3. Which of the following demonstrates the correct associations between the components of Ohm's law and their units of measure?

a. Current (Amps); Voltage (Ohms)
b. Resistance (Ohms); Voltage (Volts)
c. Current (Ohms); Resistance (Amps)
d. Resistance (Amps); Current (Volts)

Refer to the following for questions 4–5:

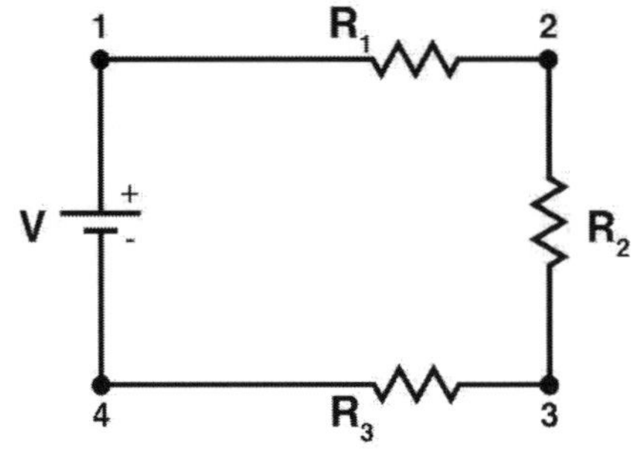

4. If the current at point 1 in the series circuit above is 3 A and the voltage drop across the first, second, and third resistors is 2 V, 3 V, and 4 V, respectively, what is the total resistance of the circuit?

a. 6 Ω
b. 3 Ω
c. 9 Ω
d. 0.33 Ω

5. If the current at point three in the series circuit above is 4 A, the resistance of R_1 is 0.5 Ω, the resistance of R_2 is 1 Ω, and the voltage drop across R_3 is 6 V, what is the size of the battery of the circuit?

a. 12 V
b. 1.5 V
c. 9 V
d. 3 V

Refer to the following for questions 6–8:

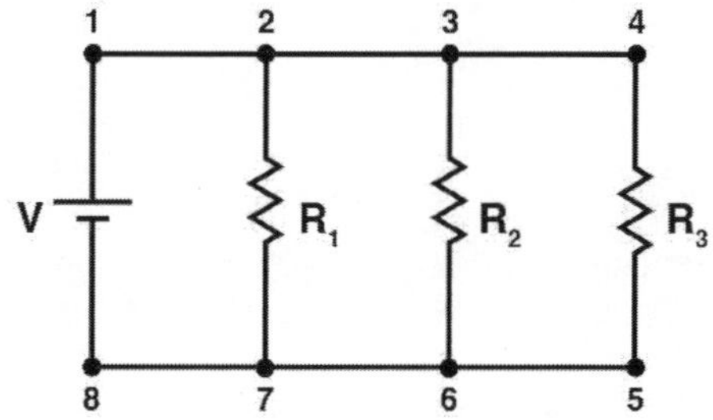

6. In the above circuit, what is the current at points 4 and 6 if the battery is 20 V, $R_2 = 4\ \Omega$, and $R_3 = 2\ \Omega$?

a. $I_4 = 10$ A; $I_6 = 15$ A
b. $I_4 = 20$ A; $I_6 = 20$ A
c. $I_4 = 10$ A; $I_6 = 10$ A
d. $I_4 = 15$ A; $I_6 = 5$ A

7. In the above circuit, what is the equivalent resistance if $R_1 = 4\ \Omega$, $R_2 = 4\ \Omega$, and $R_3 = 2\ \Omega$?

a. 10 Ω
b. 3.33 Ω
c. 1 Ω
d. 32 Ω

8. In the above circuit, if two resistors in series were in place of R_1 and 3 resistors in series were in place of R_3, what is the order of steps necessary to solve the problem?

a. Treat all resistors as if they were in parallel.
b. Find the equivalent resistance of the series resistors, then add the parallel resistors together.
c. Add all resistors together.
d. Add the series resistors together, then find the equivalent resistance of the parallel resistors.

9. If a 60-Watt lightbulb is used in a flashlight with a 9 V battery, what is the current between them?

a. 540 A
b. 6.66 A
c. 69.7 A
d. 0.15 A

10. All of the following are true regarding alternating current EXCEPT:

a. Alternating current periodically reverses direction.
b. Alternating current is used to transport electricity over land.
c. Alternating current is used to supply electricity to homes.
d. Alternating current is produced by batteries.

11. Alternating current is commonly used in which of the following places?

a. Cell phones
b. Ships
c. Homes
d. Airplanes

12. Which of the following commonly serves as a ground?

a. The earth
b. Car tires
c. A house
d. Lightning

13. Which of the following is true of p-type semiconductors?

a. They have an excess of electrons.
b. When an electric field is applied, a positive pole is formed.
c. They can result from silicon being doped with antimony.
d. They can result from antimony being doped with boron.

14. What is the purpose of a diode?

a. To serve as a high-functioning resistor
b. To step up or step down input voltage
c. To allow current to pass in only one direction
d. To create a magnetic field

15. Transistors are used in all of the following applications except:

a. Radio
b. Television
c. Computer memory chips
d. Light bulbs

Auto Information

1. What is the correct order of the steps in the four-stroke engine cycle?

a. Intake, power, compression, exhaust
b. Intake, compression, power, exhaust
c. Intake, exhaust, compression, power
d. Intake, compression, exhaust, power

2. What component generates electricity for a vehicle to use while it runs?

a. Battery
b. Engine
c. Alternator
d. Starter motor

3. In older vehicles, what was the function of the carburetor?

a. Mix air and fuel before combustion
b. Supply electricity to the spark plugs
c. House the combustion reaction
d. Filter exhaust before it reached the tail pipe

4. Spark plugs use electricity to create a spark in the:

a. Transmission
b. Motor
c. Alternator
d. Engine

5. Which of the following can lead to spark plug fouling?

a. Driving on the highway
b. Driving long distances
c. Driving on dusty roads
d. City driving

6. Which of the following will occur as a result of failing piston rings?

a. Engine smoking
b. Car won't start
c. Backfiring
d. Poor fuel economy

7. Which of the following is true about the exhaust system?

a. The exhaust manifold converts pollutants to water vapor and carbon dioxide.
b. The muffler collects gas byproducts from the engine for transport to the manifold.
c. The catalytic converter primarily dampens engine noise.
d. Exhaust flows from the combustion chamber through the exhaust valve, to the exhaust manifold, to the catalytic converter, to the muffler, and out the tail pipe.

8. Which of the following is NOT a function of motor oil?

a. Lubricate the engine
b. Prevent corrosion
c. Fuel the engine
d. Prevent overheating

9. What happens when the thermostat gets stuck open?

a. The engine will overheat.
b. The engine will run cold and have bad gas mileage.
c. The engine will flood with coolant and will stall.
d. The air conditioning system will freeze and eventually fail.

10. A transaxle is found most commonly in which drivetrain configuration?

a. Rear wheel drive (RWD)
b. Front wheel drive (FWD)
c. All wheel drive (AWD)
d. Four-wheel drive (4WD)

Shop Information

1. Which of the following describes the process of cutting wood parallel to the grain?

a. Cross cut
b. Rip cut
c. Bevel cut
d. Miter cut

2. What type of chisel is this?

a. Mortise chisel
b. Paring chisel
c. Beveled edge chisel
d. Japanese bench chisel

3. What type of wrench is this?

a. Ratcheting wrench
b. Socket wrench
c. Combination wrench
d. Torque wrench

4. Which of the following describes correct pairs?

a. Allen wrench: hexagon; Phillips-head: simple wedge
b. Allen wrench: cross; Phillips-head: simple wedge
c. Flat head: hexagon; Phillips-head: cross
d. Flat head: simple wedge; Allen wrench: hexagon

5. Which of the following correctly describes the difference between welding and soldering?

a. Soldering uses much higher heat than welding.
b. Soldering is used in jobs that are much larger in size.
c. Welding involves melting of the base metal.
d. Welding is commonly used to connect electrical components on a circuit.

6. Which of the following is true of rivets?

a. They support shear and tensile loads.
b. They support tensile loads only.
c. They support compressive loads only.
d. They support compressive and shear loads.

7. The pliers below are called:

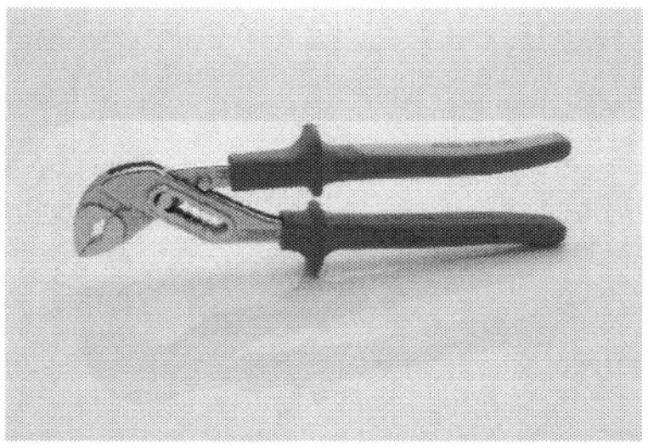

a. Diagonal pliers
b. Slip joint pliers
c. Tongue and groove pliers
d. Crimping pliers

8. Which tool can be considered a combination of a clamp and pliers?

a. G-clamp
b. Vice-grips
c. Tongue and groove pliers
d. Speed clamp

9. What is the difference between drilling and boring?

a. Drilling produces blind holes, which do not pass completely through a workpiece; boring does not.
b. Boring produces blind holes, which do not pass completely through a workpiece; drilling does not.
c. Only boring can be done using hand tools.
d. Drilling creates new holes in workpieces; boring enlarges existing holes.

10. Which of the following is the most portable?

a. Miter saw
b. Oscillating saw
c. Table saw
d. Vertical band saw

Mechanical Comprehension

1. A cannon fires off a ship up towards a mountain range. Neglecting air resistance, where will the velocity of the projectile be greatest?

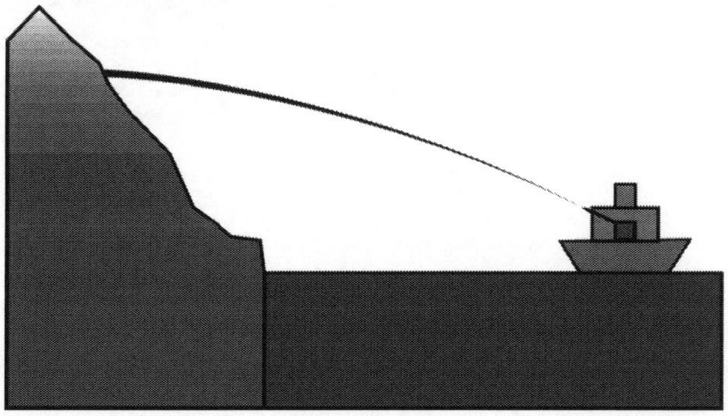

a. Exiting the muzzle
b. Halfway to the mountains
c. As it impacts the mountains

2. These pulleys are connected by belts. Which pulley travels the fastest?

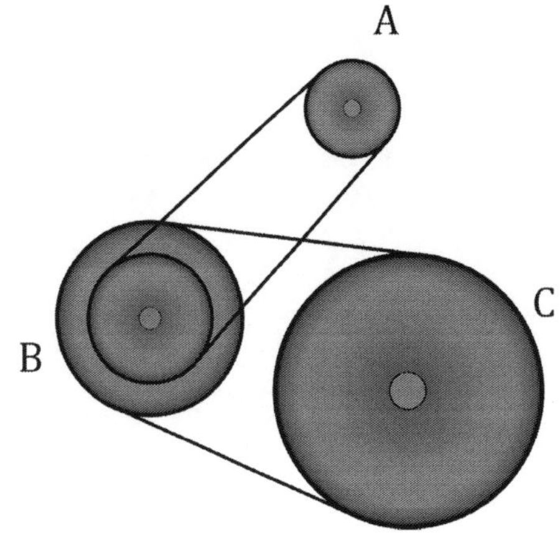

a. Pulley A
b. Pulley B
c. Pulley C

3. If Gear A is traveling at 10 rpm, how many times will Gear C rotate in 3 minutes?

a. 1.7 times
b. 3 times
c. 30 times

4. Where should the fulcrum be located to balance this beam?

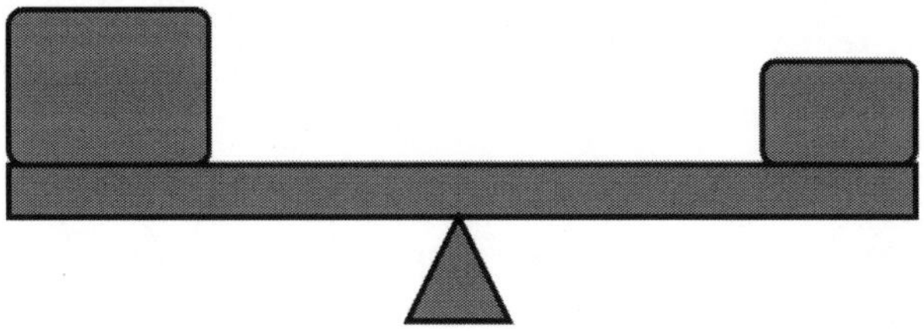

a. Closer to the large mass
b. Closer to the small mass
c. Exactly between the two masses

5. Assuming that there is no frictional force involved, which orientation will require more force to pull?

a. With the rope at an angle to the table
b. With the rope parallel to the table
c. Both orientations are equal

6. The larger piston has four times as much horizontal area as the smaller piston. If the small piston is compressed 8 inches, how far will the larger piston move?

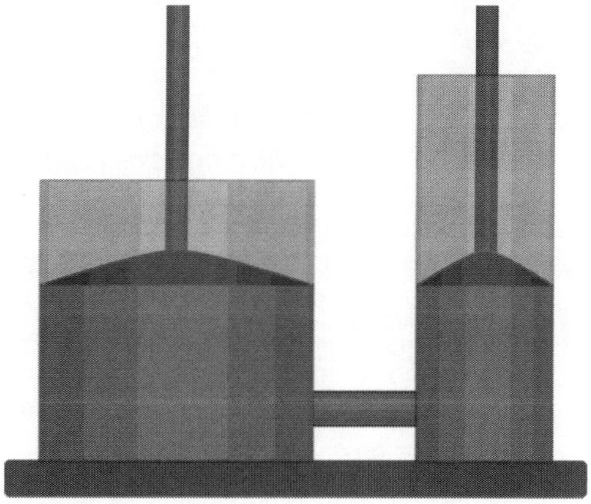

a. 8 inches
b. 2 inches
c. 32 inches

7. A wing in flight has a set of pressures causing the overall forces on the top and bottom of the wing. Where will the total force on the wing point?

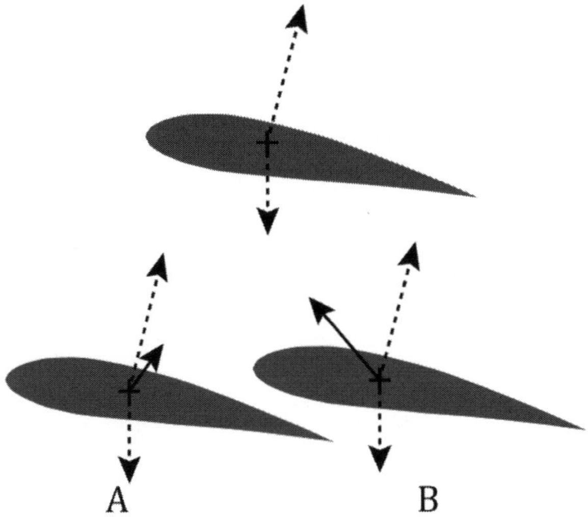

a. Up and to the right
b. Up and to the left
c. Neither A nor B

8. River water enters a section where the water spreads out into a wide, deep area. Is the water likely to speed up, slow down, or remain at a constant speed?

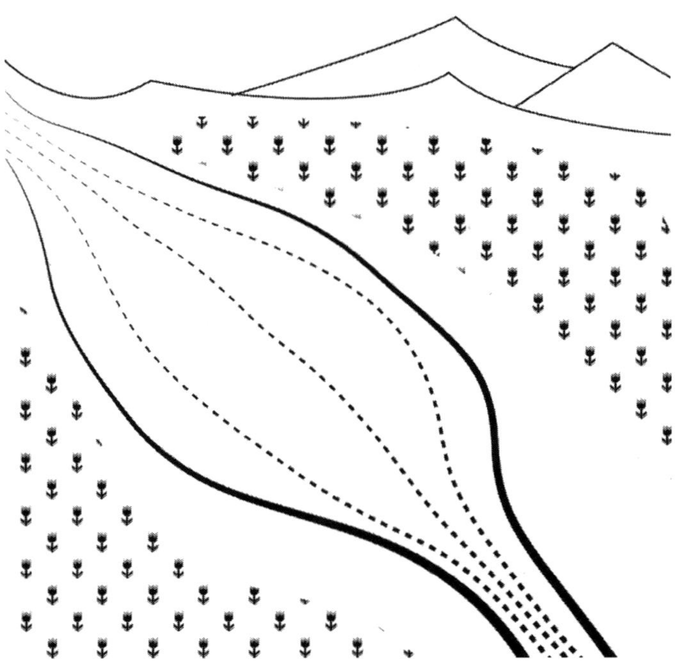

a. Speed up
b. Slow down
c. Remain at a constant speed

9. A magnet is placed in the middle of two identical, anchored magnets. Which direction will the magnet go?

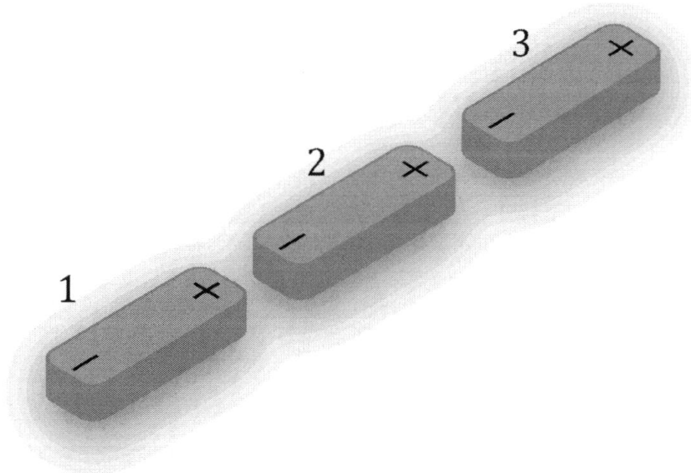

a. It will move towards magnet 1.
b. It will move towards magnet 3.
c. The magnet won't move.

10. A solid substance melts at −21 °C. If the object is known to change phase at 81 °C, will the object be a solid, liquid, or gas at 90 °C?

a. Solid
b. Liquid
c. Gas

11. If the resistors in the circuits are identical, which circuit will have the greatest overall resistance?

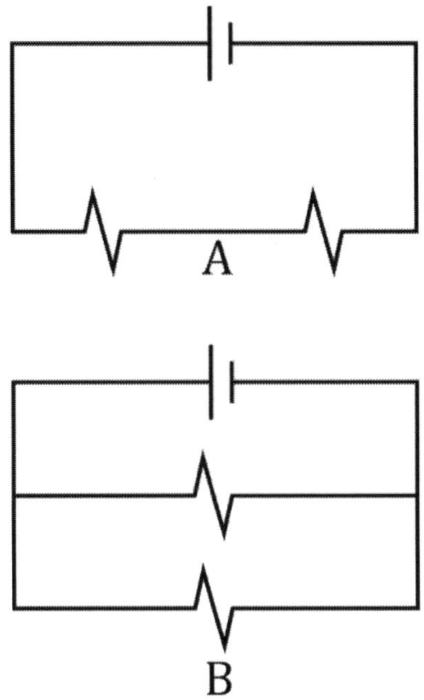

a. Circuit A
b. Circuit B
c. Same overall resistance

12. A pendulum swings back and forth once per second. The pendulum is shortened by removing half of the string. The new frequency is 1.4 Hz (Hz = 1/sec). How often will the pendulum swing back and forth in a minute?

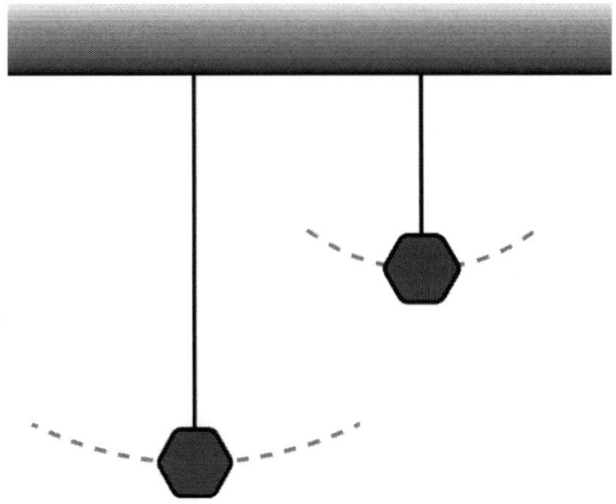

a. 84 times
b. 92 times
c. 72 times

13. Two identical pistons are connected by a pipe. What is the mechanical advantage of the piston system?

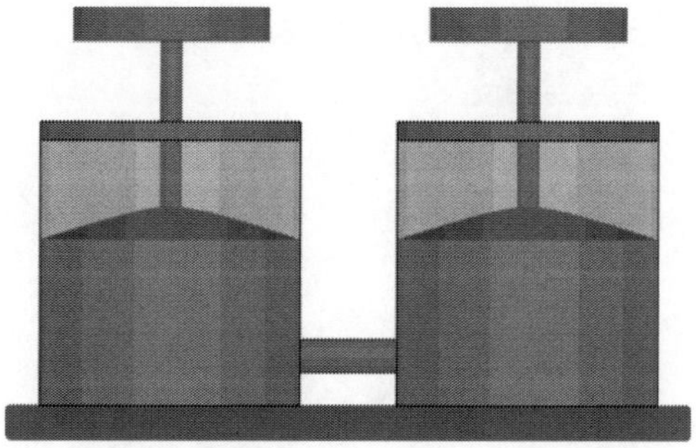

a. 0.5
b. 1
c. 2

14. A ball is thrown horizontally off a cliff at the same time that an identical ball is dropped off the cliff. How long after the dropped ball hits the ground will the thrown ball hit the ground?

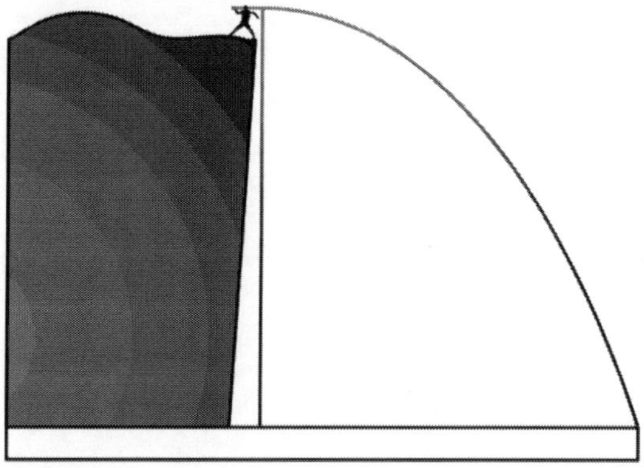

a. Approximately 1 second after
b. Approximately 2 seconds after
c. At the same time

15. The cam shown below rotates at 5 rpm. How many times will the follower (needle) move up and down in a minute?

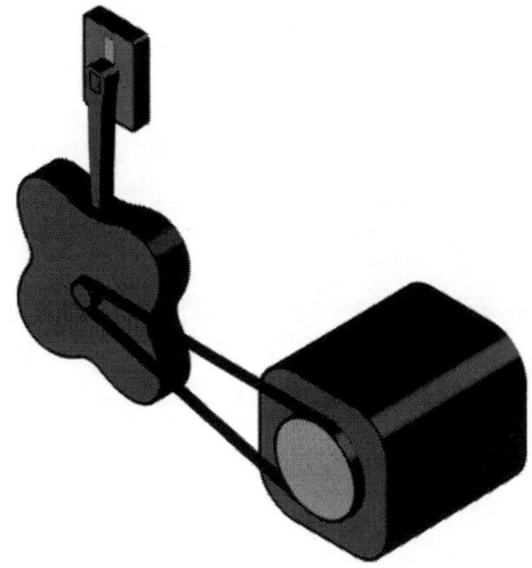

a. 20
b. 72
c. 140

Assembling Objects

1. Which of the following configurations represents how the following objects might appear if they are rearranged?

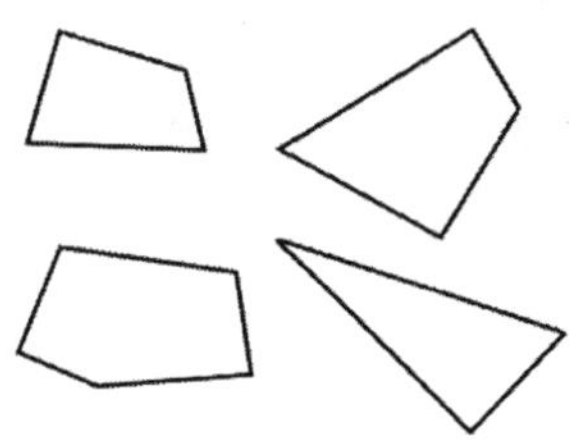

a.

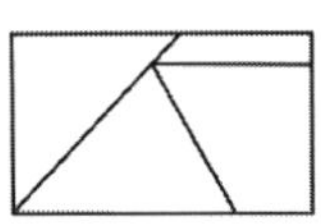

b.

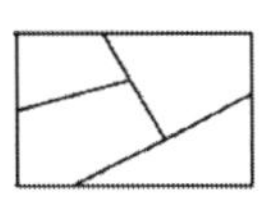

c.

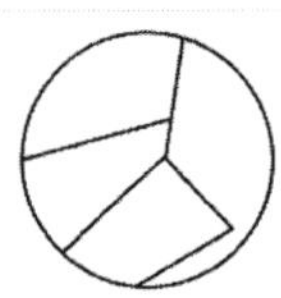

d.

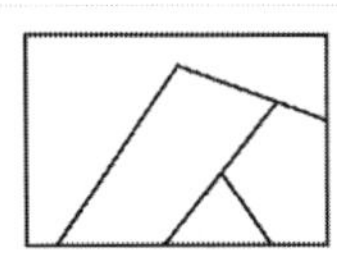

2. Which of the following configurations represents how the following object might appear if its components are rearranged?

a.

b.

c.

d.

3. Which of the following configurations represents how the following objects might appear if they are rearranged?

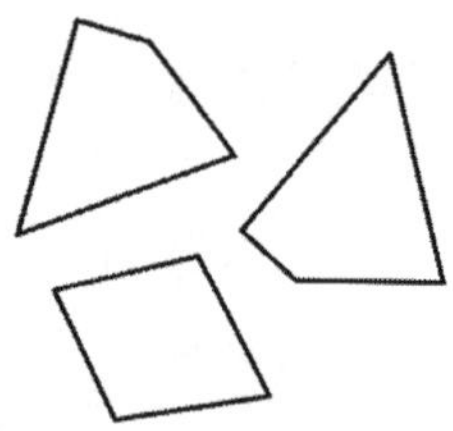

a.

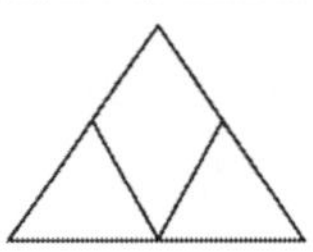

b.

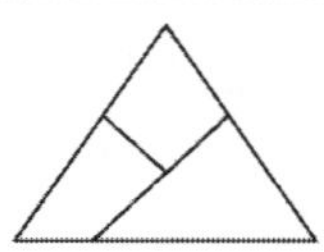

c.

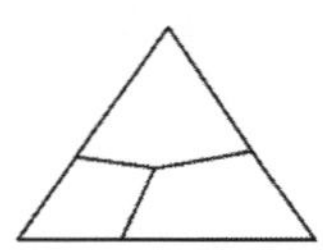

d.

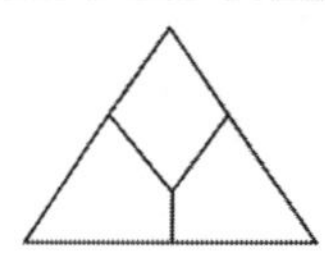

4. Which figure best shows how the objects might be connected if a line is drawn from one point to the other?

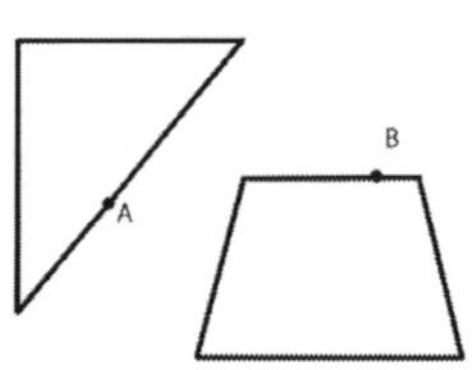

a.

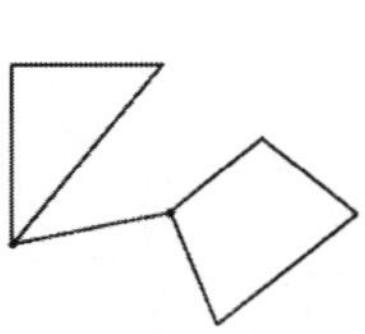

b.

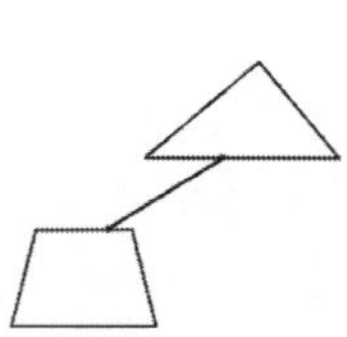

c.

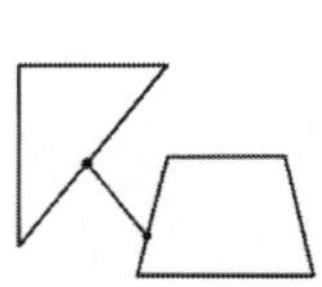

d.

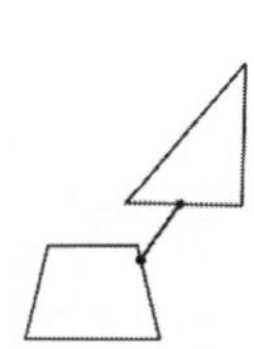

5. Which of the following configurations represents how the following object might appear if its components are rearranged?

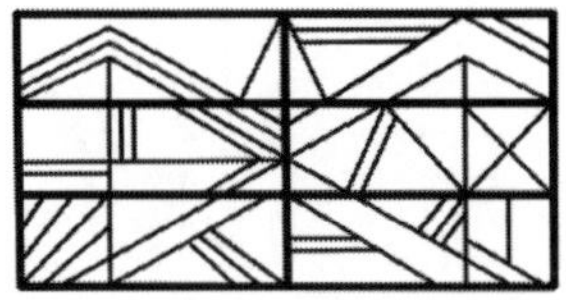

a.

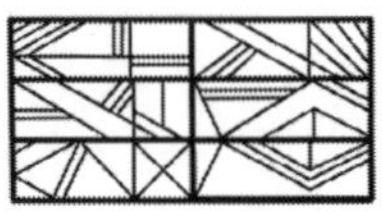

b.

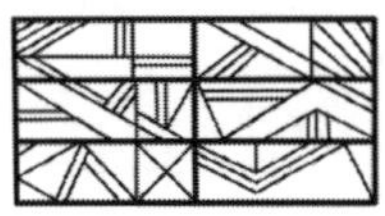

c.

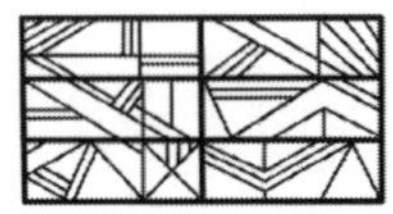

d.

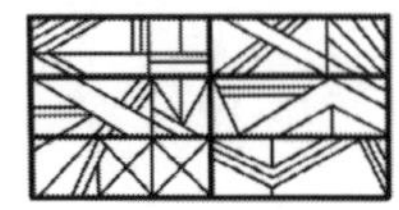

6. Which of the following configurations represents how the following objects might appear if they are rearranged?

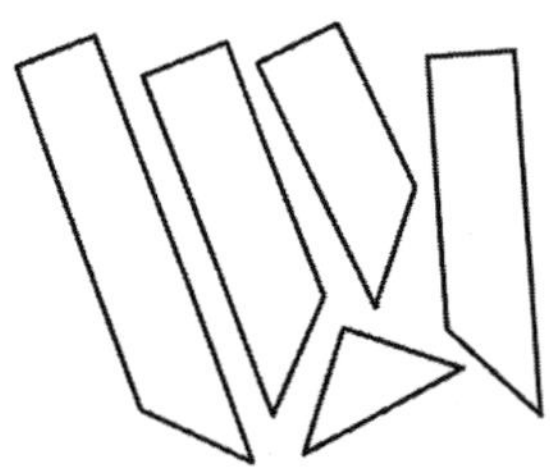

a.

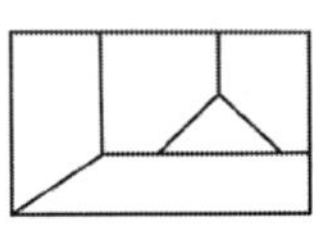

b.

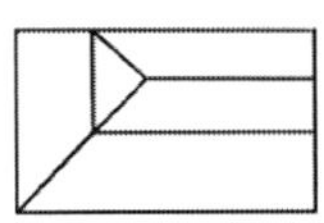

c.

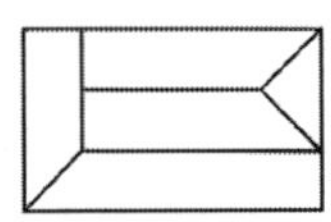

d.

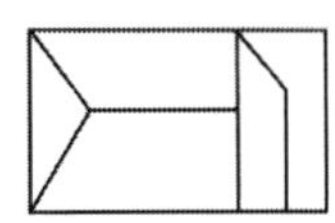

7. Which figure best shows how the objects might be connected if a line is drawn from one point to the other?

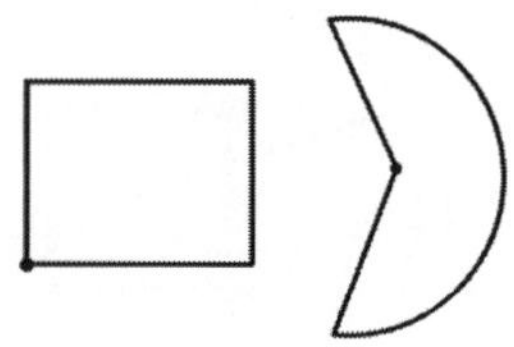

a.

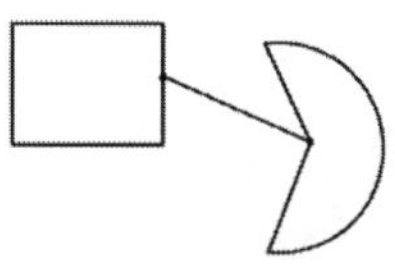

b.

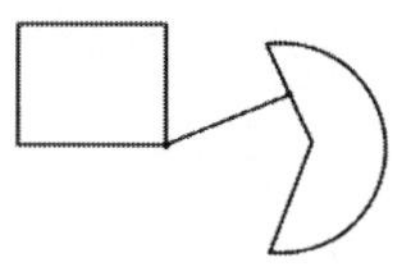

c.

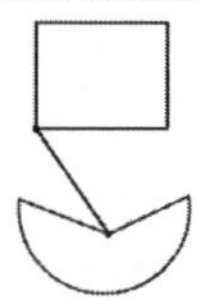

d.

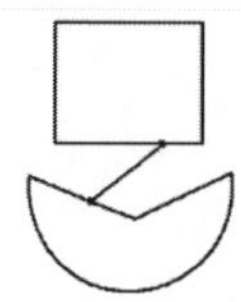

8. Which of the following configurations represents how the following objects might appear if they are rearranged?

a.

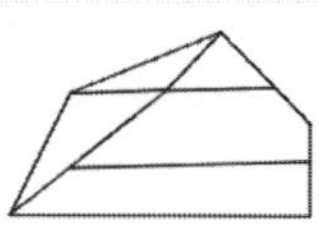

b.

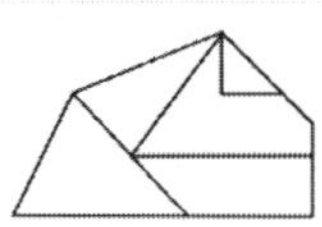

c.

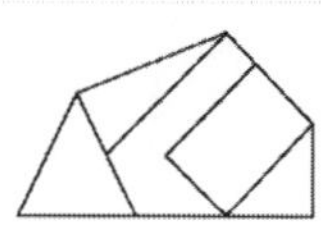

d.

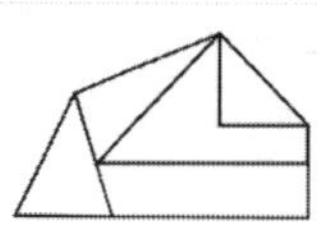

9. If the objects below are translated along the path indicated by the line, keeping in mind that a dotted line corresponds to a place on the side of the object that cannot be seen, how might the final image appear? (Note: the images may not be rotated.)

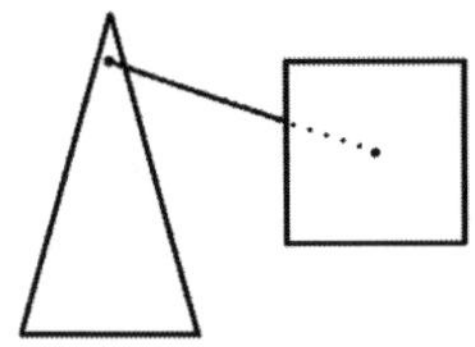

a.

b.

c.

d.

10. Which figure best shows how the objects might be connected if a line is drawn from one point to the other?

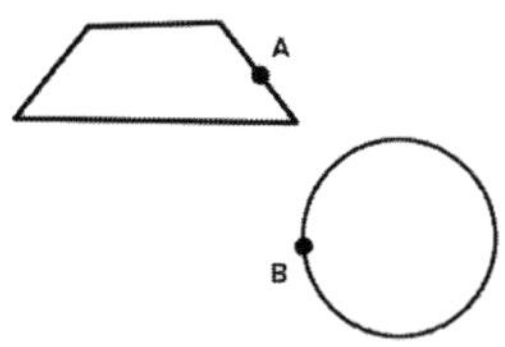

a.

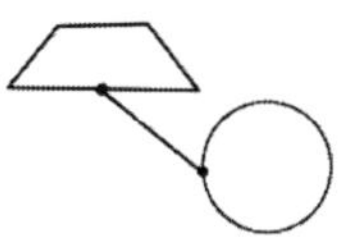

b.

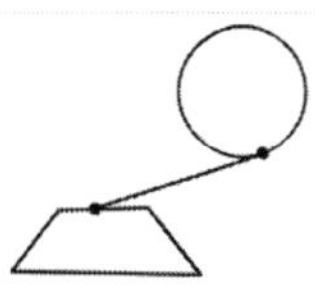

c.

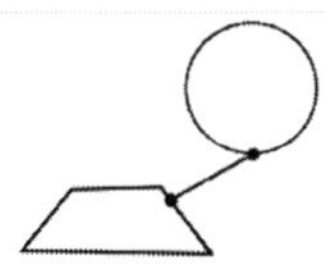

d.

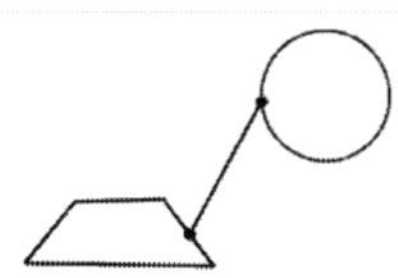

11. Which of the following configurations represents how the following objects might appear if they are rearranged?

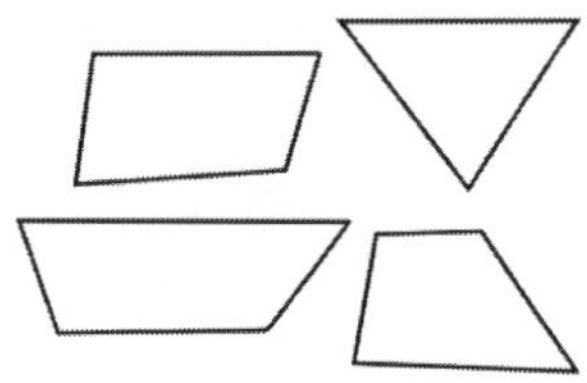

a.

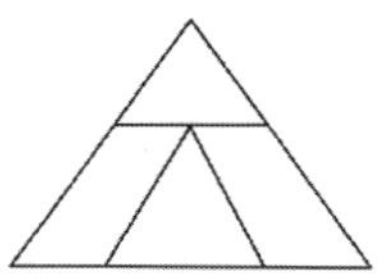

b.

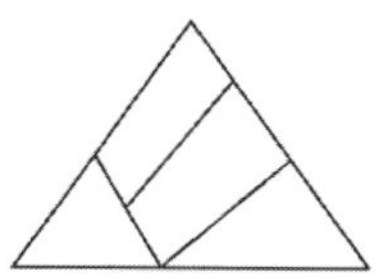

c.

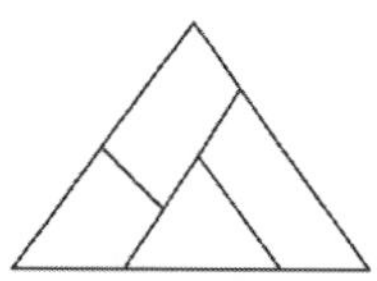

d.

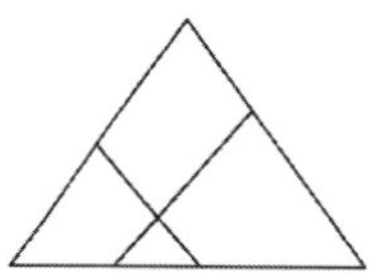

12. Which of the following configurations represents how the following objects might appear if they are rearranged?

a.

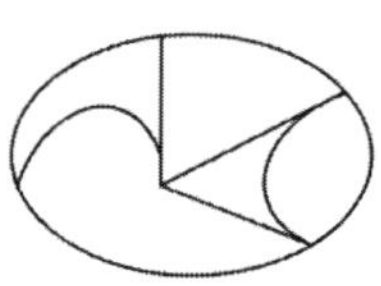

b.

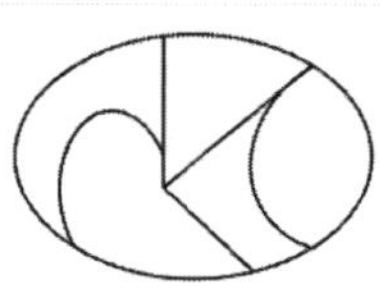

c.

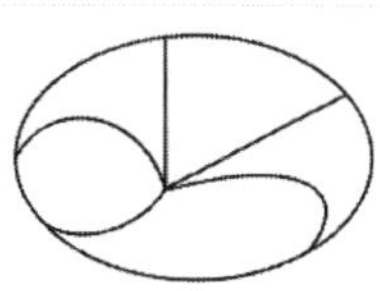

d.

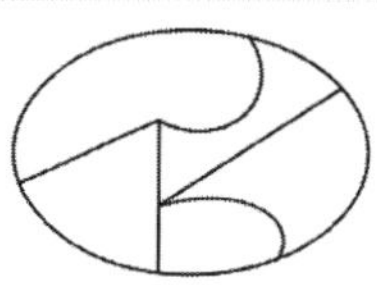

13. Which figure best represents what might result if the shapes shown on the left are cut out of the shape on the right?

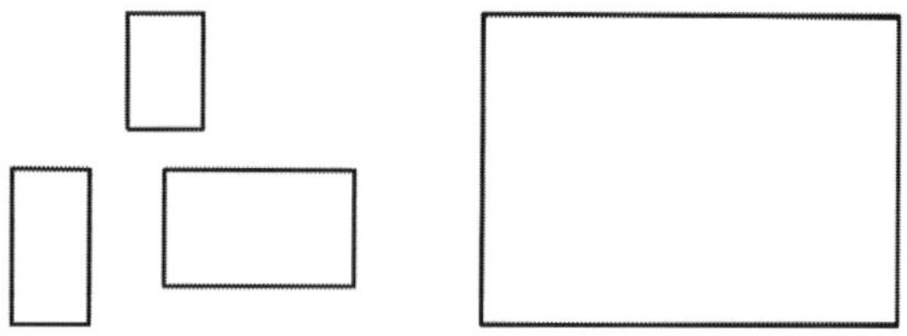

a.

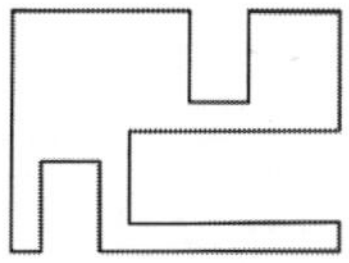

b.

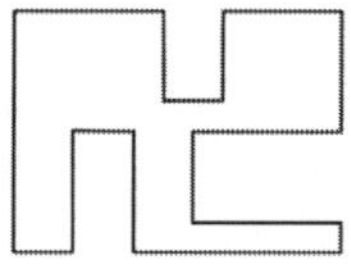

c.

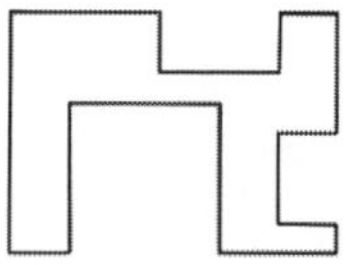

d.

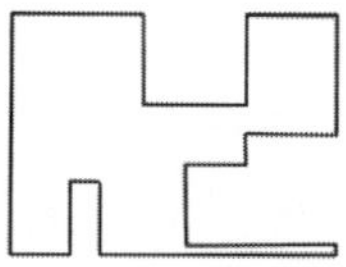

14. Which of the following configurations represents how the following objects might appear if they are rearranged?

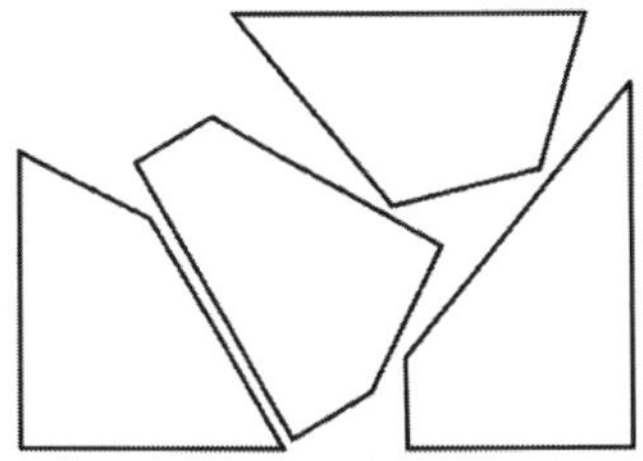

a.

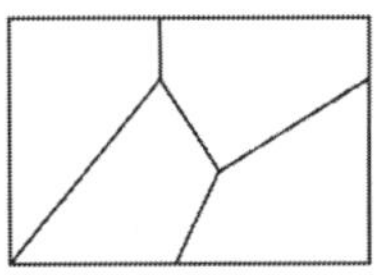

b.

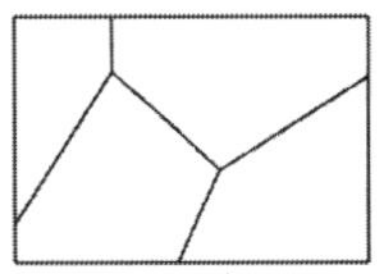

c.

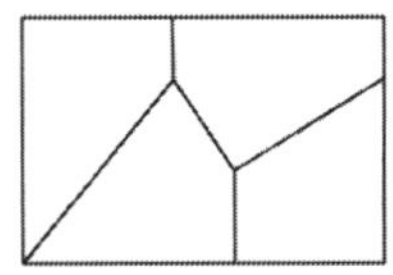

d.

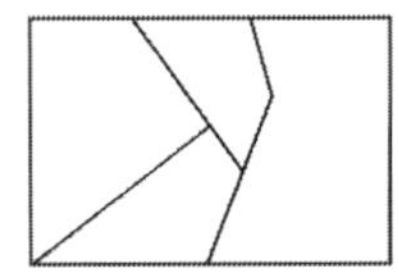

15. Which of the following configurations represents how the following object might appear if its components are rearranged?

a.

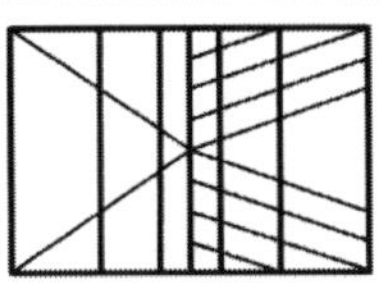

b.

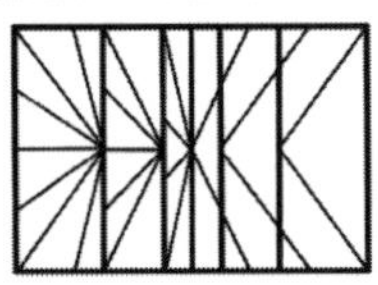

c.

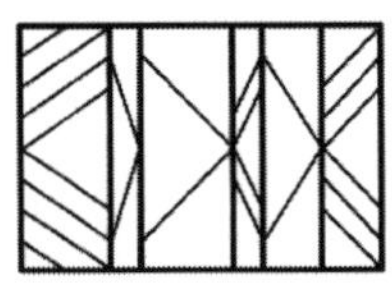

d.

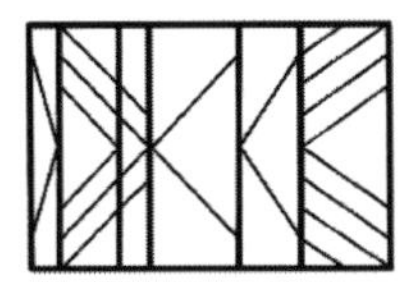

Answer Key and Explanations

General Science

1. D: The name for a substance that stimulates the production of antibodies is an *antigen*. An antigen is any substance perceived by the immune system as dangerous. When the body senses an antigen, it produces an antibody. *Collagen* is one of the components of bone, tendon, and cartilage. It is a spongy protein that can be turned into gelatin by boiling. *Hemoglobin* is the part of red blood cells that carries oxygen. In order for the blood to carry enough oxygen to the cells of the body, there has to be a sufficient amount of hemoglobin. *Lymph* is a near-transparent fluid that performs a number of functions in the body: It removes bacteria from tissues, replaces lymphocytes in the blood, and moves fat away from the small intestine. Lymph contains white blood cells.

2. D: The cellular hierarchy starts with the cell, the simplest structure, and progresses to organism, the most complex structure.

3. B: A hypertonic solution is a solution with a higher particle concentration than in the cell, and consequently lower water content than in the cell. Water moves from the cell to the solution, causing the cell to experience water loss and shrink.

4. A: The immune system consists of the lymphatic system, spleen, tonsils, thymus and bone marrow.

5. D: The rate at which a chemical reaction occurs does not depend on the amount of mass lost, since the law of conservation of mass (or matter) states that in a chemical reaction there is no loss of mass. Increased temperature, surface area, and the presence of catalysts would result in the increase in rate of a chemical reaction in many cases.

6. B: Boyle's law states that, for a gas at a constant mass and temperature, pressure and volume are inversely related: $PV = C$, where C is a constant.

7. C: Prokaryotic cells are simpler cells that do not have membrane-bound organelles, whereas eukaryotic cells have several membrane-bound organelles.

8. A: A ribosome is a structure of eukaryotic cells that makes proteins.

9. B: Gametes are haploid and carry only one allele per gene. Remember that a zygote receives one allele from each parent, so each allele cannot be used more than one time. Therefore, it is impossible for an AaBb zygote to have an aa parent gamete; it would be impossible for the lowercase a to appear twice in the gamete.

10. B: An apple turning brown is an example of a chemical change; in this case, oxidation. During a chemical change, one substance is changed into another. Sublimation of water refers to the conversion between the solid and the gaseous phases of matter, with no intermediate liquid stage. This is a phase change, not a chemical reaction. Dissolution of salt in water refers to a physical change since the salt and water can be separated again by evaporating the water. Pulverized rock is an example of a physical change where the form has changed but not the substance itself.

11. D: The temperature of a substance during the time of any phase change remains the same. In this case, the phase change was from liquid to solid, or freezing. Latent heat of fusion, in this case, is energy that is released from the substance as it reforms its solid form. This energy will be released and the liquid will turn to solid before the temperature of the substance will decrease further. If the substance were changing from solid to liquid, the heat of fusion would be the amount of heat required to break apart the attractions between the molecules in the solid form to change to the liquid form. The latent heat of fusion is exactly the same quantity of energy for a substance for either melting or freezing. Depending on the process, this amount of heat would either be absorbed by the substance (melting) or released (freezing).

12. A: The typical result of mitosis in humans is two diploid cells. *Mitosis* is the division of a body cell into two daughter cells. Each of the two produced cells has the same set of chromosomes as the parent. A diploid cell contains both sets of homologous chromosomes. A haploid cell contains only one set of chromosomes, which means that it only has a single set of genes.

13. A: Boron does not exist as a diatomic molecule. The other possible answer choices, fluorine, oxygen, and nitrogen, all exist as diatomic molecules. A diatomic molecule always appears in nature as a pair: the word *diatomic* means "having two atoms." With the exception of astatine, all of the halogens are diatomic. Chemistry students often use the mnemonic BrINClHOF (pronounced "brinkelhoff") to remember all of the diatomic elements: bromine, iodine, nitrogen, chlorine, hydrogen, oxygen, and fluorine. Note that not all of these diatomic elements are halogens.

14. B: The freezing point of sea water is lower than that of fresh water as sea water is denser. It is denser because it has more dissolved salts. The freezing point changes with salinity, pressure, and density, but can be as low as –2 °C (28.4 °F), compared with 0 °C (32 °F) for fresh water.

15. B: Water can stabilize the temperature of living things because of its high specific heat capacity, which means that it takes a while to heat or cool. This ability to minimize changes in temperature protects the body from sudden temperature shifts that could disrupt normal physiological processes. While water does help decrease body temperature through evaporation, this is not a comprehensive description of water's overall role in temperature regulation.

Arithmetic Reasoning

1. D: There are 16 empty chairs. This gives $\frac{2}{5}$ of the total enrollment. So, the full class must be:

$$\text{Class} = \frac{5}{2} \times 16 = 40 \text{ students}$$

Another option is to use proportions.

$$\frac{2}{5} = \frac{16}{x}$$

First, cross multiply to get: $2x = 80$. Then, divide each side by 2 to solve for x. So, $x = 40$, which means there are 40 students in the entire class.

2. C: To calculate his new hourly rate, add his raise to his original hourly rate.

$$\$15.23 + \$2.34 = \$17.57$$

Therefore, the man's new hourly rate is $17.57.

3. B: First, find the total before taxes.

$$\$7.50 + \$3.00 = \$10.50$$

Then, calculate 6% of the total.

$$\$10.50 \times 0.06 = \$0.63$$

Finally, add the tax to find how much he pays in all.

$$\$10.50 + \$0.63 = \$11.13$$

Therefore, he pays $11.13.

4. A: To find the total number of passengers, multiply the number of planes by the number of passengers each plane can hold.

$$6 \times 300 = 1{,}800$$

Therefore, 1,800 people can travel on 6 planes.

5. D: First, calculate 13% of 540.

$$540 \times 0.13 = 70.2$$

This can be rounded to 70. Then, add this value onto the original number of workers.

$$540 + 70 = 610$$

After the expansion, the company will employ 610 people.

6. B: The woman has four days to earn $250. To find the amount she must earn each day, divide the amount she must earn by 4.

$$\$250 \div 4 = \$62.50$$

Therefore, she must earn $62.50 each day.

7. C: A quick estimation of the number of feet the mountain climber climbs is found by rounding each day's climb to the nearest hundred feet and finding the sum. 480 rounds to 500, 610 rounds to 600, 295 rounds to 300, and 303 also rounds to 300.

$$500 + 600 + 300 + 300 = 1{,}700$$

Therefore, she climbed approximately 1,700 feet.

8. C: First, figure out how many points the first woman will earn.

$$3 \times 5 = 15$$

Then, figure out how many points the second woman will earn.

$$6 \times 5 = 30$$

Finally, add these two values together.

$$30 + 15 = 45$$

Therefore, the two women will have a combined total of 45 points.

9. D: Knowing that the chef can make 25 pastries in a day and that there are 7 days in a week, the weekly number can be calculated by multiplying 25 by 7.

$$25 \times 7 = 175$$

Therefore, the chef can make 175 pastries in a week.

10. D: To find the number of apartments on each floor, divide the total number of apartments by the number of floors.

$$65 \div 13 = 5$$

Therefore, there are 5 apartments on each floor.

11. C: The number of pieces of fruit that the vendor has is equal to the sum of the numbers of individual types of fruit. The number equals $52 + 88 + 48 + 45$, or 233 pieces of fruit.

12. C: First, figure out how much the second child contributed.

$$\$24 - \$15 = \$9$$

Then, calculate how much the first two children contributed in total.

$$\$24 + \$9 = \$33$$

Finally, figure out how much the third child will have to contribute.

$$\$78 - \$33 = \$45$$

Therefore, the third child will have to contribute $45.

13. B: Currently, there are two men for every woman. If the number of women is doubled, then the new ratio is $2 : 2$. This is equivalent to $1 : 1$.

14. B: To find the amount of interest she will earn, multiply the amount of money in her bank account by 5% as a decimal.

$$\$450 \times 0.05 = \$22.50$$

Therefore, she will earn $22.50 in interest for the month.

15. A: To find the number of cars remaining, subtract the number of cars that were sold from the original number.

$$476 - 36 = 440$$

Therefore, there are 440 cars left at the end of the week.

Word Knowledge

1. C: When something is described as challenging, it usually means that it is difficult or demanding.

2. D: When something is concluded, it means that it is finished or completed.

3. C: To say something was done instantly means that it was done immediately and without hesitation.

4. A: Something that is costly is expensive. It costs a lot of money.

5. B: A response is also commonly known as an answer. A response to a question carries the same meaning as an answer to a question.

6. A: Something that is being observed is being watched. Binoculars are used to see things more clearly, so it makes sense that the man would be observing or watching eagles with binoculars.

7. D: The word difficulty implies hardship. When it is said that somebody is having difficulties with another person or thing, it usually means they are experiencing problems.

8. A: When it is said that someone is generous, it usually means they are giving and unselfish.

9. B: A teacher provides instruction and information to an individual or group of individuals. An instructor functions in the same capacity, that is, in the practice of teaching.

10. A: A residence is a place where a person lives; the term is often used to refer to someone's home.

11. C: Something that is described as gigantic is extremely large, or huge, in size.

12. D: An opportunity is a chance to do something. For example, saying someone was given the *opportunity* to go to school or saying somebody was given the *chance* to go to school conveys the same meaning.

13. C: To say that something is done frequently implies that it is done regularly or often.

14. D: Saying that somebody purchased something and saying they bought something conveys the same meaning.

15. A: Entire is an amount. It usually means the whole amount. For example, if someone says they ate an entire apple, it is the same as saying they ate a whole apple.

Paragraph Comprehension

1. A: The passage states: "During interphase, all of the genetic material within the cell is replicated. Then, the strands that contain the genetic material, which are known as chromatin, become compacted and condensed." According to the passage, the material in the cell is copied (replicated) before the chromatin becomes compacted into strands.

2. B: The conclusion that many people do not practice healthy eating can be made based on two points in the passage. First, we are told that many people are obese. Second, it is stated that healthy eating is more important to maintaining a healthy weight than exercise activity. Therefore, if a large number of people are overweight, and eating unhealthy foods is the major contributor to obesity, it can be concluded that many people do not practice healthy eating.

3. B: The author is relying on experiences that were reported by others. This is evident through the use of such phrases as "he said that he was later told" and "she says the job went to a less qualified applicant."

4. D: The passage directly states that *Beowulf* is important because "it is often viewed as the first significant work of English literature," making D the correct answer choice.

5. B: The purpose of the passage is to convince the reader that cats are better pets than dogs. This is stated in the opening sentence when the author states "Cats are by far superior pets compared to dogs." Also, the remainder of the passage describes the advantages of cats as pets. Any time cats are compared to dogs, cats are described as superior pets.

6. A: After the malaria parasites infect the red blood cells, symptoms like fever occur. The passage states that "There, they multiply, and soon they infect red blood cells. Malaria symptoms like fever will begin to be experienced at this point."

7. D: The main idea in this passage is that water sports don't have to be dangerous. The passage states "Many people feel that summer time water sports are dangerous. While accidents do occur, the vast majority are preventable." Also, the rest of the passage focuses on outlining what precautions can be taken to ensure that water sports are less risky.

8. D: This can be concluded based on the section of the passage that states "Today, with blogs, virtually anybody can put their work out there for others to view. It's as easy as setting up your blog, naming it, and posting anything you want."

9. D: Many people still do not buy organic food because it is too expensive. The passage states "the price of organic foods still prevents many people from eating them on a regular basis."

10. A: It is reasonable to conclude that the author mentioned Cindy because it would strengthen the argument that birth order affects personality traits. The passage states that oldest children are more responsible and perform better in school. Since Cindy was on the Dean's list (good academic performance) and did her chores as a child (a sign of responsibility), it is reasonable to assume that Cindy was an oldest child.

Mathematics Knowledge

1. A: To calculate the value of this expression, substitute –3 for x each time it appears in the expression.

$$3(-3)^3 + (3(-3) + 4) - 2(-3)^2$$

According to the order of operations, any operations inside of parentheses must be done first.

$$3(-3)^3 + (-9 + 4) - 2(-3)^2$$
$$3(-3)^3 + (-5) - 2(-3)^2$$

Then, simplify any exponents.

$$3(-27) + (-5) - 2(9)$$

Next, perform any multiplication.

$$-81 - 5 - 18$$

Finally, subtract from left to right.

$$-81 - 5 - 18 = -104$$

2. B: To solve for a variable using a system of equations, one of the variables must be canceled out. To eliminate x from these equations, use the elimination method. Start by multiplying the top equation by 3.

$$3(2x - 6y = 12)$$
$$6x - 18y = 36$$

Then, add the two equations to eliminate x.

$$\begin{aligned} 6x - 18y &= 36 \\ \underline{+\ (-6x + 14y} &\underline{= 42)} \\ -4y &= 78 \end{aligned}$$

Solve for y by dividing both sides by –4.

$$\frac{-4y}{-4} = \frac{78}{-4}$$
$$y = -19.5$$

Therefore, the value of y is –19.5.

3. D: To solve for x, first isolate the variable by subtracting 8 from both sides.

$$-4x + 8 \geq 48$$
$$-4x \geq 40$$

Then, divide both sides by –4 to solve for x. When an inequality is divided by a negative number, the sign must change directions.

$$\frac{-4x}{-4} \geq \frac{40}{-4}$$
$$x \leq -10$$

4. C: Lines that are perpendicular to each other have negative reciprocal slopes. The slope of the original equation is $-5x$. The negative reciprocal of this is $\frac{x}{5}$. The value of the y-intercept is not important for the purpose of answering this question. The only equation with a slope of $\frac{x}{5}$ is $y = \frac{x}{5} + 27$, so this is the correct answer.

5. C: $9y$ is contained in all parts of the expression $9x^2y - 18xy - 27y$. Therefore, $9y$ can be factored out.

$$9y(x^2 - 2x - 3)$$

$(x^2 - 2x - 3)$ can also be factored.

$$(x - 3)(x + 1)$$

The final factored form of the expression is $9y(x - 3)(x + 1)$.

6. C: To solve for x, simply add 6 to both sides.

$$x - 6 = 0$$
$$x - 6 + 6 = 0 + 6$$
$$x = 6$$

7. A: To find the slope of the line, use the slope formula.

$$m = \frac{y_2 - y_1}{x_2 - x_1}$$

Substitute $(-3,18)$ for (x_1, y_1) and $(5,2)$ for (x_2, y_2).

$$m = \frac{2 - 18}{5 - (-3)} = \frac{2 - 18}{5 + 3} = \frac{-16}{8} = -2$$

Therefore, the slope of the line is –2.

8. D: First, gather the like terms on opposite sides of the equation.

$$-3q + 12 \geq 4q - 30$$
$$12 \geq 7q - 30$$
$$42 \geq 7q$$

Then, divide both sides by 7 to solve for q.

$$\frac{42}{7} \geq \frac{7q}{7}$$
$$6 \geq q$$

The inequality can be flipped to match the formatting of the answer choices, giving the inequality $q \leq 6$.

9. A: Besides the \$600 he has remaining, Chan has paid out a total of 85% (30% + 30% + 25%) of his bonus for the expenses described in the question. Therefore, the \$600 represents the remaining 15%. Remember that 15% can be written as $\frac{15}{100}$. To determine his total bonus, solve $\frac{15}{100}x = 600$. So, $x = \frac{100}{15} \times 600 = 4{,}000$, and Chan's total bonus is \$4,000.

10. B: One side of a square is 56 cm. All of its sides are equal, and the perimeter is the sum of all sides.

$$56 \text{ cm} + 56 \text{ cm} + 56 \text{ cm} + 56 \text{ cm} = 224 \text{ cm}$$

Therefore, the perimeter is 224 cm.

11. D: To simplify the expression, use the exponent rule $(x^m)^n = x^{m\times n}$.

$$(3x^{-2})^3 = (3)^3(x^{-2})^3 = 27x^{-6}$$

12. B: The perimeter of a figure is the sum of all its sides. Since a rectangle's width and length will be the same on opposite sides, the perimeter of a rectangle can be calculated by using the following formula.

$$P = 2w + 2l$$

Substitute the numbers given in the question.

$$P = 2(7) + 2(9)$$
$$P = 14 + 18$$
$$P = 32$$

Therefore, the perimeter of the rectangle is 32 cm.

13. D: There are three feet in a yard. In feet, the lot is $3 \times 3 = 9$ feet wide, and $4 \times 3 = 12$ feet long. So, its area is $9 \text{ ft} \times 12 \text{ ft} = 108 \text{ ft}^2$.

As an alternate way of solving the problem, first find the lot's area in square yards: $3 \text{ yd} \times 4 \text{ yd} = 12 \text{ yd}^2$. Then, convert square yards to square feet: since there are 3 feet in a yard, there are $3^2 = 9$ square feet in a square yard. So, the lot's area in square feet is $12 \times 9 = 108$ square feet.

14. D: To find a midpoint, use the midpoint formula to calculate the average of the two sets of points.

$$\text{midpoint} = \left(\frac{x_1 + x_2}{2}, \frac{y_1 + y_2}{2}\right)$$

Substitute $(-20,8)$ for (x_1, y_1), and substitute $(5,3)$ for (x_2, y_2).

$$\text{midpoint} = \left(\frac{-20 + 5}{2}, \frac{8 + 3}{2}\right)$$
$$\text{midpoint} = \left(\frac{-15}{2}, \frac{11}{2}\right)$$
$$\text{midpoint} = (-7.5, 5.5)$$

Therefore, the midpoint is $(-7.5,5.5)$.

15. A: First, find the total number of pens purchased.

$$5 \times 3 = 15$$

Then, find the total number of pencils purchased.

$$3 \times 7 = 21$$

Finally, express the number of pens to the number of pencils purchased as a ratio.

$$15 : 21$$

This ratio can be simplified by dividing both sides by 3.

$$5 : 7$$

Therefore, the ratio of the number of pens to the number of pencils is $5 : 7$.

Electronics Information

1. D: Voltage is the potential energy difference between two charged terminals, and current is the rate of flow of charge past a given point.

2. C: Using Ohm's law, $V = I \times R$ and the given current ($I = 4$ A) and resistance ($R = 3\ \Omega$):

$$12\text{ V} = 4\text{ A} \times 3\ \Omega$$

3. B: Resistance is measured in ohms, current in amps, and voltage in volts. Ohmmeters, Ammeters, and Voltmeters can take readings of those respective measurements.

4. B: This series circuit can be solved 2 ways. First, by looking at the circuit as a whole:

$$\Delta V_{total} = \Delta V_1 + \Delta V_2 + \Delta V_3$$
$$\Delta V_{total} = 2\text{ V} + 3\text{ V} + 4\text{ V} = 9\text{ V}$$

$$I_{total} = I_1 = I_2 = I_3 = I_4$$
$$I_{total} = 3\text{ A}$$

Ohm's Law: $\Delta V_{total} = I_{total} \times R_{total}$

$$R_{total} = (9\text{ V})/(3\text{ A}) = 3\ \Omega$$

Alternatively, the resistance of each resistor could be found and summed:

$$R_{R_\#} = \Delta V_{R_\#}/I_{R_\#}$$
$$R_{R_1} = (2\text{ V})/(3\text{ A}) = 0.66\ \Omega$$
$$R_{R_2} = (3\text{ V})/(3\text{ A}) = 1\ \Omega$$
$$R_{R_3} = (4\text{ V})/(3\text{ A}) = 1.33\ \Omega$$

$$R_{total} = R_{R_1} + R_{R_2} + R_{R_3}$$
$$R_{total} = 0.66\ \Omega + 1\ \Omega + 1.33\ \Omega = 3\ \Omega$$

5. A: Using Ohm's law with a circuit in series:

$$I_{total} = I_1 = I_2 = I_3 = I_4$$
$$I_{total} = 4\text{ A}$$

$$R_{total} = R_{R_1} + R_{R_2} + R_{R_3}$$
$$R_{total} = 0.5\ \Omega + 1\ \Omega + 1.5\ \Omega = 3\ \Omega$$

Ohm's Law: $\Delta V_{total} = I_{total} \times R_{total}$

$$\Delta V_{total} = 4\text{ A} \times 3\ \Omega = 12\text{ V}$$

6. A: $I_4 = 10$ A; $I_6 = 15$ A. Because the battery is 20 V, $R_2 = 4\ \Omega$, $R_3 = 2\ \Omega$, and the resistors are in parallel:

$$\Delta V_{battery} = \Delta V_2 = \Delta V_3 = 20\text{ V}$$

$$I_4 = I_{R_3} = \Delta V_{R_3}/R_3 = (20\text{ V})/(2\ \Omega) = 10\text{ A}$$

$$I_{R_2} = \Delta V_{R_2}/R_2 = (20\text{ V})/(4\ \Omega) = 5\text{ A}$$

$$I_6 = I_{R_2} + I_{R_3} = 10\text{ A} + 5\text{ A} = 15\text{ A}$$

7. C: 1 Ω. If $R_1 = 4\ \Omega$, $R_2 = 4\ \Omega$, and $R_3 = 2\ \Omega$, equivalent resistance (R_{eq}) can be found using:

$$\frac{1}{R_{eq}} = \frac{1}{R_1} + \frac{1}{R_2} + \frac{1}{R_3}$$
$$\frac{1}{R_{eq}} = \frac{1}{4} + \frac{1}{4} + \frac{1}{2}$$
$$\frac{1}{R_{eq}} = \frac{4}{4}$$
$$R_{eq} = 1$$

8. D: To solve a circuit with both series and parallel components, first add resistors that are found in series, then solve for the equivalent resistance of the parallel resistors. For example, in the pictured circuit, add the two resistors that would be in series in place of R_1 and add the three resistors that would be in series in place of R_3 before solving for equivalent resistance of the simplified resistors.

9. B. Using $P = I \times V$ to solve for current (I), where $P = 60$ watts and $V = 9$ V:

$$I = (60\ W)/(9\ V) = 6.66\ A$$

10. D: Alternating current is produced by generators, periodically changes direction of flow, can be transported over long distances without losing power, and is used to supply electricity to homes. Direct current is produced by batteries, flows only in one direction, and is used on ships and airplanes.

11. C: Direct current is used in ships, planes, and cell phones. Alternating current is used in homes to power appliances and lights.

12. A: The earth commonly serves as a ground because it can infinitely donate or accept electrons without mathematically significant changes to its net charge. In cars, the negative terminal of the car battery serves as the ground. Lightning rods allow for the high-voltage current of lightning to ground to the earth safely. Home wiring is also grounded to the earth.

13. B: P-type semiconductors have a shortage of electrons; when an electric field is applied, a positive pole forms (example: silicon doped with boron). N-type semiconductors have an excess of electrons as a result of the doping process; when an electric field is applied, a negative pole forms due to the buildup of negatively charged electrons (example: silicon doped with antimony).

14. C: Diodes allow current to pass in only one direction. P-n junction diodes are made up of fused p- and n-type semiconductors and are considered solid-state diodes because electricity flows through solid material rather than a vacuum.

15. D: Transistor applications include radio, television, computer chips, and early hearing aids.

Auto Information

1. B: Most gasoline engines operate with reciprocating pistons in cylinders, and most automobiles in the United States utilize the four-stroke cycle. Four piston strokes make up the four-stroke cycle: intake, compression, power, and exhaust. In one cycle, the piston moves down and back up twice.

2. C: While the battery is used to start the vehicle, the alternator converts mechanical energy from the motor running to create electricity and recharges the battery as it turns. The battery supplies power to the starter to start the engine and it provides power for the spark plugs to cause ignition.

3. A: Carburetors (in older vehicles) and fuel injectors (in newer vehicles) mix air and fuel before combustion. Fuel injectors complete the process with the help of a computer, and allow for greater fuel efficiency.

4. D: Combustion occurs in the engine, and in gasoline engines, a spark from a spark plug ignites the fuel-air mixture in the cylinder to begin combustion.

5. D: One of the most common ignition problems is spark plug fouling, which occurs when carbon builds up at the ignition point; it will cause engine misfiring and increased carbon emissions. Driving at highway speeds is good for spark plugs because the increased temperature of the engine helps burn off the excess fuel or ash. Spark plug fouling is more common with prolonged idling and city driving because the engine doesn't get as hot.

6. A: Failing piston rings will result in engine smoking because oil from the crankcase will leak into the combustion chamber and smoke when combusted.

7. D: Exhaust from the combustion chamber is released by the exhaust valve towards the exhaust manifold, which collects gas byproducts from each cylinder and helps with noise control. Through the exhaust pipe, gas travels to the catalytic converter, which filters out pollutants and converts them to water vapor and carbon dioxide. From the catalytic converter, exhaust travels through the exhaust pipe to the muffler, which further reduces noise. From the muffler, the tail pipe releases gas away from the vehicle.

8. C: Motor oil is not consumed by the engine and is not used in combustion, so it does not act as fuel. It does lubricate the gears and prevent overheating and corrosion.

9. B: The thermostat helps control engine temperature by sending coolant either to the engine or to the radiator if it needs to be cooled further. A thermostat stuck open will cause the engine to run cold and result in bad gas mileage; a thermostat stuck closed will cause the engine to overheat.

10. B: Front wheel drive (FWD) is found in most modern economy or compact cars; the transaxle combines the functionality of the transmission, front axle, and differential into one component.

Shop Information

1. B: Ripping wood is the process of cutting it parallel to the grain. Cross cuts are perpendicular to the grain. Bevel cuts are angled across the depth of the wood, and miter cuts are angled across the wide face of the workpiece.

2. C: Beveled edge chisels have three beveled edges; mortise chisels only have one. Japanese bench chisels are less beveled than Western chisels, and paring chisels, while beveled, are very thin and nearly flexible.

3. A: At least one end of the ratcheting wrench contains a ratcheting device so that loosening or tightening doesn't require a complete circular motion or removing and resetting the wrench if something is in the way. These wrenches are helpful in tight spaces. Manual and digital torque wrenches help prevent overtightening because they can be calibrated in accordance with manufacturer specifications. Socket wrenches have a drive (the square-shaped fitting) attached to a ratchet on one end; various sockets can be attached to the drive to accommodate different size bolt heads. A combination of box-ended and open-ended wrenches, combination wrenches have an open and a closed end.

4. D: The Phillips-head screwdriver forms a cross at the end of the screwdriver; The flat head screwdriver is a simple wedge shape; Allen wrenches are hexagonal.

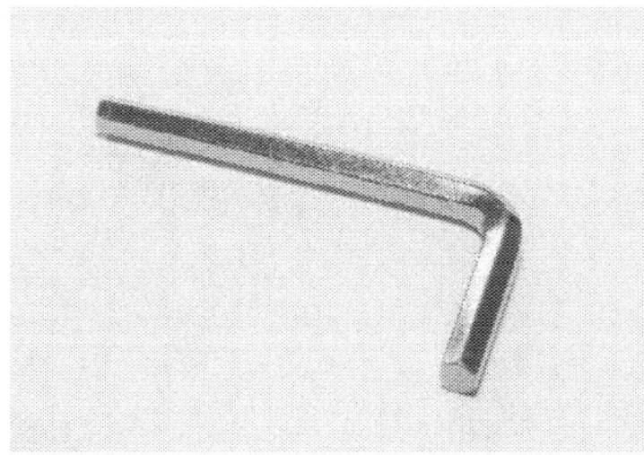

5. C: Soldering involves applying heat measuring roughly 600–840 °F, is commonly used in electrical circuits, and is usually used in relatively smaller jobs than welding. Welding uses extreme heat (6500 °F) to melt the base metal to fuse the two work pieces; soldering joins two separate metals with an alloy.

6. A: Rivets support tensile loads (force that occurs in opposite directions along the same axis) and shear loads (force that produces sliding, which is a failure in the plane parallel to direction of force). The most common modern applications include residential gutter construction, HVAC duct work, and aircraft manufacturing.

7. C: Various grooves on the upper jaw of tongue and groove pliers (also called Channel Locks) allow for an adjustable, locking fulcrum and a highly versatile tool. Diagonal pliers, also called wire cutters, have acutely angled jaws that enable cutting of wire and nails. Crimping pliers have specialized jaws to allow for breaking plastic coating on wire and crimping wires together; this makes them ideal for telecommunications technicians. Slip joint pliers are highly versatile, smaller than tongue and groove pliers, and the adjustable fulcrum allows the corrugated jaws to lock at varying widths.

8. B: Vise-grips (which can also be spelled vice-grips), also known as locking pliers, are part clamp and part pliers. With handles, corrugated jaws, and a fulcrum between the two like pliers, they can also be locked into a clamped position. A lever in one of the handles allows for the release of the clamping action.

9. D: Drilling creates new holes in workpieces; boring enlarges existing holes. Both processes can pertain to either blind or pass-through holes in a workpiece.

10. B: Oscillating saws are the smallest and most portable of the given list. Vertical band saws and table saws are stationary, and miter saws are able to be mounted to a workbench.

Mechanical Comprehension

1. A: The velocity is made up of two components: the x and y components. The x component does not change during flight, but the weight of the projectile decreases the positive y component of the velocity; thus, the total velocity will be greatest before the y component has decreased.

2. A: Because the linear speed of two connected pulleys is the same, the pulley with the smaller radius spins faster. The largest pulley will spin slower than the middle pulley. The smallest pulley will spin faster than the middle pulley, making it the fastest pulley.

3. C: Gear A and gear C have the same number of teeth. Thus, gears A and C will have the same speed. Since gear C is rotating at 10 rpm, the total number of rotations is calculated by multiplying the rpm by the number of minutes.

4. A: Because the large mass will produce a greater torque at the same distance from the fulcrum as the small mass, the distance from the large mass to the fulcrum should be shortened. Then, the torque produced by the large mass will decrease and the torque produced by the small mass will increase.

5. A: When the rope is not parallel to the intended path of motion, the force is divided into useful force (x direction) and not useful force (y direction). If only some of the force is useful, then the man will need to apply more force to achieve the same pulling force as if the rope were parallel to the table.

6. B: Because the volume of the liquid doesn't change, when the small piston is compressed, the volume of the bigger piston increases by the amount the volume of the smaller piston decreases. As the volume is the area times the height, the height of the larger piston only needs to raise one fourth the height that the small piston moved.

7. A: The downward force decreases part of the y component of the top force but does not affect the x component of the force; thus, the resultant force is up and to the right.

8. B: Because the same volume of water has to flow through all parts of the river, the water will slow down to fill the wide section.

9. C: The negative side of magnet 2 will be attracted to the positive side of magnet 1. The positive side of magnet 2 will be attracted to the negative side of magnet 3 with the same force. Because the magnitudes of the forces are equal and the directions are opposite, the sum of the forces will be zero.

10. C: The first phase change is from solid to liquid at −21 °C. The next phase change is from liquid to gas at 81 °C. 90 °C is only slightly higher than 81 °C, making it safe to say that the substance is still a gas.

11. A: Substitute token values for the resistors to solve. Using 1 Ω resistors, the resistance of circuit A, having resistors in series, is the simple sum of the two resistors: 2 Ω. Because the resistors in circuit B are in parallel, the resistance of circuit B is the reciprocal of the sum of the reciprocals of the resistances, or $\frac{1}{\frac{1}{1}+\frac{1}{1}}$. The result is 1/2 Ω.

12. A: To find the number of swings in a given period from the frequency, multiply the frequency by the time period (after converting the time period into seconds to match the frequency). The final calculation is $\frac{1.4 \text{ swings}}{\text{second}} \times 1 \text{ minute} \times \frac{60 \text{ seconds}}{1 \text{ minute}} = 84 \text{ swings}$.

13. B: The mechanical advantage is calculated by the output force divided by the input force. Because both pistons are the same size, the output force will equal the input force, resulting in a mechanical advantage of one.

14. C: Because the horizontal component of the thrown ball's velocity will not affect the vertical component, the vertical component of the thrown ball's velocity will be identical to the dropped ball's velocity. The balls will hit at the same time.

15. A: The cam has four bumps on it. The needle will move up and down for each bump. The cam will rotate five times in one minute. The total times the needle will move up and down will be five times four, or 20.

Assembling Objects

1. B:

2. D

3. D

4. B

5. A

6. C

7. C

8. D

9. A

10. D

11. C

12. B

13. B

14. A

15. C

Image Credits

LICENSED UNDER CC BY 4.0 (CREATIVECOMMONS.ORG/LICENSES/BY/4.0/)

Leaf Spring: "Elliptic leaf spring of Galakhov" by Wikimedia user Alex Gomankov (https://commons.wikimedia.org/wiki/File:Elliptic_leaf_spring_of_Galakhov.svg)

Simple Outside Micrometer: "Micrometer caliper parts" by Wikimedia user Three-quarter-ten (https://commons.wikimedia.org/wiki/File:Micrometer_caliper_parts_0001.png)

Band Saw: "Delta bandsaw" by Wikimedia user Tiia Monto (https://commons.wikimedia.org/wiki/File:Delta_bandsaw.jpg)

LICENSED UNDER CC BY-SA 4.0 (CREATIVECOMMONS.ORG/LICENSES/BY-SA/4.0/)

Jigsaw: "Jigsaw AccuMaster" by Wikimedia user Артём В. (https://commons.wikimedia.org/wiki/File:Jigsaw_AccuMaster.jpg)

Reciprocating Saw: "AEG us 400 xe" by Wikimedia user Eladhayut (https://commons.wikimedia.org/wiki/File:AEG_us_400_xe.jpg)

LICENSED UNDER CC BY-SA 3.0 (CREATIVECOMMONS.ORG/LICENSES/BY-SA/3.0/)

Water Level: "Schlauchwaage Schematik" by Wikimedia user Obersachse (https://commons.wikimedia.org/wiki/File:Schlauchwaage_Schematik.svg)

Pipe Wrench: "Straight Pipe Wrench 3C by Wikimedia user TheAdcomGroup (https://commons.wikimedia.org/wiki/File:Straight_Pipe_Wrench_3C.jpg)

Lug Wrench: "Kreuzschlüssel" by Wikimedia user Steffen Heinz Caronna (https://commons.wikimedia.org/wiki/File:Kreuzschl%C3%BCssel.jpg)

Combination Wrench: "1933 Plomb Combination Wrench" by Wikimedia user Electron2002 (https://commons.wikimedia.org/wiki/File:1933_Plomb_Combination_Wrench.jpg)

Socket Wrench: "Socket wrench and sockets" by Wikimedia user Kae (https://commons.wikimedia.org/wiki/File:Socket_wrench_and_sockets.JPG)

Speed Clamp: "Irwin Quick-Grip bar clamp" by Wikipedia user J.C. Fields (https://en.wikipedia.org/wiki/File:Irwin_Quick-Grip_bar_clamp.jpg)

Vise-grips: "Locking Pliers" by Wikimedia user Duk (https://commons.wikimedia.org/wiki/File:Locking_pliers.jpg)

Back Saw: "Backsaw" by Wikimedia user Simon A. Eugster (https://commons.wikimedia.org/wiki/File:Backsaw.jpeg)

Chainsaw: "Chainsaw-mcculloch hg" by Wikimedia user Hgrobe (https://commons.wikimedia.org/wiki/File:Chainsaw-mcculloch_hg.jpg)

LICENSED UNDER CC BY-2.0 (CREATIVECOMMONS.ORG/LICENSES/BY /2.0/)

Dial Caliper: "Dial Caliper" by Keith Litchfield (https://www.flickr.com/photos/keithitchfield/21551991804)

Mortise Chisel: “mortising chisel” by David Numan (https://www.flickr.com/photos/57813190@N00/1841488509)

Bent Nose Pliers: “IMG_2818” by Windel Oskay (https://www.flickr.com/photos/oskay/4792522961)

C-Clamp: “Clamp compression tool on white” by Marco Verch (https://www.flickr.com/photos/30478819@N08/33917308458)

Miter Saw: “Mitre saw white” by Ewen Roberts (https://commons.wikimedia.org/wiki/File:Mitre_saw_white.jpg)

Licensed Under CC BY-SA 2.0 (creativecommons.org/licenses/by-sa/2.0/)

Vernier Caliper: “Vernier callipers” by Coshipi (https://www.flickr.com/photos/coshipi/8789583212)

Table Saw: “Table saw” by Nottingham Hackspace (https://www.flickr.com/photos/nottinghack/6843985536)

Drill Bit: “Twist Drill Bit” by andersen_mrjh (https://www.flickr.com/photos/75793838@N08/6954963717)

How to Overcome Test Anxiety

Just the thought of taking a test is enough to make most people a little nervous. A test is an important event that can have a long-term impact on your future, so it's important to take it seriously and it's natural to feel anxious about performing well. But just because anxiety is normal, that doesn't mean that it's helpful in test taking, or that you should simply accept it as part of your life. Anxiety can have a variety of effects. These effects can be mild, like making you feel slightly nervous, or severe, like blocking your ability to focus or remember even a simple detail.

If you experience test anxiety—whether severe or mild—it's important to know how to beat it. To discover this, first you need to understand what causes test anxiety.

Causes of Test Anxiety

While we often think of anxiety as an uncontrollable emotional state, it can actually be caused by simple, practical things. One of the most common causes of test anxiety is that a person does not feel adequately prepared for their test. This feeling can be the result of many different issues such as poor study habits or lack of organization, but the most common culprit is time management. Starting to study too late, failing to organize your study time to cover all of the material, or being distracted while you study will mean that you're not well prepared for the test. This may lead to cramming the night before, which will cause you to be physically and mentally exhausted for the test. Poor time management also contributes to feelings of stress, fear, and hopelessness as you realize you are not well prepared but don't know what to do about it.

Other times, test anxiety is not related to your preparation for the test but comes from unresolved fear. This may be a past failure on a test, or poor performance on tests in general. It may come from comparing yourself to others who seem to be performing better or from the stress of living up to expectations. Anxiety may be driven by fears of the future—how failure on this test would affect your educational and career goals. These fears are often completely irrational, but they can still negatively impact your test performance.

Elements of Test Anxiety

As mentioned earlier, test anxiety is considered to be an emotional state, but it has physical and mental components as well. Sometimes you may not even realize that you are suffering from test anxiety until you notice the physical symptoms. These can include trembling hands, rapid heartbeat, sweating, nausea, and tense muscles. Extreme anxiety may lead to fainting or vomiting. Obviously, any of these symptoms can have a negative impact on testing. It is important to recognize them as soon as they begin to occur so that you can address the problem before it damages your performance.

The mental components of test anxiety include trouble focusing and inability to remember learned information. During a test, your mind is on high alert, which can help you recall information and stay focused for an extended period of time. However, anxiety interferes with your mind's natural processes, causing you to blank out, even on the questions you know well. The strain of testing during anxiety makes it difficult to stay focused, especially on a test that may take several hours. Extreme anxiety can take a huge mental toll, making it difficult not only to recall test information but even to understand the test questions or pull your thoughts together.

Effects of Test Anxiety

Test anxiety is like a disease—if left untreated, it will get progressively worse. Anxiety leads to poor performance, and this reinforces the feelings of fear and failure, which in turn lead to poor performances on subsequent tests. It can grow from a mild nervousness to a crippling condition. If allowed to progress, test anxiety can have a big impact on your schooling, and consequently on your future.

Test anxiety can spread to other parts of your life. Anxiety on tests can become anxiety in any stressful situation, and blanking on a test can turn into panicking in a job situation. But fortunately, you don't have to let anxiety rule your testing and determine your grades. There are a number of relatively simple steps you can take to move past anxiety and function normally on a test and in the rest of life.

Physical Steps for Beating Test Anxiety

While test anxiety is a serious problem, the good news is that it can be overcome. It doesn't have to control your ability to think and remember information. While it may take time, you can begin taking steps today to beat anxiety.

Just as your first hint that you may be struggling with anxiety comes from the physical symptoms, the first step to treating it is also physical. Rest is crucial for having a clear, strong mind. If you are tired, it is much easier to give in to anxiety. But if you establish good sleep habits, your body and mind will be ready to perform optimally, without the strain of exhaustion. Additionally, sleeping well helps you to retain information better, so you're more likely to recall the answers when you see the test questions.

Getting good sleep means more than going to bed on time. It's important to allow your brain time to relax. Take study breaks from time to time so it doesn't get overworked, and don't study right before bed. Take time to rest your mind before trying to rest your body, or you may find it difficult to fall asleep.

Along with sleep, other aspects of physical health are important in preparing for a test. Good nutrition is vital for good brain function. Sugary foods and drinks may give a burst of energy but this burst is followed by a crash, both physically and emotionally. Instead, fuel your body with protein and vitamin-rich foods.

Also, drink plenty of water. Dehydration can lead to headaches and exhaustion, especially if your brain is already under stress from the rigors of the test. Particularly if your test is a long one, drink water during the breaks. And if possible, take an energy-boosting snack to eat between sections.

Along with sleep and diet, a third important part of physical health is exercise. Maintaining a steady workout schedule is helpful, but even taking 5-minute study breaks to walk can help get your blood pumping faster and clear your head. Exercise also releases endorphins, which contribute to a positive feeling and can help combat test anxiety.

When you nurture your physical health, you are also contributing to your mental health. If your body is healthy, your mind is much more likely to be healthy as well. So take time to rest, nourish your body with healthy food and water, and get moving as much as possible. Taking these physical steps will make you stronger and more able to take the mental steps necessary to overcome test anxiety.

Mental Steps for Beating Test Anxiety

Working on the mental side of test anxiety can be more challenging, but as with the physical side, there are clear steps you can take to overcome it. As mentioned earlier, test anxiety often stems from lack of preparation, so the obvious solution is to prepare for the test. Effective studying may be the most important weapon you have for beating test anxiety, but you can and should employ several other mental tools to combat fear.

First, boost your confidence by reminding yourself of past success—tests or projects that you aced. If you're putting as much effort into preparing for this test as you did for those, there's no reason you should expect to fail here. Work hard to prepare; then trust your preparation.

Second, surround yourself with encouraging people. It can be helpful to find a study group, but be sure that the people you're around will encourage a positive attitude. If you spend time with others who are anxious or cynical, this will only contribute to your own anxiety. Look for others who are motivated to study hard from a desire to succeed, not from a fear of failure.

Third, reward yourself. A test is physically and mentally tiring, even without anxiety, and it can be helpful to have something to look forward to. Plan an activity following the test, regardless of the outcome, such as going to a movie or getting ice cream.

When you are taking the test, if you find yourself beginning to feel anxious, remind yourself that you know the material. Visualize successfully completing the test. Then take a few deep, relaxing breaths and return to it. Work through the questions carefully but with confidence, knowing that you are capable of succeeding.

Developing a healthy mental approach to test taking will also aid in other areas of life. Test anxiety affects more than just the actual test—it can be damaging to your mental health and even contribute to depression. It's important to beat test anxiety before it becomes a problem for more than testing.

Study Strategy

Being prepared for the test is necessary to combat anxiety, but what does being prepared look like? You may study for hours on end and still not feel prepared. What you need is a strategy for test prep. The next few pages outline our recommended steps to help you plan out and conquer the challenge of preparation.

Step 1: Scope Out the Test

Learn everything you can about the format (multiple choice, essay, etc.) and what will be on the test. Gather any study materials, course outlines, or sample exams that may be available. Not only will this help you to prepare, but knowing what to expect can help to alleviate test anxiety.

Step 2: Map Out the Material

Look through the textbook or study guide and make note of how many chapters or sections it has. Then divide these over the time you have. For example, if a book has 15 chapters and you have five days to study, you need to cover three chapters each day. Even better, if you have the time, leave an extra day at the end for overall review after you have gone through the material in depth.

If time is limited, you may need to prioritize the material. Look through it and make note of which sections you think you already have a good grasp on, and which need review. While you are studying, skim quickly through the familiar sections and take more time on the challenging parts.

Write out your plan so you don't get lost as you go. Having a written plan also helps you feel more in control of the study, so anxiety is less likely to arise from feeling overwhelmed at the amount to cover.

Step 3: Gather Your Tools

Decide what study method works best for you. Do you prefer to highlight in the book as you study and then go back over the highlighted portions? Or do you type out notes of the important information? Or is it helpful to make flashcards that you can carry with you? Assemble the pens, index cards, highlighters, post-it notes, and any other materials you may need so you won't be distracted by getting up to find things while you study.

If you're having a hard time retaining the information or organizing your notes, experiment with different methods. For example, try color-coding by subject with colored pens, highlighters, or post-it notes. If you learn better by hearing, try recording yourself reading your notes so you can listen while in the car, working out, or simply sitting at your desk. Ask a friend to quiz you from your flashcards, or try teaching someone the material to solidify it in your mind.

Step 4: Create Your Environment

It's important to avoid distractions while you study. This includes both the obvious distractions like visitors and the subtle distractions like an uncomfortable chair (or a too-comfortable couch that makes you want to fall asleep). Set up the best study environment possible: good lighting and a comfortable work area. If background music helps you focus, you may want to turn it on, but otherwise keep the room quiet. If you are using a computer to take notes, be sure you don't have any other windows open, especially applications like social media, games, or anything else that could distract you. Silence your phone and turn off notifications. Be sure to keep water close by so you stay hydrated while you study (but avoid unhealthy drinks and snacks).

Also, take into account the best time of day to study. Are you freshest first thing in the morning? Try to set aside some time then to work through the material. Is your mind clearer in the afternoon or evening? Schedule your study session then. Another method is to study at the same time of day that you will take the test, so that your brain gets used to working on the material at that time and will be ready to focus at test time.

Step 5: Study!

Once you have done all the study preparation, it's time to settle into the actual studying. Sit down, take a few moments to settle your mind so you can focus, and begin to follow your study plan. Don't give in to distractions or let yourself procrastinate. This is your time to prepare so you'll be ready to fearlessly approach the test. Make the most of the time and stay focused.

Of course, you don't want to burn out. If you study too long you may find that you're not retaining the information very well. Take regular study breaks. For example, taking five minutes out of every hour to walk briskly, breathing deeply and swinging your arms, can help your mind stay fresh.

As you get to the end of each chapter or section, it's a good idea to do a quick review. Remind yourself of what you learned and work on any difficult parts. When you feel that you've mastered the material, move on to the next part. At the end of your study session, briefly skim through your notes again.

But while review is helpful, cramming last minute is NOT. If at all possible, work ahead so that you won't need to fit all your study into the last day. Cramming overloads your brain with more information than it can process and retain, and your tired mind may struggle to recall even previously learned information when it is overwhelmed with last-minute study. Also, the urgent nature of cramming and the stress placed on your brain contribute to anxiety. You'll be more likely to go to the test feeling unprepared and having trouble thinking clearly.

So don't cram, and don't stay up late before the test, even just to review your notes at a leisurely pace. Your brain needs rest more than it needs to go over the information again. In fact, plan to finish your studies by noon or early afternoon the day before the test. Give your brain the rest of the day to relax or focus on other things, and get a good night's sleep. Then you will be fresh for the test and better able to recall what you've studied.

Step 6: Take a Practice Test

Many courses offer sample tests, either online or in the study materials. This is an excellent resource to check whether you have mastered the material, as well as to prepare for the test format and environment.

Check the test format ahead of time: the number of questions, the type (multiple choice, free response, etc.), and the time limit. Then create a plan for working through them. For example, if you have 30 minutes to take a 60-question test, your limit is 30 seconds per question. Spend less time on the questions you know well so that you can take more time on the difficult ones.

If you have time to take several practice tests, take the first one open book, with no time limit. Work through the questions at your own pace and make sure you fully understand them. Gradually work up to taking a test under test conditions: sit at a desk with all study materials put away and set a timer. Pace yourself to make sure you finish the test with time to spare and go back to check your answers if you have time.

After each test, check your answers. On the questions you missed, be sure you understand why you missed them. Did you misread the question (tests can use tricky wording)? Did you forget the information? Or was it something you hadn't learned? Go back and study any shaky areas that the practice tests reveal.

Taking these tests not only helps with your grade, but also aids in combating test anxiety. If you're already used to the test conditions, you're less likely to worry about it, and working through tests until you're scoring well gives you a confidence boost. Go through the practice tests until you feel comfortable, and then you can go into the test knowing that you're ready for it.

Test Tips

On test day, you should be confident, knowing that you've prepared well and are ready to answer the questions. But aside from preparation, there are several test day strategies you can employ to maximize your performance.

First, as stated before, get a good night's sleep the night before the test (and for several nights before that, if possible). Go into the test with a fresh, alert mind rather than staying up late to study.

Try not to change too much about your normal routine on the day of the test. It's important to eat a nutritious breakfast, but if you normally don't eat breakfast at all, consider eating just a protein bar. If you're a coffee drinker, go ahead and have your normal coffee. Just make sure you time it so that the caffeine doesn't wear off right in the middle of your test. Avoid sugary beverages, and drink enough water to stay hydrated but not so much that you need a restroom break 10 minutes into the test. If your test isn't first thing in the morning, consider going for a walk or doing a light workout before the test to get your blood flowing.

Allow yourself enough time to get ready, and leave for the test with plenty of time to spare so you won't have the anxiety of scrambling to arrive in time. Another reason to be early is to select a good seat. It's helpful to sit away from doors and windows, which can be distracting. Find a good seat, get out your supplies, and settle your mind before the test begins.

When the test begins, start by going over the instructions carefully, even if you already know what to expect. Make sure you avoid any careless mistakes by following the directions.

Then begin working through the questions, pacing yourself as you've practiced. If you're not sure on an answer, don't spend too much time on it, and don't let it shake your confidence. Either skip it and come back later, or eliminate as many wrong answers as possible and guess among the remaining ones. Don't dwell on these questions as you continue—put them out of your mind and focus on what lies ahead.

Be sure to read all of the answer choices, even if you're sure the first one is the right answer. Sometimes you'll find a better one if you keep reading. But don't second-guess yourself if you do immediately know the answer. Your gut instinct is usually right. Don't let test anxiety rob you of the information you know.

If you have time at the end of the test (and if the test format allows), go back and review your answers. Be cautious about changing any, since your first instinct tends to be correct, but make sure you didn't misread any of the questions or accidentally mark the wrong answer choice. Look over any you skipped and make an educated guess.

At the end, leave the test feeling confident. You've done your best, so don't waste time worrying about your performance or wishing you could change anything. Instead, celebrate the successful completion of this test. And finally, use this test to learn how to deal with anxiety even better next time.

Review Video: Test Anxiety
Visit mometrix.com/academy and enter code: 100340

Important Qualification

Not all anxiety is created equal. If your test anxiety is causing major issues in your life beyond the classroom or testing center, or if you are experiencing troubling physical symptoms related to your anxiety, it may be a sign of a serious physiological or psychological condition. If this sounds like your situation, we strongly encourage you to seek professional help.

Online Resources

Due to our efforts to try to keep this book to a manageable length, we've created a link that will give you access to all of your online resources:

mometrix.com/resources719/afct

It's Your Moment, Let's Celebrate It!

Share your story @mometrixtestpreparation